Conrad's
Short Fiction

CONRAD'S SHORT FICTION

by

Lawrence Graver

UNIVERSITY OF CALIFORNIA PRESS
BERKELEY AND LOS ANGELES

UNIVERSITY OF CALIFORNIA PRESS
BERKELEY AND LOS ANGELES, CALIFORNIA

UNIVERSITY OF CALIFORNIA PRESS, LTD.
LONDON, ENGLAND

For my Mother and Father

Preface

Within the past decade it has become commonplace to assert that the highest level of Conrad's art exists in his short fiction. In a recent polemical introduction to his anthology for *Twentieth-Century Views*, Marvin Mudrick even goes so far as to say: "Conrad is not a novelist but a writer of novellas. His impulse exhausts, or only artificially protracts, itself beyond their length: the length of a nightmare or of a moral test, not—as novels require—of history or biography. The enduring Conrad is the Conrad who had learned his scope and his method without having yet decided to evade the force of his obsessions." Without wishing to conspire with Mudrick to proscribe four great novels from the canon of modern literature, one can admit that his argument has its seductive side. *Lord Jim* and *Under Western Eyes* begin superbly and slack off; the irony of *The Secret Agent* hardens; and *Nostromo*, even for the admiring Dr. Leavis, has its hollow moments. But "Typhoon," "The Shadow-Line," and "Heart of Darkness" are as fine as anything of their kind in English, and their flaws are venial.

My aim in this book is to describe and evaluate Conrad's achievement in short fiction and to relate it to certain conflicts in his career as a short story writer. The most obvious of these is the split between Conrad's desire to write stories of depth, originality, and daring and his wish to be a popular writer. Although this conflict is also apparent in his work as a novelist, it can be isolated and discussed with greater clarity in his career as a writer of stories because of the conditions under which the stories were written.

As a guide to selection, I have been influenced by the casual dogmatism of Ford Madox Ford, who once said:

Conrad never wrote a true short story, a matter of two or three pages of minutely considered words, ending with a smack . . . with what the French call a coup de canon. *His stories were always what for lack of a better phrase one has to call "long-short" stories. For these the form is practically the same as that of the novel. Or, to avoid the implication of saying that there is only one form for the novel, it would be better to put it that the form of long-short stories may vary as much as may the form of novels. The short story of Maupassant, of Tchekhov, or even of the late O. Henry is practically stereotyped—the introduction of a character in a word or two, a word or two for atmosphere, a few paragraphs for the story, and then, click! a sharp sentence that flashes the illumination of the idea over the whole.*

To Conrad's mind, the idea of a "long-short" story did possess a certain magical suggestiveness. In 1902, while preparing the manuscript of "The End of the Tether," he told David Meldrum of *Blackwood's:* "I want to give you an idea how the figure works. Upon the episodes, after all, the effect of reality depends and as to me I depend upon the reader *looking back* upon my story as a whole. This is why I prefer the form which needs for its development 30,000 words or so." And to the publisher himself, Conrad remarked, "I've a subject which may be treated in 30–40 thou: words: the form I like best but which I believe is in no favor with the public." Subsequently, at different times in his career, Conrad spoke of between thirty and forty thousand words as an ideal story length. Oddly enough, he would sometimes describe a work as being 30,000 words when it was, in point of fact, much longer, a habit which suggests that the figure itself had a definitive quality for him. Once, in a conversation with Lady Veronica Wedgwood, Conrad insisted that the length of "Daisy Miller" (about 25,000 words) was perfect for a short story, and that a writer who could produce one such tale each year was indeed a master.

For the purposes of this study, I have used three criteria to determine if a work should be included: (1) does it fit Conrad's own specifications of "30,000 words or so"? (2) did he publish it as one of a group of stories in any of his six collections? and (3) did he himself consider it a short story? There are four problematical works among the thirty-one possible candidates. I have included

"Heart of Darkness" (38,000), " The End of the Tether" (47,000), and "The Shadow-Line" (45,000) because they meet at least one of my tests, and have ruled out *The Nigger of the "Narcissus"* (54,000) because it meets none of them. I have, however, included a brief discussion of *The Nigger* for reasons that will become apparent in chapter 3.

For permission to quote from Conrad's published works and from manuscripts and unpublished letters, I am obliged to J. M. Dent and Sons, Ltd., acting for the trustees of the Conrad estate. The late John D. Gordan was especially kind in allowing me to read and to quote from two unusual collections that he owned: Conrad's letters to J. B. Pinker and the correspondence of various editors about Conrad's relationship with contemporary periodicals. Yale University Library, Harvard University Library, the Lilly Library at the University of Indiana, the Berg Collection of the New York Public Library, and the Rosenbach Foundation in Philadelphia have all permitted me to quote from manuscripts in their possession.

Parts of this study have appeared in different form in *Modern Fiction Studies, College English, Studies in Short Fiction, The Explicator,* and *Nineteenth-Century Fiction.*

A faculty fellowship from the University of California, Los Angeles, in the summer of 1963 allowed me to begin work on this book, and an assistant professor's leave from Williams College in the spring of 1967 made it possible for me to finish it.

I am pleased to acknowledge my debt to Ian Watt for guidance when this book first took embryonic form as a dissertation at Berkeley. Frederick C. Crews recommended changes to improve an earlier version. I am grateful, too, for the encouragement and valuable criticism of Charles Thomas Samuels, especially when it was most needed, at the end. And my wife Suzanne has been a devoted and discriminating reader of all versions, early and late.

Contents

1
First Tales

Conrad's earliest stories—"The Black Mate," "The Idiots," and "An Outpost of Progress"—all contain elements reminiscent of older writers working in acceptable forms and thus reveal the voice of a new writer who has not yet become himself. Later, when he achieved a degree of critical recognition, Conrad would occasionally try to please the public by repeating one of his own earlier successes. At other times, when this design proved defective, he would fall back on the tested formulae of comedy, adventure and romantic love. But at the beginning of his career, Conrad's idea of popularity seemed to require that he compose tales resembling those of successful writers whom he actually admired.

Behind the first two apprentice stories stand Daudet and Maupassant, both of whom had long been among Conrad's favorite authors. When *Almayer's Folly* was being set for publication in 1895, Conrad called Daudet "a youthful enthusiasm [of mine] that has survived, and even grown"; and he asked his relative Marguerite Poradowska, "You know my worship of Daudet. Do you think it would be ridiculous on my part to send him my book—I who have read all his books under every sky?"[1] When Daudet died two years later, several English periodicals were patronizing to his talent, but Conrad wrote a short article for *Outlook* which praised his honesty, animation, and open heart—his "prodigality approaching magnificence."[2] This memorial essay conveys the peculiar mixture of wistfulness, braggadocio, sentimentality, and irreverence that gives Daudet's work its special appeal. A gifted storyteller caught by the uniqueness of the moment, Daudet found the anecdotal approach to human affairs useful and satisfying, and—for Conrad—his candid good nature and tender skepticism were contagious enough to dispel criticism.

"THE BLACK MATE"

Many of Daudet's tales are based on the motif of harmless deception; at worst, deceit is inspired by knavery but never by serious double-dealing. Like the typical Daudet story, "The Black Mate" uses anecdotal reminiscence as a narrative frame, and employs deception and a trick ending to bring events to a happy close. Written in a preliminary form in 1886 (three years before the start of *Almayer's Folly*), it was an unsuccessful entry in a prize competition set by *Tit-Bits*, the magazine of jests and anecdotes. Twenty-two years later, in response to a request for fiction from the *London Magazine*, Conrad rewrote the story in its present form.* At first, he had thought of sending the editors "Razumov" (an early version of "Under Western Eyes"), but he had strong doubts about "appearing in a periodical of that sort" and finally told his agent J. B. Pinker, "I would prefer R. anywhere else but the L.M. It *won't do* there—I feel it. It's better for us I think to give them as *suitable* stuff as possible." The "suitable stuff" turned out to be the rewritten version of "The Black Mate," and a month later Conrad confessed, "I wrote the short story for the London for no other reason but that I don't want to have Rasumov mangled by fools. . . ."[3]

By choosing to retell the lighthearted story of the black mate at a time when he was struggling with the complicities of Razumov and the Russian conspirators, Conrad seems to have been looking back wistfully to a less troubled time of his life. He begins "The Black Mate" with a conventional description by a nostalgic first-person narrator of ships loading at the London docks during the 1880s. Most of the sailors are called steady, staunch, and unromantic men, whose personal characteristics are obliterated by a certain "professional stamp." But the *Sapphire's* new first-mate, Winston Bunter, stands out because of his impressive stature and ebony black hair,

---

* For a more detailed discussion of the composition of "The Black Mate," see "Conrad's First Story," *Studies in Short Fiction*, II, 2 (winter 1965), 164–69, and Jocelyn Baines, *Joseph Conrad: A Critical Biography* (London, 1960), pp. 84–85.

which has recently earned him the nickname, "Black Mate." Then, the narrator remarks in an off-hand way, "Of course I knew him. And, what's more, I knew his secret at the time, this secret which —never mind just now." And at key points in the story he continues to make such teasing remarks as "a life with a mystery," "a certain secret action," and "but [more] of that later."

The narrator's main story concerns Bunter and the *Sapphire's* Captain Johns, a humorless, mean-spirited man, with little respect for craft or tradition, who believes that sailors over forty should be poisoned and that the world is governed by the power and presence of ghosts. At the same time, there is a secondary thematic strand, typical of Conrad, that runs through the tale: a theme embodying a nostalgic view of the past and the community of the maritime life. After establishing these two lines, one of action and the other of idea, the narrator becomes an actor in his own drama and spends an evening with Bunter aboard the ship (a narrative technique reminiscent of Daudet's *Lettres de mon Moulin*). In this way he is able to emphasize the mate's anxiety about the disclosure of his secret on the coming voyage. Yet even at this point, the secret remains obscure; and in his desire to heighten the suspense, the narrator commits what is, by Conradian standards, an uncharacteristic act. Neglecting the drama of a violent trial at sea, he emphasizes a detail which, though trivial in itself, is crucial for the artificial plot. During heavy weather off the Cape of Good Hope, furniture is toppled and bottles spilled in Bunter's cabin; the narrator, however, ignores the sea drama and talks mysteriously of two drawers unexpectedly overturned.

Although the original narrator is not on the voyage of the *Sapphire*, he reports its course as if he had been and continues to tease the audience by presenting an extended debate between Bunter and Johns on the subject of ghosts. Bunter inflames the Captain by refusing to become a true believer; exasperated by his personal loss (which is still obscure), he tells Johns, "You don't know what a man like me is capable of." Two days later, after a bad fall from a ladder, Bunter grudgingly tells the captain "You were right!" and admits having seen a ghost. Johns is triumphant. When he learns in addition that Bunter's hair has suddenly turned white from shock, he is awed by the dazzling power of supernatural forces and tries to convince the mate to hold a seance. On returning to England, Bunter reveals the heart of the matter to his wife and the narrator. He had originally dyed his prematurely white hair in order to get the mate's position on the *Sapphire* after a number of unsuccessful attempts to find another job. When the storm smashed the bottles of dye in his drawers, he was terrified of being exposed; and although the fall from the ladder had been accidental, it did provide a perfect ruse to protect his secret. He invented the story of the ghost and then, as his dye ran out, reinforced the trick by displaying his "new" white hair. Bunter's story ends happily; his wife inherits enough money for them to retire and Captain Johns goes through life muttering about a "murderous, gentlemanly ruffian" who had a manifestation from "beyond the grave."

Conrad's first story leans heavily on sentimental irony, steady suspense, mechanically developed characters, a colloquial style, a whimsical plot, and a surprise ending—traits which are found in Daudet, in *Tit-Bits*, and in the *London Magazine*, but rarely in Conrad's best work. The central situation of "The Black Mate" is simply not very engaging, and even Conrad's dexterity and forced high-spirits cannot disguise the fact from the reader. Since Bunter's predicament involves among other things solitude, deception, and a delicate point of honor, it does have certain superficial resemblances to the dilemmas of Jim, old Whalley, and the Scandinavian Falk. But in those instances Conrad is far more deliberate in developing the moral consequences of his theme. Deceit in "The Black Mate" is at bottom cheerful and Bunter is Conrad's only mischievous hero, a man whose well-being is momentarily menaced by nothing more terrible than broken bottles and the tedium of a captain's conversation. Obviously, "The Black Mate" is a sport in the Conrad canon and few readers today would be able to recognize the author of *Nostromo* in its tentative pages. It is the only one of Conrad's forty-two works of fiction in which money allows a man and a woman to live happily ever after.

"THE IDIOTS"

"The Idiots"—a sport of another kind—was written in May 1896 during Conrad's honeymoon in Brittany. He had come to Ile Grande to finish *The Rescuer*; but when work stalled on that ill-fated project, he began writing short stories to lighten the tension and help pay the bills. Frustrated by his deadlock with the history of the younger Lingard, Conrad chose, quite uncharacteristically, to use fictional materials immediately at hand. Brittany, close to Normandy, brought Maupassant to mind; and Conrad produced an austere tale of peasant misfortune in the manner of the man universally considered master of these country matters.

The single-mindedness of Maupassant had impressed Conrad from the start of his career. Writing to Marguerite Poradowska in 1894, he confessed being "too much under the influence of Maupassant. I have studied *Pierre et Jean*—thought, method, and everything—with deepest discouragement. It seems to be nothing at all, but the mechanics are so complex that they make me tear out my hair."[4] Some time later, he sent Edward Garnett "that amazing masterpiece *Bel-Ami*," the technique of which "gives to one acute pleasure. It is simply enchanting to see how it's done."[5] While preparing the statement of critical principles later to be published as the preface to *The Nigger of the "Narcissus,"* Conrad drew upon the ideas in Maupassant's introduction to *Pierre et Jean*.[6] And, finally, between 1902 and 1914 he was indirectly involved in two different translations of Maupassant done by Elsie Martindale Hueffer* and Ada Galsworthy, wives of close friends. For Mrs. Hueffer, Conrad provided advice on idiom, choice of word, and syntax; for Mrs. Galsworthy, he wrote a short preface which later appeared in *Yvette and Other Stories* (1914).

Conrad spoke of being "saturé de Maupassant" and "un peu responsable" for the Martindale rendition. At times, he was rather involved in the project, raising questions and critical issues. "What," he once asked Elsie Hueffer, "does Ford mean in the

* Wife of Ford Madox Ford.

preface about Maupassant being or even seeming a rhetorician in the last sentence of *Chair-mender*. This is either perverseness or carelessness—or I don't know what rhetoric is. To me it's sheer narrative—sheer report—bare statement of facts about horses, dogs, the relations of doctor to chemist and tears in the bargaining eyes."[7] Placed alongside the preface to *Yvette*, these remarks to Ford's wife help define the nature of Conrad's relationship to Maupassant. He admired the older writer for his straightforward narrative skill and obvious ethical clarity; but when Conrad came to make a final judgment, he praised him for those highly generalized traits that exist in almost any serious writer: a devotion to art, a refusal to use hollow catch phrases, and a contempt for heavy measures of charm, sentiment, and buffoonery. In some ways Conrad's portrait of Maupassant resembles Conrad, for the figure that emerges from the preface to *Yvette* is a moralist who never lets outward fascinations "turn him away from the straight path, from the vouchsafed vision of excellence."[8] In more specific and telling ways, however, Maupassant and Conrad are very different. The first is a cynic, a critic of man's animal nature, and a great master of the surface world; the second, a skeptic, a critic of man's idealism, and a master of the world of shadows.

But strapped for a subject in Brittany in the spring of 1896, Conrad found inspiration in the stories of Maupassant. Borrowing his long-suffering peasants, his accustomed reticence, and one of his favorite narrative devices, Conrad wrote "The Idiots," which even he later dismissed as an "obviously derivative piece of work."[9]

"The Idiots" is composed in four parts. A three page introduction in which the narrator sees idiot children at a Breton roadside is followed by parts two and three, in which he first tells the history of their luckless parents and then focuses on the night the wife murdered the husband and fell to her death. The story concludes with a brief epilogue in which the restoration of order in the village is shown to have richly ironical overtones. Anyone who remembers Maupassant's "Mother Savage," "The Model," or "The Corsican Bandit" will recognize Conrad's debt. In each of those stories, a first-person narrator arrives on the scene, learns of a violent peasant tragedy, and closes with an incisive comment on the ironies of circumstance.

At the start, Conrad's narrator succeeds in sounding like Maupassant by trying objectively to record his first sight of the idiots. Even when drawn to figurative language, his similes reflect common experience: branches look as if they were perched on stilts and small fields resemble "the unskillful daubs of a naive picture." No effort is made by Conrad to individualize the speaker himself, a fact that immediately separates the invented voice of this story from the reflective narrators of the later fiction. The only attempt to sketch character in the early pages again suggests the economical example of Maupassant. After the narrator asks the carriage driver: "More idiots? How many are there, then?" the old man replies: "There's four of them—children of a farmer near Ploumar here. . . . The parents are dead now. . . . The grandmother lives on the farm. In the daytime they knock about on this road, and they come home at dusk along with the cattle . . . . . . It's a good farm."[10] Turning on the split between human and material values, the irony neatly reveals the driver's lack of compassion and reinforces an earlier description of his pleasure in showing off the idiots as a local tourist attraction.

Although the setting, the grim situation, and the narrative method are reminiscent of Maupassant, there are elements in the introduction that undercut the desire for conciseness and objectivity, and show Conrad's own voice beginning to break through. Since his fundamental method is both dramatic and meditative, Conrad can rarely report an act of violence without commenting on it. Thus the typical grandiloquence of such phrases as "the inexplicable impulses of their monstrous darkness," occasionally violates the reporter's detachment. The idiots, at one moment frail creatures, are suddenly transformed into "an offence to the sunshine, a reproach to empty heaven, a blight on the concentrated and purposeful vigour of the wild landscape." The contradictory claims of rhetoric and reticence—just barely evident at the start—will later become the most damaging flaw in the story.

In the second section, however, this weakness has not yet grown serious. During his description of the Bacadou marriage, Conrad is able to maintain a reasonable degree of neutrality and interest. He explains how Jean-Pierre Bacadou returns from the army to find his parents' farm falling into ruin. Worried about the absence of men to work the land, he marries quickly in hope of sons; but when his wife delivers idiot twins and then an idiot boy, Jean-Pierre is reduced to a desperate rage. At the insistence of his mother-in-law, the anticlerical peasant goes sheepishly to Mass; but the prayer is answered by the birth of still another imbecilic child. Rage turns to brutality and he begins regularly to beat Susan, his unfortunate wife.

Although the strident fiddler and the terrified birds at the Bacadou wedding also performed at the marriage of Charles Bovary, the stories of Maupassant continue to be the main source for this peasant tragedy. The laconic narration and the casual flashes of black humor echo any number of Maupassant's descriptions of Norman life. Yet up to this point one's major uneasiness about the story is less a matter of unoriginality than of development. As their hopelessness increases, the Bacadous, sullen and incommunicative, are reduced to animals at the mercy of a genetic fallacy, and Conrad is unable to give them the slightest power of self-determination. Had Maupassant written "The Idiots," the story would have ended quickly with the murder scene and a few terse reflections on life at the lowest levels. But Conrad goes after bigger game, and a creditable imitation turns into a pretentious and implausible melodrama.

The most serious sign of trouble comes in the paragraphs that introduce the third section of the story. As a preparation for the violent murder, Conrad begins to describe the Breton landscape as if it were the heath in *Lear*. The bay of Fougère resembles an immense black pit "from which ascended mutterings and sighs as if the sands down there had been alive and complaining." Black boughs lie naked, gnarled, and twisted, "as if contorted with pain"; and summer streams rush toward the sea "with the fury of madness bent on suicide." Given this anthropomorphism, one might expect some kind of titanic confrontation; but instead of dramatizing the gruesome stabbing of Jean-Pierre, Conrad has Susan report it during a protracted scene with her mother. In the confusion of their final interview, the entire affair seems more ludicrous than heartrending. Susan, covered with mud, cannot spit out her words; when she does, her mother doesn't quite take them in; and after the deed registers, the old lady starts thinking about her friendly relations with the police before she rejects her daughter as incorrigible. The confusion of tone is compounded by the subsequent collapse of Conrad's narrative method. Although the speaker is described as a tourist who has gathered the facts from neighbors ten years after the events, he can by the close of the story describe the solitary heroine's most intimate thoughts as she faces death. Fleeing the condemnation of her mother, Susan runs out alone toward the beach, appalled by rocks, water, and "the unbroken stillness of the night." At first, she imagines Jean-Pierre chasing her; but calmed by her distance from the village she describes the murder in a monologue of which the narrator can never have learned. Moments later, at the edge of a cliff, Susan mistakes a would-be rescuer for her husband; and when he says, "I am perfectly alive," she shrieks and jumps into the sea.

If this climax were not preposterous enough, the 300-word epilogue that follows mocks it further by returning to Maupassant's terseness and irony. In a carefully composed vignette, Madame Levaille watches four workmen carry her daughter's body on a hand-barrow, while the powerful Marquis of Chavanes passes on horseback. After the old woman remarks dispassionately that her only child cannot be buried in consecrated ground, the Marquis reassures her: "I shall speak to the Curé. She was unquestionably insane, and the fall was accidental." And then as the story ends, he trots off thinking: "I must get this old woman appointed guardian of those idiots, and administrator of the farm. It would be much better than having here one of those other Bacadous, probably a red republican, corrupting my commune."

The connection between the corruption of the aristocracy and the fate of the Bacadous has never been satisfactorily established in the story, and the irony—neat enough in itself—seems too mild to close out a drama of idiocy, delirium, and murder. Years later, Conrad was to find a much richer ironical perspective for a similar drama, the stabbing of the amorous Adolf by Winnie Verloc in *The Secret Agent.*

Looking back at "The Idiots" with a knowledge of Conrad's later fiction, one can see a number of obsessive preoccupations behind the borrowed mask. Characters revealed at moments of extreme exasperation, a hero enslaved by destructive illusion, a denouement of exile, bloodletting, and suicide—all these are motifs with which the reader of *Victory* or *Nostromo* is well acquainted. But unlike Heyst, Monygham, or Emilia Gould, the people in "The Idiots" display neither resiliency nor thoughtfulness, and they are victimized without ever being tested.

"AN OUTPOST OF PROGRESS"

The case of "An Outpost of Progress" is more involved. Here, the debt to others is partial rather than pervasive, and there is enough authentic Conradian material to make this a more absorbing tale than "The Idiots." Like *Almayer's Folly* and *An Outcast of the Islands,* "Outpost of Progress" is an ironical study of human vulnerability, especially among those who belong to what Conrad liked to call the fellowship of the stupid, the lazy, and the ineffectual. Two ivory dealers named Kayerts and Carlier go berserk at their trading station under the Congo sun. Originally, the men had come to Africa with hopes and fine slogans; but as their stay in the jungle lengthens, they become more and more irritable. After their supplies run out, they quarrel savagely over a few remaining lumps of sugar; and in a brutal climax Kayerts shoots his unarmed associate and plans to bury him as a fever victim. Unhappily, before he can dispose of the corpse, he hears the whistle announcing the long-awaited visit of his boss, the Managing Director of the Great Civilizing Company. When the director reaches the settlement, he finds Kayerts hanging from a wooden cross with his swollen tongue pointed in his direction.

Here, as in *The Secret Agent,* Conrad chooses to treat shallow characters and a violent situation ironically; and since "An Outpost of Progress" is a work of ruthless belligerence, its interest rests less in the people than in the quality of the narrator's attack. The targets themselves are worth aiming at (greed masquerading as philanthropy and colonizers shielded from their natural impulses by the dead hand of custom), and the assault is carried off with verve and decisiveness. But, since Conrad insists from the start that Kayerts and Carlier live "incapable of independent thought . . . like blind men in a large room," they are crushed under an irony too easily assumed.

Then, too, some of this irony comes from Flaubert and some from Kipling. The use of irony to expose the transparent postures of the fat Kayerts and the thin Carlier closely resembles Flaubert's choice of weapon and victims in *Bouvard et Pécuchet*, a classic revelation of bourgeois stupidity and pretension. In fact, one episode in "An Outpost of Progress" parallels a fine scene in Flaubert's novel. Once settled in their posts, Kayerts and Carlier find novels left by their predecessor; and "in the centre of Africa they made the acquaintance of Richelieu and of d'Artagnan, of Hawk's Eye and of Father Goriot. . . . They discounted their virtues, suspected their motives, decried their successes; were scandalized at their duplicity or were doubtful about their courage." Similarly, Bouvard and Pécuchet mention Richelieu and read Dumas and Balzac in an uncomprehending way. Kayerts' daughter Melie has the same name as the provocative maid from whom Pécuchet—in one of his rare acts of sexual aggressiveness—contracts gonorrhea. In Conrad's tale, Melie is "a little girl with long bleached tresses and a rather sour face."*

The influence of Kipling and the limitations of Conrad's own irony can be seen by glancing at the opening paragraph of "An Outpost," a 600-word expository block that sets the tone for the events to follow. That Conrad worked carefully on this passage (the longest first paragraph in all of his fiction) is clear from his side of an exchange with Edward Garnett: "You are right in your

* Conrad's admiration for Flaubert and his knowledge of his works is discussed by Jocelyn Baines on pp. 145–148 of his biography.

criticism of *Outpost*. The construction is bad. . . . It's very evident that the first 3 pages kill all the interest. And I wrote them of set purpose!! I thought I was achieving artistic simplicity!!!!!!"[11]

The information conveyed in the opening paragraph is straightforward enough. Two white men named Kayerts and Carlier have been placed in charge of an African trading post by the managing director of the Great Trading Company, with a native, Makola, as the third member of the staff. But in addition to the bare facts of case, enough negative criticism is conveyed through the narrator's tone of voice to support Garnett's complaint that human interest is forfeited from the beginning. By the close of the first paragraph, two patterns of irony emerge clearly and remain rigid for the rest of the story. First, there is the simple contrast based on a physical or moral reversal. Makola, who insists that his real name is Henry Price, is neat, taciturn, and unflappable, while his slovenly white superiors are easily moved to tears or suspicious enmity. The pragmatic director makes a rousing speech about opportunities offered by a station 300 miles from its neighbors; but the moment the ship moves away, he calls both the men and the station "useless."

Despite broad hints of imminent disaster, the mood at the start is humorous. Much of this humor comes from Conrad's second ironical device, a blunt form of rhetorical irony reminiscent of Kipling in his Indian stories. Makola, Conrad tells us, "spoke English and French with a warbling accent, wrote a beautiful hand, understood bookkeeping, and cherished in his innermost heart the worship of evil spirits." To place the disparate element about evil spirits at the end of a sentence concerned with such civilized accomplishments as handwriting, elocution, and the keeping of accounts is inevitably to evoke a comparison with the master of the method, the Kipling of stories like "The Man Who Would Be King."

For most readers in the 1890s, this playful mixture of the jaunty and the macabre would have been Kipling's unmistakable signature. The first connections between Conrad and his younger contemporary had been made by reviewers of *Almayer's Folly*, who excused the absence of "plot and petticoats" in the hope that Conrad might yet become the Kipling of the Malay Archipelago. Although he resented both the strictures and the comparison, Conrad enjoyed Kipling's early work and in 1898 told a cousin writing from Poland, "Among the people in literature who deserve attention the first is Rudyard Kipling."[12] Earlier in the same year, in answer to Arthur Symon's charge that *Captains Courageous* and *The Nigger of the "Narcissus"* were devoid of ideas, Conrad wrote an essay defending himself and Kipling. But it seems to have been rejected by the *Outlook* and subsequently lost.[13] Toward the end of his career, Conrad took a strong dislike to Kipling's politics and to his journalistic vivacity; but in the early days, he felt that in comparison with other fiction of the period Kipling's *"ébauches* appear . . . finished and impeccable."[14]

Inevitably, men who were writing of the English in India and of the English in Africa and Borneo were going to touch on some of the same subject matter. But the similarities between "The Man Who Would Be King" and "An Outpost of Progress" are too close to be wholly accidental. Aside from the occasional tonal likeness, both stories describe the breakdown of two European egoists who had hoped to get rich quickly in a primitive society, and both end with scenes of slaughter and crucifixion. At the close of Kipling's tale, Peachey Carnehan pulls the dried, withered head of his friend Dravot from a paper bag, an act similar in grotesque impact to Kayerts' suicide on the cross. Conrad's use of high-spirited gallows humor to treat squalid materials seems like an attempt to capitalize on a fictional fashion which Kipling had established by himself.

Throughout "An Outpost of Progress," Conrad keeps falling back on humor typical of Kipling, particularly euphemistic substitution to mask the ugly facts of life. Not far from Kayerts' bungalow was "another dwelling place. . . . In it, under a tall cross much out of the perpendicular, slept the man who had seen the beginning of all this . . ."—his shiftless predecessor who succumbed to fever. After a while, these examples of verbal irony (which at least require a certain deftness in placing) degenerate into direct sarcasm. Makola is a "neat, civilized nigger"; Carlier becomes "sagacious" and "a pioneer of trade"; and when the steamer's whistle summons

Kayerts to his death, it is the voice of "progress and civilization" which rings in his ear.

These jokes and predictable contrasts mirror Conrad's self-delight, for they appear with little variation on every page of the story. Yet the broadness of this irony might be excusable, if it were not for a half dozen passages of reflection in which points already established through action or irony are repeated in candid expository prose. The pattern is typical: first, a brief description of a scene; then, a long, self-evident stretch of generalized, repetitive commentary. The brevity of one matched by the banality of the other makes development of an idea or a dramatic action impossible.

Static and derivative, "An Outpost of Progress" reveals a writer handling materials that he has not yet made his own. When he turned back to the Congo experience two years later, Conrad produced "Heart of Darkness." But in the meantime, he had discovered Marlow, and then Kurtz.

*   *   *

Working within modes used by other nineteenth-century writers helped Conrad define the nature and limits of his own talent. Daudet might be able to create vivid tales from casual anecdotes, but Conrad lacked his simplicity and charm. Mechanical contrivance, which in the Frenchman's hands had its spirited side, was for Conrad a fatal invitation to melodrama. In Maupassant's stories Conrad could see a master of tact and selection find drama in "the obscure trials of ignorant hearts," but he was learning that his own flamboyance made such subjects potentially dangerous. To treat the drab and the inarticulate, Conrad would have to use the filter of a sophisticated irony or the services of a narrator himself involved in the action. The surprise ending, so skillfully employed by Daudet and Maupassant, was not suited to the kind of moral drama that Conrad was eventually to write. In his stories the turn of events occurs early enough for the actors to reflect on it; or if it comes at the close, the narrator had been commenting on it all along. Kipling's cheerful grotesquerie was, for Conrad, an unsuitable voice; his own farce would have to be more sinister and less consoling.

Flaubert's irony was a model only in the sense that it taught the virtues of reticence and restraint.

Although the full significance of Conrad's apprentice period cannot be understood until we discuss the work of his maturity, certain generalizations are clear. His experiments with the modes of Daudet, Kipling, and Maupassant taught Conrad that there were certain subjects and narrative methods that he had best leave alone. "My thought," he once told Garnett, "is always multiple"; and generally speaking, the movement in his next tales would have to be away from directness and simplicity, a pursuit of exemplary situations in which moral patterns become increasingly more intricate. The main technical problem would be to find the most satisfactory distance from the melodramatic events of the story, and the development of an actor-narrator will be the first of several strategic advances. Needless to say, this flight from directness runs counter to the demands of editors and readers and is responsible for the conflict that is the subject of the chapters to follow.

2
Coming to *Blackwood's*

Since several of Conrad's earliest stories were written with specific periodicals in mind, they cannot be fully understood without some knowledge of his relationship to the contemporary magazine market, an especially involved history that begins with the writing of *The Rescue* in the spring of 1896. For some time, the failure of his books to sell had made Conrad anxious about his future as a writer. Although *Almayer's Folly* and *An Outcast of the Islands* were generously praised by the critics, their combined sale was considerably less than five thousand copies. After making a false start on a third novel, *The Sisters*, Conrad decided to offer in his next book larger quantities of love and adventure, two time-honored ingredients of popular fiction. As he explained to Fisher Unwin: "If the virtues of Lingard please most of the critics, they shall have more of them. The theme of it shall be the rescue of a yacht from some Malay vagabonds and there will be a gentleman and a lady cut out according to the regulation pattern."[1] The following year he candidly told Edward Garnett, "all my ambition is to make it good enough for a magazine—readable in a word."[2]

During the summer, "in the intervals of squirming," when work on the Lingard novel would not progress, Conrad began writing short stories, the first of which was "The Idiots." Since he knew little about the periodical market, he called on Unwin and Garnett for advice. In the beginning, the two names mentioned most frequently were the *Savoy*, which had recently asked Garnett for a Conrad contribution, and *Cosmopolis*, which was distributed by Unwin's own firm. The *Savoy*, an inexpensive version of the *Yellow Book*, was one of the liveliest of the short-lived decadent magazines published at the end of the century; but Conrad felt the personality of Arthur Symons unsympathetic, and told Unwin, "I would rather wait longer and fare better." *Cosmopolis*, on the other hand, was a magazine with a rising and respectable reputation. Like the recent *Botteghe Oscure*, it accepted work in English, French, and German from prominent avant-garde European writers. Henry James published "The Figure in the Carpet" in the first issue; and Kipling, Tolstoi, Nietzsche, Anatole France, and Mallarmé appeared at odd intervals. Despite the fact that Andrew Lang conducted a literary chronicle marked mainly by his inability to tell good fiction from bad, the general standards were unusually high. Most important of all, perhaps, was the magazine's policy of reporting the latest literary events in six nations, for this guaranteed an audience of inquisitive writers and artists. In fact, Conrad's long friendship with R. B. Cunninghame Graham started when the Scottish writer came upon an early Conrad serial in *Cosmopolis*.

Although Conrad feared *Cosmopolis* might reject "The Idiots," he accepted Unwin's suggestion that it should be submitted. At the same time, however, matters were complicated by the efforts of Garnett who, through E. V. Lucas, had interested the *Cornhill* in Conrad's work. Garnett sounded a note that must have satisfied his older friend: "*The Cornhill* is a very good magazine for your work to appear in, no doubt they will pay you well, or at any rate fairly well. . . . The publishers Smith & Elder are rich, and probably a determined effort will be made to push the Magazine now that the old Editor James Payn has resigned."³ Four days later the official letter arrived:

Dear Sir,

I am instructed by the new editor of the Cornhill Magazine, Mr. St. Loe Strachey, to say that if you ever write short stories or sketches we should be most happy to give them our most sympathetic consideration. With regards to serials, we are unfortunately already 'booked' up to 1899, but shorter contributions will always be acceptable. As a general rule 6000 or 8000 words represents the maximum length for such contributions, but in exceptional cases we can sometimes publish a story of 12000 words in two instalments. A page of The Cornhill contains about 450 words, and the rate of remuneration is one guinea a page.

It is perhaps advisable, to prevent any misunderstanding to say that the Editor cannot pledge himself in advance to accept any contribution; though he thinks, to judge from the remarkable brilliancy and power of your published work that it is very unlikely he should decline anything you sent him.

Faithfully yours,
Charles L. Graves[4]

By early the next day, Conrad was convinced and told Unwin, "I think the Cornhill is not a bad mag to appear in—and, if you have not placed 'The Idiots' yet, we might try there."[5] But the story had already been sent to Cosmopolis where it had the rare fortune of being rejected not once but twice; when it finally did go to the Cornhill it was refused still another time. In all likelihood, the editors wanted a more typical work and one that was closer to their original estimate of 6,000 words. At last, Conrad agreed to send the story to the Savoy and explained to Unwin: "I must live. I don't care much where I appear since the acceptance of such stories is not based on their intrinsic worth. . . . But in that case there is no particular gratification in being accepted here rather than there. If the Savoy thing asks for my work—why not give it to them. I understand they pay tolerably well (2 g's per page)."[6] Conrad's initial hesitation at publishing his naturalistic story in the Savoy was probably well founded; for even now a reader receives a jolt when, after experiencing the somber mood of "The Idiots," he turns the page to find Beardsley's deliciously decadent illustration "The Death of Pierrot." Conrad was temperamentally out of place in the Savoy; and despite his seeming nonchalance about being printed "here rather than there," he did develop preferences among publishers and would not send any other work to the Savoy.*

Although Cosmopolis and the Cornhill had rejected "The

* Admittedly, Conrad's expression of preferences sometimes sounds contradictory. Much depended on fees and the pressure of day-to-day dealings with editors.

Idiots," they still seemed interested in Conrad's future fiction; so when he had further trouble with *The Rescuer* in July and August, he wrote two tailor-made stories, "An Outpost of Progress" and "The Lagoon," the first of which appeared in *Cosmopolis* in June–July 1897 and the second in *The Cornhill* in January of the same year.

At first glance, *Cosmopolis* would seem to have been an admirable place for Conrad to publish his short stories, but unhappily he soon began quarreling with the editors. After they had refused "The Idiots," he seemed agreeable enough to write another, "if I only had an idea of what they considered suitable." But when they began to complain about the length of "An Outpost of Progress," he told a friend: "It is too long for one number, they say. I told the unspeakable idiots that the thing halved would be as ineffective as a dead scorpion. There will be a part without sting—and the part with the sting,—and being separated they will be both harmless and disgusting."[7] However, Conrad was soon quieted by the fact that *Cosmopolis* was to pay him £2/10 a page, more than he had yet received for any of his writings. He was eager to sell other stories to the magazine; but as things developed, he did not have the chance.

Conrad had just as little respect for the editors at the *Cornhill* as he did for those at the *Savoy* and *Cosmopolis*: "I've sent a short thing to the *Cornhill*. A malay tells a story to a white man who is spending the night at his hut. It's a tricky thing with the usual forests river—stars—wind sunrise, and so on—and lots of second-hand Conradese in it. I would bet a penny they will take it. There is only 6000 words in it so it can't bring in many shekels. . . ."[8] Conrad was right about the "shekels"; *Cornhill* paid twelve and a half guineas, considerably less per page than he received for "The Idiots" and "An Outpost." Yet because of Garnett's urging, Conrad had hoped to stay on good terms with the editors and to publish other stories in the *Cornhill*. In addition to the unsuccessful attempt to sell *The Rescuer*, he tried to persuade Reginald Smith to make room for *The Nigger of the "Narcissus"*; but Smith again felt Conrad's work was too long and turned it down. Garnett resumed his role as Conrad's unofficial agent and finally convinced W. E. Henley to print *The Nigger* in the *New Review*.*

COMING TO *BLACKWOOD'S*

Although the *Cornhill* was the first magazine in which Conrad showed any real interest (and which in turn showed interest in him), it was in *Blackwood's Edinburgh Magazine* that he published his most representative work, and it was *Blackwood's* that provided the rare blend of editorial harmony, attractive fees, and discriminating response which was perfect for Conrad's needs at the moment.** Once again it was Edward Garnett who was responsible for pointing Conrad in the right direction. "It is destined by Providence for *Blackwood's*," Garnett said one day about "Karain"; and after some delay and preliminary haggling, the story was accepted. "All the good moments," Conrad wrote to his friend, "the real good ones in my new life I owe to you. . . . You sent me to Pawling—you sent me to Blackwood's—when are you going to send me to heaven?"9

Much to Conrad's surprise and delight, Blackwood asked for first refusal on any new short story. "This, coming from Modern Athens, was so flattering that for a whole day I walked about with my nose in the air. Since this morning, however, it occurred to me that Blackwood won't help me to write the stories,—and with me, I see, the trouble is not in the publishing: it is in the writing."10 The long, involved, and especially fruitful relationship between Conrad and the editors of *Blackwood's* was to be important both in the publishing and in the writing. Conrad had a genuine respect for the magazine, repeatedly saying that *Blackwood's* was the only monthly he cared to read.

He expressed enormous relief that he could write "for *Maga* in-

---

* Because of its reputation for quality, Conrad would most likely have sent other stories to the *New Review*; but it stopped publishing in 1898. He did, however, submit essays to its successor, *Outlook*.

** My summary of Conrad's relationship with *Blackwood's* is indebted to William Blackburn's introduction to *Letters to Blackwood* and to his carefully edited text.

stead of for 'the market'—confound *it* and all its snippetty works."[11] "My ambition had never been to see myself drawn, quartered and illustrated in a Magazine run for the Million by a Millionaire,"[12] and "I had much rather work for *Maga* and the House than for the 'market': were the 'market' stuffed with solid gold throughout."[13] Once he appeared in the magazine regularly, Conrad could feel secure of its continued patronage and he did not have to play the selling game any longer. In 1899 he told Sir Algernon Methuen, who showed an interest in publishing his fiction, that "*Blackwood's* is the only periodical *always* open to me—and is the only one for which I really care to work."[14] Although *Blackwood's* circulation was never high—ranging between 3,000 to 10,000 copies a month— Conrad preferred it to magazines of greater popularity. He could easily have published elsewhere but elected to stay with *Maga*. David Meldrum, the publisher's assistant, once wrote to Blackwood: "I gently hinted that his price for *Maga* was high, and he showed me an offer of £50 for a short story which he declined in a popular magazine—*Pearson's*. He wants to have his stories in a good magazine."[15] Conrad's first fee from *Blackwood's* was £40 for "Karain"; and later he received £2/10 per 1,000 words for "Youth" and "Heart of Darkness," less, in fact, than he had earned for his earlier stories (see p. 25). *

Still another congenial factor in the relationship was William Blackwood's desire to be more than just a stone-faced editor facing a temperamental author across a desk. A respectable confidence quickly developed between writer and publisher, and they exchanged notes about composition, family matters, and Conrad's personal finances. Blackwood agreed to innumerable advances on material yet to be written and soon became involved in complicated insurance policy loans that Conrad had made. Given the fact that Conrad's need for money was always far greater than his selling value to the magazine, it is a wonder the friendship lasted five years before the first serious sign of strain. The older man comes off quite well—few editors would have been as patient or understanding in

* Successful writers like Kipling or Hall Caine could command £15 or more for 1,000 words of short fiction.

dealing with so exasperating a personality. Conrad was always asking for favors—money, sympathy, or an extension of time—and
Blackwood was always accommodating.

Finally, Conrad tried even Blackwood's tolerance. At a time when
his output was exceptionally small, he asked for a loan against
future copyrights, and was bluntly told that the firm carried him
at a loss.[16] The estrangement brought forth from the injured Conrad a letter which in its statement of artistic conviction is one of
the most eloquent he ever wrote. But this should not lead anyone
to question Blackwood's decision. Reasonable expediency allowed
him no other choice; and in later years, when Conrad came round
to see this, he spoke of his former editor with considerable respect.
As late as 1911, Conrad was still reminding people what it meant
for his career to have been published in *Blackwood's*. "I regret
Maga. One was in decent company there and had a good sort of
public. There isn't a single club and messroom and man-of-war in
the British Seas and Dominions which hasn't its copy of Maga. . . ."[17]
And in 1912, when Austin Harrison was wondering if *Chance* was
too experimental for the *English Review*, Conrad told him: "One
thing occurs to me: that is that in 1899 B'Wood's Maga: accepted
my *Lord Jim* a much closer knit and more complicated work with
remote psychology—sailors, malays, and so on—whereas *Chance* is
English in personages and locality, much easier to follow and understand. It was a very new form then; and yet old Maga had the
audacity to take it up when we all were much less 'advanced' than
we are now and Conrad was a practically unknown writer."[18]

Conrad was indeed lucky. Aside from the friendship of Blackwood, he found in David Meldrum a most perceptive reader, who
was enthusiastic about his work from first acquaintance. In his
capacity as Blackwood's London advisor, Meldrum often prepared
short reports on manuscripts. As early as 1897, he had written of
"Karain," "this is a capital story—extremely strong and good on the
literary side";[19] and some years later he wrote, "I knew Conrad was
good—in fact 'Youth' I hold to be the most notable book we have
published since George Eliot."[20] In 1900, when Blackwood was
troubled by the enormous length of *Lord Jim* (which started as a

20,000-word sketch and grew to a 140,000-word novel), Meldrum consoled him with this thought: "In the annals of *Maga* half a century hence it will be one of the honourable things to record of her that she entertained 'Jim.' "[21]

Reasonable fees, an intelligent audience, and a sympathetic set of editors—these are rare features to find in a magazine at any time. Certainly, it could not have been the regular diet of *Blackwood* fiction that made the magazine attractive to Conrad. The stories and short novels appearing month after month in *Maga* were entertaining, conventional, artless, and optimistic—the kind most periodical editors would be delighted to publish. The typical novel was a romance or adventure story set in the English provinces, Scotland, or in the mountains of some far-off land; and its point was to feed the reader's desire for exciting events, exotic landscapes, or the slightly eccentric in personal behavior.

The short stories in *Blackwood's* were even more stereotyped than the novels, falling almost always into one of five categories: the supernatural tale ("The Land of Suspense: A Story of the Seen and the Unseen"); dialect sketches ("Owd Lads" and "Th' Ploughin' o' th' Sunnyfields"); the exotic or violent adventure tale ("The Sequel of Black Murdo," "Death in the Alps," or "Hawaghy Wa'l Bint: An Egyptian Idyl".); the conventional O. Henry or Maupassant story with the surprise ending ("A Victim of Circumstance"); and the charming romantic sketch ("Jo Reggelt: A Hungarian Love Story"). These pieces offered nothing more than superficial, and for the most part derivative, storytelling.

Although Conrad read many of these pieces and wrote courteous notes to Edinburgh, such fiction could hardly have drawn him to the magazine. The appeal of *Blackwood's* must have been made on the strength of its general articles and its "clubable," conservative point of view. Conrad once described himself as "plus royaliste que le roi—more conservative than Maga,"[22] and it seems likely that it was this congruity of interests and attitudes that made the association a happy one. *Maga* presented a peculiar blend of the foreign and the familiar that coincided in a most extraordinary way with Conrad's own set of interests. Given his background and temperament, how could he fail to respond to a magazine that published within the course of a few years such articles as "The Negroes of the Congo," "Franklin and the Arctic," "Disobedience in Action," "The Philosophy of Impressionism," "The German Peril," "The Zionists," "Smollett and the Old Sea Dogs," "From Bulawayo to the Victoria Falls," and finally "The Carlists: Their Case, Their Cause, Their Chief"?

Although *Blackwood's* was a good many miles away from the avant-garde, it did provide Conrad with a steady outlet for his work in a periodical that he considered of high quality, and it tolerated his slow writing pace. The eventual quarrel with the editor had an unfortunate effect on Conrad's short stories, forcing him further into a role he found singularly distasteful—the popular writer desperately trying to gauge public taste and play the selling game. In later years Conrad made concessions to the demands of the popular magazines which seriously marred his stories; and he was forced in several instances to prepare one version of a tale for the pulp market and another for publication in book form. As far as such complicated works as *Nostromo* are concerned, the contention of Jocelyn Baines that Conrad was lucky to outgrow the restrictions of *Blackwood's* is perhaps correct; but the effect on the later short stories is certainly less fortunate. There is no simple explanation for the inferior quality of the later tales, but certainly Conrad's failure to find a congenial magazine was an important factor. *Blackwood's* provided an enviable publishing situation, for Conrad could have his money, his art, and appreciation as well. He was never again so fortunate.

At the beginning of his career, Conrad was rarely forced to tamper with his work for commercial reasons. However, after years of illness and financial strain, he was literally worn down and began making serious concessions to the demands of the market. He spoke of all his art becoming "artfulness in exploiting agents and publishers"; and his letters to his agent J. B. Pinker are filled with comments such as this: "Conrad will accommodate the story to the requirements of serial publication. . . . I could arrange certain passages in shorter form. Of course it would take some suggestiveness from the writing but in a serial a quality like that is lost anyhow."[23]

This bitterness developed only after many years of unhappy experiences in the periodical market. In the 1890s, however, Conrad's attitude toward serial fiction was less scornful. In a sense, the beginning of his career as a short story writer had been accidental, since he wrote stories only during delays in his longer works. But he became confirmed in his new role when he found that a 10,000-word story could often earn more than a novel. The following figures offer a revealing comparison:

Story and No. of Words	Sum Paid by Magazine for 1st Publication	Novel and No. of Words	Sum Paid by F. Unwin for Book Rights
"The Idiots" (10,000)	£42 (*Savoy*)	*Almayer's Folly* (64,000)	£20
"An Outpost of Progress" (9,750)	£50 (*Cosmopolis*)	*An Outcast of the Islands* (107,000)	£50 plus 12% on a 1st edition of 3,000 copies at 6s. each, which did not sell out
"The Lagoon" (5,700)	£12½ (*Cornhill*)		
"Karain" (14,500)	£40 (*Blackwood's*)		

Even by 1900, when his critical reputation had been established by the early Malayan novels, *The Nigger of the "Narcissus"* and *Tales of Unrest*, Conrad's popular appeal was limited; and Blackwood's did not see the need for more than 2,100 copies of the first printing of *Lord Jim*. Gradually, Conrad began to serialize his novels as well as his stories and then, of course, it became more profitable to write the longer works.

"THE LAGOON"

If "The Black Mate," "The Idiots," and "An Outpost of Progress" were derivative from Daudet, Flaubert, Maupassant, and Kipling, Conrad's fourth story, "The Lagoon," has the distinction of being the first tale in which he borrowed from himself. When the editors

of the *Cornhill* requested something more characteristic of his
exotic style, Conrad tried to reproduce the tangled landscape of his
Malayan novels, complete with "forests river—stars—wind sunrise . . . and lots of second-hand Conradese." "The Lagoon," told
in the same breath as *An Outcast of the Islands*, is more of a mood
piece than any of Conrad's other stories; and it is his only work of
fiction to take its title from a physical place rather than from an
individual, a natural phenomenon, or an ironical description of a
human situation. Although at 5,500 words his shortest story, it seems
overextended, suffering from what Conrad once called "the suspicious immobility of a painted scene."

A white man comes by small boat to spend the night at the house
of his young Malay friend Arsat. As he approaches he finds the
native caring for his dying wife; and while the two men wait sadly
for her life to end, Arsat tells the story of their great love. Some
years before, with the help of his devoted brother, he had run off
with a girl who had been the servant of his ruler; but unhappily
the trio had been quickly overtaken by pursuing guards. At the last
moment, having heard his brother shout for help, Arsat failed to
respond, choosing instead to escape with the girl. Ever since that
time, he has been stricken with self-doubt and remorse at his
brother's sacrifice; and now, freed by the death of his wife, he talks
of returning home to avenge the murder.

Neither the theme nor the setting of "The Lagoon" is particularly
distinctive. The subject of impulsive betrayal and permanent remorse is treated with greater suggestiveness in many of Conrad's
other works; while the jungle is a more brilliant and threatening
actor in his first two novels, not to mention "Heart of Darkness."
Yet for several reasons, "The Lagoon" has had its share of
fascinated readers. In 1897, thanking an acquaintance for a note
of praise, Conrad called it his favorite short story, written to please
himself; but the context of the remark (and other biographical
evidence) suggests that it came more from a sense of politeness
than from critical conviction. Fifteen years later, Max Beerbohm
based a clever parody on the adjectival excesses of its style. More
recently, because of its convenient length, the story has been an-

thologized many times; and Albert Guerard has called it an important, though flawed work, in which the traces of Conrad's personal accent can be heard for the first time. Then, too, the story has puzzled many readers because it closes on an ambiguous note. Since Arsat is free at the end to avenge his brother's killing and says quite plainly, "I am going back now," several critics have insisted that the final scene is the prelude to his act of redemption. According to this view, Arsat can prove his courage by dying honorably, and the end of the story is rich with the possibility of salvation. However, other readers, finding such optimism unconvincing, insist that the story ends more bleakly; for even if Arsat does return, he will receive little consolation from his act.[24] The price for betrayal has already been exacted.

If one reads "The Lagoon" with all the pertinent facts in mind, there seems no question that the darker reading is more convincing. The pertinent facts in this instance are both external and internal, facts about composition and structure. When Conrad was preparing the original version of "The Lagoon" for publication in book form, he made several verbal changes, one of which provides a clue to the tale's ultimate meaning. In the closing lines, with Arsat standing immobile, staring at the sun, the *Cornhill* version ends: "he was still looking through the great light of a cloudless day into the darkness of the world." In the book, however, the final line reads: "he looked beyond the great light of a cloudless day into the darkness of a world of illusions."[25] In all likelihood, Conrad revised the magazine version of "The Lagoon" in order to strengthen the thematic unity of the five stories in *Tales of Unrest*; for the idea of destructive dreams is central to four of the five pieces, and in the fifth, "Karain," a trick ending turns defeat into an unconvincing victory. "Illusions," then, is the last word of the story and of the book, both of which are concerned with the crippling nature of moral blindness.

By failing to understand the moral implications of his fatal choice and by thinking that a simple act of revenge will provide final retribution, Arsat remains a permanent victim of his inadequate dreams. This reading can be further supported by evidence from the story itself. Perhaps the most singular fact about the setting of "The Lagoon" is that it has an ominous life of its own, changing and growing more persuasively than the characters, functioning throughout as an ironical commentator on the actions of the human figures. At first, Conrad presents a land "from which the very memory of motion had forever departed." The lagoon is stagnant, the forest somber and full, the entire land caught in "an immobility perfect and final." In a "profound and dumb stillness," the "motionless and shadowy" Arsat tells the white man his story, "without a stir, without a gesture." At the very end, as he finishes, Arsat speaks in "a dreamy tone" of seeing "clear enough to strike," but he does not move.

Thomas Moser has argued that when Arsat finishes his narration, a breeze comes up and the landscape comes to life, suggesting the possibilities of redemption.[26] Admittedly, there are several carefully composed contrasts to the deadly stillness of Arsat's surroundings: the native polers think of him living among actively malevolent ghosts, while the white man fears that the country wears a "mask of unjustifiable violence." Moreover at the story's close, the sun rises, the "whisper of unconscious life" grows louder, and a white eagle soars magnificently into the blue sky. But this is an ironic contrast, for Arsat is left standing paralyzed, looking beyond the light and into a dark world of illusion. The way in which the light-and-dark motif works in "The Lagoon" (the searching sun illumines reality, while the darkness fosters illusion) suggests that, though Arsat achieves a degree of relief by telling his story to the white man, he is merely substituting one illusion for another. Even if he goes back to avenge his brother (and this, in context, is uncertain), the return will be in no sense triumphant. It is worth noting, too, that the word "return" occurs at critical moments in every story in *Tales of Unrest*; and in four of the five cases no return, physical or metaphorical, is possible. The Bacadous are defeated by biology, Kayerts and Carlier by innate stupidity, and Arsat by a defective moral sense (although some impatient readers may feel he is overwhelmed by the landscape).

Although the setting is the protagonist of "The Lagoon," there is another figure in the story worth watching, if not for his own sake, at least for his role in the development of Conrad's narrative technique. The white man, who listens to Arsat's story and appears to embody a moral position simply by standing around, is a shadowy precursor of a later, more familiar, figure. For the most part, he is merely a pair of eyes reporting and reflecting the physical scene; virtually every time he appears, Conrad follows with the words "he looked," "he gazed," "he saw," and so on. However, at one or two points in the story he seems ready to reveal some secret about that "unquiet and mysterious country of inextinguishable desires and fears"; but finally his reflections emerge as pure rhetoric, and we learn nothing from him that we had not already learned from the omniscient narrator.

"KARAIN"

Just after finishing "The Lagoon," Conrad wrote his first masterpiece, *The Nigger of the "Narcissus,"* in which a symbolic setting is subservient to a significant human action and in which the figure of the narrator (despite the notorious solecisms) is handled with impressive sophistication. And following *The Nigger*, he wrote his fifth short story, "Karain," a work which he claimed was "something like the Lagoon but with less description."[27] Although "Karain" looks small next to *The Nigger*, it is more ambitious than its Malay predecessor; for it solves some of the technical problems raised by the earlier stories and in many formal ways is the most accomplished piece in *Tales of Unrest*. There is a faint note struck in "The Lagoon" that is heard more fully in "Karain" and that eventually becomes a major theme in Conrad's work. In the earlier story, the reader is made vaguely aware that Arsat's tale of love and betrayal is to evoke a moral response from the white listener. In "Karain: A Memory," this response is perhaps the most important part of the story, and only recently have critics noticed its place in the development of Conrad's fictional technique.[28]

"Karain" is still another tale of duplicity, guilt, and illusion; but in this instance the illusions prove to be salutary. Karain and his friend Matara have spent many months hunting for Matara's sister and her perfidious lover, a Dutch planter. During the chase, under conditions of great hardship, Karain is sustained by an image of the lovely girl and troubled by Matara's intention to murder her. At last, when the couple is discovered, Matara gives Karain the only rifle and they plan an ambush, in which Karain is instructed to shoot the planter while Matara stabs the girl. But when Matara raises the knife for the kill, Karain shoots him instead of the Dutchman. When the girl fails to recognize him, Karain goes off disconsolate and torn by guilt, haunted by the ghost of his native friend. Some time later, after telling the story to three white men, he is given a talisman which exorcises the evil spirit and permits him to return to rule his people.

Although a simple plot summary of this kind might provide a fair notion of a story like "The Lagoon," it does not begin to convey the quality of "Karain." By placing the Malay story in a complex narrative frame, Conrad attempts to give it a universality that "The Lagoon" never achieves. The first clue to his intentions can be found in the title "Karain: A Memory," for it is in the memory of the white narrator that the Malay lives. The story opens with a deliberate, often charming contrast between past and present. The feeling of nostalgia for a better time is firmly established. Today's air is murky, yesterday's is exotic and perfumed; modern Englishmen are befogged and timid, their native contemporaries are frank, loyal, and courageous.

When Karain, now an impressive chieftain, comes aboard the narrator's ship to exchange greetings with the white friends who sell him firearms, he is described as being slightly larger than life, a tall, splendid figure, "made important by the power he had to awaken an absurd expectation of something heroic." For the first twenty-eight pages (half of the story), the narrator juxtaposes his description of Karain with remarks about the theatrical nature of heroism. In a bemused, nostalgic, ironical tone of voice, he longs for the old days when "we were imaginative enough to look with a kind of joyous equanimity on any chance there was of being quietly hanged somewhere out of the way of diplomatic remonstrance."

Although this narrator is not named, the voice belongs to Charlie Marlow, who will make his debut a year later in "Youth." For the first time in a Conrad story, the narrator has moved forward to share the stage with the central character in the drama; and from this point on, it is necessary to watch the teller as well as the tale.

One day, Karain comes aboard soaking wet. Pursued by the ghost of Matara, he has fled from his people and, in the central portion of the story, explains the murder to the white men. His story is interrupted when a crew member named Jackson, accidentally touching his guitar, fills the cabin with a plaintive resonance whose "confused vibrations died out slowly." One becomes aware of Jackson for the second time (he had been in the cabin earlier), and the interruption is similar to the calculated breaks Marlow and the narrator make in "Youth" and "Heart of Darkness." The resonance of the guitar itself is another metaphor for the atmospheric effect Conrad later called the kernel and the haze; and the appearance of Jackson at this point is a deliberate foreshadowing of the role he will play at the close of the story.

Haunted by the ghost of his friend, Karain wants asylum in the West. Once refused, he asks for a charm to keep off the demon, and the three Westerners feel like judges at the "gate of Infernal regions" called on "to decide the fate of a wanderer coming suddenly from a world of sunshine and illusions." Hollis decides to enjoy a joke at the native's expense. He decorates a sixpenny coin in ribbon and passes it off as a talisman. As the satisfied Karain walks off, the narrator repeats an image used earlier: "he left us, and seemed straightway to step into the glorious splendour of his stage, to wrap himself in the illusion of unavoidable success." Here, too, the narrator addresses the reader for the first time: "I wonder what they thought; what he thought . . . what the reader thinks?"

But the story does not end there. Seven years later, the narrator meets Jackson in the Strand.

"Do you remember Karain?"
I nodded. . . .
"I wonder whether the charm worked—you remember Hollis'

charm, of course. If it did . . . never was a sixpence wasted to better advantage! Poor devil! I wonder whether he got rid of that friend of his. Hope so. . . . Do you know, I sometimes think that—"
I stood still and looked at him.
"Yes . . . I mean, whether the thing was so, you know . . . whether it really happened to him. . . . What do you think?"
"My dear chap," I cried, "you have been too long away from home. What a question to ask! Only look at all this."

At this point, the narrator describes the commotion of the London Street, and Jackson replies:

"Yes; I see it. . . . It is there; it pants, it runs, it rolls; it is strong and alive; it would smash you if you didn't look out; but I'll be hanged if it is yet as real to me as . . . the other thing . . . say, Karain's story."
I think that, decidedly, he had been too long away from home.[29]

It is possible to see in this exchange the early development of Conrad's technique for treating moral discovery in terms of multiple consciousnesses. The experience has affected Jackson as well as the narrator, and the story's frame is a simplified version of that used in "Heart of Darkness." The reader is supposed to feel that Jackson's uneasiness offers a clue to the ultimate reality of the story. The theatrical posturings of Karain and his naive faith in charms are perhaps more real than the confusions of a crowded city street.

The theme of "Karain"—that illusions have the power to conquer remorse and guilt—connects it with all the other stories in *Tales of Unrest*; but it is, of course, the only one of the five stories that has a lighthearted ending. The native part of the tale is successful because the unsophisticated mentality reacting to a set of crucial actions is forcefully handled. But dissatisfaction arises from Conrad's ambitious attempt to establish a link between the primitive and civilized, between East and West. Somehow the gibes are always too playful, and certain exchanges are impossible to take seriously. Karain, for instance, says: "With you I will go. To your land—To your people. To your people, who live in unbelief; to whom day is day, and night is night—nothing more. . . . To your land of unbelief, where the dead do not speak, where every man is wise, and alone—and at peace!" "Capital description," murmured Hollis, with the flicker of a smile."[30] Strained passages such as this (and there are several) are reminiscent of inferior Kipling and W. W. Jacobs, a fact that Conrad seems to have known: "I am glad you like 'Karain,' " he once wrote to Cunninghame Graham, "I was afraid you would despise it. There's something magazine'ish about it. Eh?"[31]

There certainly is something magazinish about "Karain." Conrad begins to tell a serious tale of murder and remorse, but deliberately takes the edge off by using a slick, humorous ending to evade the full complexities of his theme. Hollis' "magic" coin is a Jubilee sixpence minted in 1888 to celebrate Victoria's fifty years as sovereign, and at times Conrad seems to be catering to a stock patriotic response: "She commands a spirit, too—the spirit of her nation; a masterful, conscientious, unscrupulous, unconquerable devil . . . that does a lot of good—incidentally . . . a lot of good. . . ."[32] Since "Karain" was written only four months before the celebration of Victoria's *sixtieth* jubilee in mid-June 1897, perhaps Conrad had hoped to capitalize on the excitement. In one sense, he succeeded very well. "Karain" was the first story he sold to *Blackwood's*, which must have been attracted by the royal high-jinks and topicality. The crafty Karain opens several conversations with pious references to the grand and invincible white queen; and the Kiplingesque ending, though ironical, is good-hearted enough to please the average magazine reader. Although it is possible to point to some larger Conradian ironies hidden behind the humor and to say that Conrad is having his little jest at the expense of the English as well as the Malays, these are not the main impressions of the story. We remember Victoria and her jubilee, not the suggestions of dark and horrible voids, or Jackson's musings on appearance and reality. As Albert Guerard has said, Lord Jim in his crime is one of us; Karain in his is only a slightly ridiculous, superstitious native.

In the last analysis the anecdote is more memorable than the serious theme in "Karain." Yet at the same time there is something admirably experimental about the story, something of the artist's testing things out in an effort to discover some of the possibilities of his material. Conrad's self-consciousness is well known, and a remark he made to William Blackwood some time after the publication of "Karain" has relevance to the early story. Speaking of his narrative method, Conrad told his publisher, "All my endeavors shall be directed to understand it better, to develop its great possibilities, to acquire greater skill in the handling—to mastery in short."[33] And it is in stories like "Karain"—with all its shortcomings —that this method was being explored.

"THE RETURN"

If Conrad's first Malayan tales are signposts showing where he was eventually to go, the last story of the early group is an excellent example of an artistic road not taken. One of the strangest works in the Conrad canon, "The Return" caused unbelievable mental anguish in composition, incurred the immediate displeasure of Edward Garnett, never appeared in serial form, and has recently been called "Conrad's worst story of any length, and one of the worst ever written by a great novelist."[34] Begun in early May 1897 just after the completion of "Karain," "The Return" treats the breakup of an upper-middle-class marriage, and is one of Conrad's few attempts to be what Ford called "a straight writer."

From the opening pages, the unfamiliar material proved intractable, and Conrad spoke of "groping through," of feeling "helpless" and "bewitched." Comparing the tale to an old man of the sea, he frantically told Blackwood, "I can't shake it off—but I am doing my best to murder it."[35] After it was finished, Conrad exchanged heated letters with Garnett, sometimes defending the story, but more often despairing of its existence. On September 27: "The work is vile—or else good. I don't know. I can't know. But I swear to you that I won't alter a line—a word—not a comma—for you. There! And this for the reason that I have a physical horror of that story. I simply won't look at it any more. It has embittered five months of my life. I hate it." [36] On September 29: "I've tried with all my might to avoid just these trivialities of rage and distraction which you judge necessary to the truth of the picture. I counted it a virtue, and lo and behold! You say it is a sin. Well! Never more! It is evident that my fate is to be descriptive and descriptive only. There are things I *must* leave alone."[37] After a few months, however, Conrad became less intense and was able to joke with Garnett: "You have missed the symbolism of the new gospel. . . . I've missed fame by a hair's breadth. And then we could have hired some chinaman of letters to explain that the whole story is transcendental symbolico-positivist with traces of illuminism."[38]

Many years later, describing the tale as "a left-handed production," Conrad suggested that there were sound psychological reasons for its composition.[39] His friend Ford added spice to the legend by claiming that in Conrad's eyes "The Return" was something "slightly obscene at which one could only peep in secret."[40] Why Conrad would write "The Idiots" and "The Return" within eighteen months of his own marriage is a question which can safely be left to his biographers.* But there are other questions that are more relevant to a study of his development as a writer.

In May 1897 Conrad was fresh from the serial success of *The Nigger of the "Narcissus"* and reasonably satisfied—despite difficulties—with "Karain" and the early promise of *The Rescuer.* The sudden, dramatic shift of subject and point of view in "The Return" is clearly provocative and even puzzling. Yet there are some possible answers. Since he had established contact with two rather sophisticated literary magazines, *Cosmopolis* and the *New Review,* and since he had just read, with admiration, *The Spoils of Poynton,* Conrad may have felt this an opportune moment to correct his popular journalistic stereotype, to alter his image as an exotic romancer, the Kipling or Stevenson of the Malay Archipelago. (At

---

* See Bernard Meyer, *Joseph Conrad: A Psychoanalytic Biography* (Princeton, 1967), for the most recent speculation.

present, when Conrad is so firmly established as a classic writer, it is hard to realize how many misconceptions and slanted judgments he had to face in his first decade as a novelist. For instance, in 1899— after he had published four books—the *Academy* felt obligated to set right a mistaken notion: "It has been stated that Mr. Joseph Conrad makes the first draft of his stories in a weird language compounded of Yiddish and other ingredients, and then translates it into English. Mr. Conrad does nothing of the kind. . . ."[41])

In July 1897, with "The Return" half done, Conrad was asked by *Blackwood's* for first refusal of any new work; yet, after agreeing about "Karain," he specifically excluded the new story from future negotiations, seemingly anxious to publish it where fiction was given greater pride of place. Once the tale was finished, Conrad asked Garnett whether he should send it to the *Yellow Book* or to *Chapman's Magazine,* a new monthly devoted only to fiction and designed by Chapman and Hall to do for short stories what their *Fortnightly Review* did for Victorian essays.

At first, the editor of *Chapman's* seemed interested, suggesting that the story might be printed in the Christmas number. He soon found it too long for one issue, however; and when Conrad refused under any circumstances to divide it, discussions were broken off. By early November, once it appeared that no one was especially anxious to print "The Return," Conrad defended it as "too good for any blamed magazine. . . . Fossils won't care for it. . . . I think it much too good to be thrown away where the *right people* won't see it."[42] By January 1898, both Unwin and Conrad had given up trying to serialize the story and agreed to publish it as the one new piece in *Tales of Unrest.* Conrad seemed to take the editorial resistance as proof of the story's boldness: " 'The Return' is not a tale for puppy dogs nor for maids of thirteen. I am not in the least ashamed of it. Quite the reverse."[43]

Admittedly, "The Return" is not a tale for maids or puppy dogs— nor, as time has proven, for critics.[44] Weakened by lifeless dialogue, an unconvincing setting, and tiresome characters, it is an extravagantly self-indulgent story, a work that would have been perhaps bearable only at one-third its length. But if we admit its weaknesses and instead study "The Return" as an object lesson, the experience can be useful and even illuminating.

In a characteristically vivid oversimplification, Conrad once divided human beings into two groups, the idiots and the convicts: "One must drag the ball and chain of one's selfhood to the end. It is the price one pays for the devilish and divine privilege of thought; so that in this life it is only the elect who are convicts—a glorious band which comprehends and groans but which treads the earth amidst a multitude of phantoms with maniacal gestures, with idiotic grimaces. Which would you be: idiot or convict?"[45] The typical idiot, with no dark spots on his soul, moves untroubled through life, accepting its gifts and its sorrows as they come. If circumstances permit, he is capable of heroic action; but his heroism is instinctive, rarely meditated, and never analyzed. His opposite, blessed and damned with reflective consciousness, is Conrad's convict.

Although Conrad wrote mainly about the glorious band of convicts, he did on occasion celebrate an heroic idiot; for example, Singleton in *The Nigger of the "Narcissus"* and MacWhirr in "Typhoon." And it was of the former that Conrad said, "he is simple and great like an elemental force. . . . Nothing can touch him,—he does not think." From time to time, however, Conrad dealt with another specimen of idiot—the man with neither consciousness nor heroic potential. Usually, Conrad recognized that such figures should be treated indirectly, condemned at a distance; and when they were, they became (like the hollow men and the papier-mâché Mephistopheles) triumphs of the satirist's art. But when Conrad failed to hold them at scalpel's point and made them major characters in a story, they were reduced to the stature of conventional melodramatic villains.

Alvan Hervey in "The Return" is such a figure. Successful, self-absorbed, and unthinking, he is compared to a "high-priest," who guards those rites and formulas which conceal "the black doubts of life." His career has been a series of petty triumphs over weak

opponents and needy men; while his marriage, built on social pro-
scriptions, has been a shallow fraud. Like Captain MacWhirr, who
sailed over the surface of the ocean ignorant of life, Hervey and
his wife "skimmed over the surface . . . like two skilful skaters . . .
disdainfully ignoring the hidden stream, the stream restless and
dark; the stream of life profound and unfrozen." Frightened of
the unexpected, they live among people who fear emotion, ec-
centricity, and failure far more than war or dreadful disease, people
for whom "all joys and sorrows are cautiously toned down into
pleasures and annoyances."

One afternoon, Hervey returns home to find a note from his
wife telling him she has run off with another man. Shattered by the
revelation, he collapses helplessly into a chair, but soon starts thinking about the social amenities and the impropriety of marital
scandal. When his wife returns and admits that she does not have
the courage to leave permanently, he has in his small way a spiritual
awakening, recognizing at last that "there can be no life without
faith and love—faith in a human heart, love of a human being."
But his wife refuses to share his new knowledge; as the story ends,
he leaves never to return.

Certainly, on its face, this is a suitable subject for fiction; however, the problem with "The Return" is not in the subject but in
the narrative method. Conrad once claimed that his desire in "The
Return" was to present "the gospel of the beastly bourgeois" and
to produce the effect of ice-cold artifice in Hervey's speeches. But
instead of dramatizing Hervey's shallowness, Conrad holds it up
for immediate disapproval. Thus Hervey is damned by relentless
(and tiresome) moral description, alienated from both our interest
and our sympathy before he has a chance to act. One is convinced
of his vacuity on the second page of the story; yet "The Return"
hobbles fitfully along for seventy pages more. And yet, once again,
it is an instructive failure, a revealing example of Conrad trying a
straightforward, analytical method and finding it uncongenial.
Obviously, he recognized that the technique was not suited to his
temperament. Although he had similar things to say about society

people in *The Rescue*, "Heart of Darkness," "The Informer," "The
Planter of Malata," and *Victory*, he never again said them in the
narrative form of "The Return."

*   *   *

Tales of Unrest is inchoate yet typical Conrad—inchoate in the
sense that it is marked by daring, diffuseness, energy, uncertainty,
and all the other signs of the apprentice hand; yet typical in that
most of the stories are based on memory and reminiscence, make
use of situations of murder and mayhem to examine problems of
conduct, and are enlivened by Conrad's theatrical sense of history.
Although in none of the early stories does Conrad achieve more
than a partial success, one can nevertheless trace a development
in his experiments. This development is generally a matter of trying
a form and finding it in one way or another restrictive: naturalistic
reporting by an omniscient narrator in "The Idiots"; direct ironic
commentary with a surprise ending in "An Outpost of Progress";
and an inward analytical method in "The Return." But in two
stories, at least, the development is clearly positive. "The Lagoon"
suggests that a symbolic setting can, if held in check, amplify theme;
while "Karain" shows that the use of several narrators can add
moral complexity to a melodramatic situation.

These first efforts can also lead toward a fuller definition of the
representative Conrad story. If Conrad is judged by the achievements of his contemporaries, he can hardly be called a short story
writer at all. "I know," he once told William Blackwood, "what I
am aiming at—and it is not pure story telling"; and this, of course,
seems to contradict what nearly every commentator on the genre
insisted was its prime function. Conrad was preoccupied with other
things, with psychological states and ideal values. Since he had no
desire to glorify the moment or to exploit the ironies of coincidence
and circumstance, he could not write *short* stories; in fact, none of
his finest works is less than 10,000 words long. But perhaps the
most obvious fact about Conrad's fiction is that it combines a raw
and melodramatic subject matter with an especially self-conscious

concern for moral analysis. Nearly all his works are explored melo-
dramas, often opening with mechanical stratagems and then set-
tling down to an investigation of the dilemmas of people caught in
extreme situations. One way of emphasizing Conrad's originality is
to recall Edith Wharton's insistence that "situation is the main concern of the short story, character of the novel." One distinguishing
feature of Conrad's best short stories is that they are about both.

Some years ago, Elizabeth Bowen wrote a memorable description
of the short stories of Hardy and James that is appropriate to those
by Conrad. She called their stories "side issues from the crowded
imagination" and went on to say: "They show, *qua* the short story,
no urgent aesthetic necessity; their matter does not dictate their
form. Their shortness is not positive; it is non-extension. They are
great architects' fancies, little buildings on an august plan. They
have no emotion that is abrupt and special; they do not give mood
or incident a significance outside the novelist's power to explore."[46]
In much the same way, Conrad's stories are also "novelist's short
stories"; their form is protean and does not follow a presribed
model. Many times during his lifetime, Conrad spoke out against
mechanistic fiction, tales cut from a book of patterns, and in his
own work used forms that would do fullest justice to the nature
of the particular subject. Yet *Tales of Unrest* suggests that Conrad
was working toward a *kind* of story form, fluid yet subject to control, which will be described at length in the following chapters.

There is still one question that should be raised in any attempt
to account for Conrad's stumbling in his earliest stories. How, after
works so steady as *Almayer's Folly* and *The Nigger of the "Narcissus,"* can the flaws in "Karain" be explained? And how can one
account for the fact that the actual plot or *donnée* of "The Lagoon" or "The Return" is very simple, while the finished product is
obviously padded and overblown? One possible answer is that Conrad made a distinction between a serious work on a Malayan theme
like *Almayer's Folly* and a more lighthearted piece like "Karain,"
seeing the first as a book aimed at a mature audience and the second as a slight magazine piece. It is impossible to have the last word
on a problem that is essentially one of intention; but my own view

is that at this stage in his career Conrad could not treat any work purely as a piece of commercial property. Despite his playful references to trading his soul for shekels, he did not actually become a victim of the public taste (and of his own desperate need for money) until later in his career. In a letter to a Polish friend, written just after he finished "The Return," Conrad defines his attitude toward popularity at this moment in his life:

I married about 18 months ago and since then I have worked without interruption. I have acquired a certain reputation—a literary one—but the future is still uncertain because I am not a popular author and I shall probably never become one. That does not depress me in the least as I have never had any ambition to write for the all-powerful masses.... I have gained the appreciation of a few chosen spirits and I shall eventually create my own public— limited of course, but large enough for me to earn my living. I do not dream of making a fortune and anyway it is not something to be found in an inkwell. However, I must confess that I dream of peace, of a little recognition and of devoting to Art the rest of a life that would be free from financial worries.[47]

When this letter and the early tales were written, the troublesome conflict between the demands of Conrad's complex artistic temperament and the single-minded requirements of the magazine market had not yet become critical. Although two of the stories were summarily written with specific writers and magazines in mind, the failures in *Tales of Unrest* are mainly of judgment and execution. "An Outpost of Progress" has a forced ending, "Karain" dissolves into a trivial anecdote, and "The Lagoon" is overwritten; yet there is no need to dismiss them as mere potboilers. They are too intense and varied to come from the hand of a writer primarily concerned with money.

3
The Major Stories

Although Conrad managed to complete only "Youth" and three short articles in 1898, the year marks the end of his apprenticeship and the beginning of a seven-year period in which he produced some of his finest stories and novels. In May he wrote "Youth" and probably started *Lord Jim*; during the summer, he continued working on the novel and on the middle sections of *The Rescue*; in September, he met Ford Madox Ford and collaborated on *The Inheritors*; and by Christmas, he had written the early pages of "Heart of Darkness." *Lord Jim*, which begins the period, and *Nostromo*, which ends it, are among his most ambitious novels; and the stories in the two collections that fall between are among his finest achievements in the genre of short fiction.

One way to approach the increasing maturity of these works is to suggest that in writing *The Nigger of the "Narcissus"* (1896–1897), Conrad made several important discoveries about the essential subject matter of his novels and stories. To explain the nature of these discoveries, Conrad himself offers a useful starting point.

EGOISM VS ALTRUISM

On August 24, 1901, vexed by several misleading statements appearing in a review of *The Inheritors*, his collaboration with Ford, Conrad wrote a long letter to the correspondence columns of the *New York Times*. To my knowledge this letter has never been reprinted, and I quote a substantial portion of it here not only because it obviously deserves renewed currency, but because it has helped shape the interpretations of Conrad's stories offered in the remaining chapters of this study. After a few traditional courtesies, Conrad goes directly to the main point:

It may perhaps be permissible to point out that the story is not directed against "some of the most cherished traditions and achievements of Englishmen." It is rather directed at the self-seeking, at the falsehood that had been (to quote the book) "hiding under the words that for ages had spurred men to noble deeds, to self-sacrifice, and to heroism." And, apart from this view, to direct one's little satire at the tradition and the achievement of a race would have been an imbecile futility—something like making a face at the great pyramid. Judge them as we may, the spirit of tradition and the body of achievement are the very spirit and the very body not only of any single race, but of the entire mankind, which, without the vast breadth and colossal form of the past would be resolved into a handful of the dying, struggling feebly in the darkness under an overwhelming multitude of the dead. Thus our Etchingham Granger, when in the solitude that falls upon his soul, he sees the form of the approaching Nemesis, is made to understand that no man is permitted to "throw away with impunity the treasure of his past—the past of his kind—whence springs the promise of the future."

This is the note struck—we hoped with sufficient emphasis—among the other emotions of the hero. And, besides, we may appeal to the general tone of the book. It is not directed against tradition; still less does it attack personalities. The extravagance of its form is meant to point out forcibly the materialistic exaggeration of individualism, whose unscrupulous efficiency it is the temper of the time to worship.

It points it out simply—and no more; because the business of a work striving to be art is not to teach or to prophecy, (as we have been charged, on this side, with attempting,) nor yet to pronounce a definite conclusion.

This, the teaching, the conclusions, even to the prophesying, may be safely left to science, which, whatever authority it may claim, is not concerned with truth at all, but with the exact order of such phenomena as fall under the perception of the senses. Its conclusions are quite true enough if they can be made useful to the furtherance of our little schemes to make our earth a little more habitable. The laws it discovers remain certain and immovable for the time of several generations. But in the sphere of an art dealing with a subject-matter whose origin and end are alike unknown there is no possible conclusion. The only indisputable truth of life is our ignorance. Besides this there is nothing evident, nothing absolute, nothing uncontradicted; there is no principle, no instinct, no impulse that can stand alone at the beginning of things and look confidently to the end. Egoism, which is the moving force of the world, and altruism, which is its morality, these two contradictory instincts of which one is so plain and the other so mysterious cannot serve us unless in the incomprehensible alliance of their irreconcilable antagonism. Each alone would be fatal to our ambition. For in the hour of undivided triumph one would make our inheritance too arid to be worth having and the other too sorrowful to own.

Fiction, at the point of development at which it has arrived, demands from the writer a spirit of scrupulous abnegation. The only legitimate basis of creative work lies in the courageous recognition of all the irreconcilable antagonisms that make our life so enigmatic, so burdensome, so fascinating, so dangerous—so full of hope. They exist! And this is the only fundamental truth of fiction. Its recognition must be critical in its nature, inasmuch that in its character it may be joyous, it may be sad, it may be angry with revolt, or submissive in resignation. The mood does not matter. It is only the writer's self-forgetful fidelity to his sensations that matters. But, whatever light he flashes on it, the fundamental truth remains, and it is only in its name that the barren struggle of contradictions assumes the dignity of moral strife going on ceaselessly to a mysterious end—with our consciousness powerless but concerned sitting enthroned like a melancholy parody of eternal wisdom above the dust of the contest.[1]

At first glance, this familiar mixture of eloquence, vague generalization, and heightened commonplace resembles many of Conrad's famous expository statements: several of the pieces in *Notes on Life and Letters*, the twenty author's notes to his collected works, or even the more formidable preface to *The Nigger of the "Narcissus."* Moreover, such essays as these—not Conrad's fiction—prompted E. M. Forster's complaint that "the secret casket of his genius contains a vapour rather than a jewel; and that we need not try to write him down philosophically, because there is, in this particular direction, nothing to write. No creed, in fact. Only opinions." Yet by looking closely at the statements in this forgotten letter, one can discover that Conrad is trying not only to describe a familiar rhythm in human life but also an important unifying theme in his own fiction. If he is not offering a creed, he is at least setting forth some revealing ideas about his response to the mysteries of human character and conduct.

The passage expresses Conrad's belief that the main role of the writer is to recognize and to describe the irreconcilable antagonism between egoism, the moving force of the world, and altruism, its essential morality. To be sure, on its face this is hardly a novel idea. In one sense or another, much of the great literature of the world can be discussed in such polarities, and the ethical struggle described here has been analyzed by countless thinkers from the beginning of human history. Yet, in fiction, Conrad treats this theme in a fresh and distinctive way, and after 1897 it is the foundation on which all his major work is built. There is, in fact, a correlation between the way the theme is handled and the success of a particular novel or story. In Conrad's best work, the conflict between egoism and altruism is elaborately developed; in his worst, it is either inchoate or nonexistent.

Conrad seems to have adopted the definitive terms for his argument from Schopenhauer and Nietzsche, and not from the earlier classical philosophers who wrote extensively on the same problem. While older writers used such pairings as self-interest *versus* benevolence, self-love *versus* charity, and so on, Schopenhauer and

Nietzsche placed the discussion within a more modern framework from which Conrad clearly borrowed. In his volume, *Ethical Reflections*, Schopenhauer expresses the problem in its most succinct form: "The question as to whether morality is something real is the question whether a well-grounded counter principle to egoism actually exists. As egoism restricts concern for welfare to a single individual, *viz.* the man's own self, the counter principle would have to extend it to all other individuals."[2] And then, in the concluding sections of the revised edition of *The World as Will and Idea*, Schopenhauer uses several different terms: ego, eros, and selfishness to set off against love or sympathy. Nietzsche, choosing to quarrel with a writer who had meant a great deal to him, insisted on equating sympathy with pity and later with altruism. Seeing altruism as a threat to the will to power, Nietzsche called it a morality of decadence, emphasizing its contemptuous and condescending elements, its weak-minded sentimentality.

Without being systematic, Conrad's novels and stories are a set of responses to Schopenhauer's questions: Does a well-grounded counterprinciple to egoism actually exist? and if so, what is its nature? But before discussing the exact nature of that response, it would be useful to define in a preliminary way the varieties of egoism and altruism as they appear in Conrad's fiction.

As the great force of energy in the Conradian universe, egoism—self-interest or the instinct of self-preservation—is responsible for every creative as well as every destructive act, for acts of sanctity and acts of damnation, for all good and evil: "*C'est égoïsme qui sauve tout,—absolument tout, tout ce que nous abhorrons, tout ce que nous aimons.*"* Although the possibilities for the expression of egoism in human life are infinite, Conrad comes back again and again to similar patterns of response. Although he admits the creative component of human egoism, he does not usually deal—as Joyce or Lawrence so memorably do—with the artist, the saint, or the affirmative rebel. Rather, he is continually preoccupied with five different kinds of restrictive or self-destructive egoists, each of

---

* Conrad's entire letter to R. B. Cunninghame Graham (Feb. 8, 1899), from which this sentence is taken, is relevant to the subject. See Jean-Aubry, I, 268–270.

whom he felt was exemplary for his generation and for the new century.

When Marlow, anxiously nearing Kurtz, is startled by the young Russian harlequin, he confesses admiration and envy for a young man so "gallantly, thoughtlessly alive, to all appearance indestructible solely by virtue of his few years and his unreflecting audacity:"

He surely wanted nothing from the wilderness but space to breathe in and to push on through. His need was to exist, and to move onwards at the greatest possible risk, and with a maximum of privation. If the absolutely pure, uncalculating, unpractical spirit of adventure had ever ruled a human being, it ruled this be-patched youth. I almost envied him the possession of this modest and clear flame. It seemed to have consumed all thought of self so completely, that even while he was talking to you, you forgot that it was he—the man before your eyes—who had gone through those things.[3]

Because his primal energies are directed against the objective challenge of the natural world, the harlequin represents the natural or instinctive egoist in Conrad's fiction. Basically uninterested in other human beings, his major goal in life is to test his courage against the inexorable challenge of his physical environment, an encounter in which success depends not on money, reputation, or power over people, but on the hero's self-reliance and adaptability. In those rare moments when he does become involved with other people, he is essentially childlike, passive, or withdrawn, and may—in fact—be threatened with the loss of his spontaneity. In different forms, this clear and modest flame burns often in Conrad's stories. Young Marlow in "Youth," full of ignorance and hope, determines to prove his strength against the sea on the battered *Judea*, which in his imagination "was not an old rattletrap carting about the world a lot of coal for a freight—[but] endeavor, the test, the trial of life."

In his capacity for selfless dedication, the natural egoist is potentially heroic, yet his heroism is of a distinctly limited kind.

There is, as Marlow admits in *Lord Jim*, a "magnificent vagueness," "a glorious indefiniteness" in the egoism of adventurers "that is their own and only reward." Glamorous, perhaps even spectacular, such a hero is also quite vulnerable, even at times, a fool. His purity depends on his living in a world of casual connection, a private world devoid of meaningful relationships with other people. Although the harlequin and young Marlow are in many ways different men, they are among the most personally appealing of Conrad's egoists because they share that kind of single-minded self-concern which is never a threat to the well-being of others.

Simplicity is also a characteristic of Conrad's second kind of egoist, but in this instance the trait inspires astonishment rather than envy or admiration. The simple-minded, unimaginative egoist is often a respected member of society with a strong instinct for self-preservation and an unthinking trust in the routine organization of civilized life. Displaying in his self-righteous rectitude, the "semi-conscious egoism of all safe, established existences," he can occasionally escape calamity in spite of himself, for his survival is due almost entirely to fool's luck. To Conrad's mind, such blustering self-confidence makes these men ludicrous; not only are they blind to the meaning of ordinary experience, they comically make virtues out of their most obvious deficiencies. Of this type, perhaps the most famous instances are the Captains Mitchell and MacWhirr. "Fussy Joe" Mitchell, the delightfully pompous superintendent of the Oceanic Steam Navigation Company in *Nostromo*, blunders his way through the political upheavals of Costaguana and lives to be the nation's unofficial bourgeois historian, offering a version of anarchy that is stereotyped and ironically incorrect; while the "fortunate" MacWhirr, "ignorant of life to the last," triumphantly leads his stricken ship through a typhoon.

A third distinct egotistical type in Conrad's fiction is the man driven primarily by desire for money, sex, or power. This figure, who appears first as the protagonist of *Almayer's Folly* and then turns up in one disguise or another in all of Conrad's novels, is defined not so much by his actions as by the quality or intensity of his desires. Almayer and Willems; the members of the Eldorado

Exploring Expedition in "Heart of Darkness"; Montero, Sotillo, Gemacho, and Fuentes (the operatic generals of Costaguana); De-Barral in *Chance* and Travers in *The Rescue*—they are all rapacious egotists, grasping, inordinately greedy men whose greatest imaginative feats rest in conjuring up women, political power, or "in a flash of dazzling light great piles of shining guilders." Despite a certain individual narrowness of range, Conrad's gallery of rapacious egotists has great variety. Beginning with casual cut-throats like Babalatchi and Ricardo, it moves on to include truculent malingerers like Donkin, and achieves one of its finest moments with Mr. Brown, a buccaneer so audacious and scornful of the human race that he seemed to be "moved by some complex intention." In a sense, these men resemble the simple-minded egotists in that they are less important as figures in their own right than they are in relationship with characters of greater magnitude. Just as MacWhirr must have his Jukes and Mitchell his Nostromo, so the full extent of DeBarral's cupidity is properly felt only through its effect on his daughter; and Mr. Brown would be a squalid adventurer if he had not helped destroy Lord Jim.

Although closely related to materialists like Almayer, the characters in the last two categories are distinguished by a more complex intention and a different capacity for image-making. Instead of envisioning only wealth and beautiful women, they dignify their desires by raising them to the level of abstract ideas. An obsessive egoist like Charles Gould in *Nostromo* idealizes the existence and value of his San Tomé mine and finally becomes its victim. Knowledgeable and without sentimentality when he first comes to Costaguana, Gould seems to have a clearer sense of the fatal duplicities of South American public life than any other foreigner in Sulaco. Becoming obsessed, however, with a desire to absolve his guilt at the death of his father, he gradually sees the mine itself as a formidable weapon in the war to achieve "a better justice." His passion both for the weapon and its putative power leads him to blur important moral distinctions; and by adopting a pose of taciturnity to avoid introspection, he gradually learns to accommodate every manifestation of political evil.

If Charles Gould were an ordinary industrialist with a capacity for hard work, success, and self-deception, he would have been a figure of minor interest for Conrad. But he towers above his kind because of his inability to act "without idealizing every simple feeling, desire, or achievement. He could not believe his own motives if he did not make them first a part of some fairy-tale." It is the potency of the fairy tale that gives Gould his impressive magnitude as a character. Having begun as a reliable interpreter of Costaguanan life, he ends as one of the most deluded figures in its history, never learning one of Conrad's fundamental lessons—that the universal city must be built on foundations more permanent than material interests. Admittedly, Gould achieves a tarnished success, but only after sacrificing the love of his wife and his own peace of mind to his messianic mission. Thus the bold and practical administrator is transformed into a compulsive idealist, the man whose "fits of abstraction depicted the energetic concentration of a will haunted by a fixed idea." And, as Conrad insists, "a man haunted by a fixed idea is insane. He is dangerous even if that idea is the idea of justice; for may he not bring the heaven down pitilessly upon a loved head?" Hallucinations of a similar kind, though of different degree, are acted out in the lives of Kurtz and Nostromo.

The last familiar egoist who appears regularly in Conrad's novels has traits in common with Gould and his kind, but is different in several important respects. Whereas an obsessive egoist like Gould begins with a set of fixed notions about society and acts from an ideal conception of his role as the chosen savior, the sequestered egoist has an ideal conception of his own worth which at first tempts him to reject society and turn his back on the world. Razumov, Axel Heyst, and Martin Decoud are the most obvious examples of the latter type, for their common egoism is a product of a belief that intellectual detachment is possible. For instance, the superior distance of Decoud is based on scorn. During his formative years, Decoud's ironical sense of mixed motives and human frailty had been so highly developed that he was inevitably forced into the role of the mocking observer. However, on his return to Costaguana, he is seduced by love and an unformulated ambition into playing a public role for which his early training has been unsatisfactory. Retaining his defense of complete knowledgeability and sophistication, he can at almost any moment analyze with devastating exactitude the moral pretensions of other people; and at times, he is able to view his own motives even more harshly. For a while, his skepticism makes him seem invulnerable to self-deception; but, of course, the irony has always been double-edged: "he had pushed the habit of universal raillery to a point where it blinded him to the genuine impulses of his own nature." Having become the victim of an ideal conception of his own skepticism, he commits suicide when surrounded by the emptiness of the Golfo Placido. It is almost as if his fate had been designed to prove Kierkegaard's adage that irony is an abnormal growth; like the enlarged liver of the Strasbourg goose, it ends by killing the individual.

These, then, are the five kinds of egoists in Conrad's fiction. In the representative plots of his novels and stories, such figures are brought into elaborate and irreconcilable conflict with characters who represent, to one degree or another, the altruistic impulse in human nature. These altruists also reappear from book to book and can be broadly typed, although not as specifically as the egoists.

If Conrad finds egoism the most obvious force of energy in the universe, then altruism (its essential morality) is something mysterious, just short of miraculous, and he invariably speaks of it with reverence. Yet despite the vagueness that steals into his prose whenever the word appears, Conrad would probably have accepted the preliminary description offered by Schopenhauer in *The World as Will and Idea*:

Thus genuine goodness of disposition, disinterested virtue, and pure nobility, do not proceed from abstract knowledge. Yet they do proceed from knowledge; but it is a direct intuitive knowledge, which can neither be reasoned away, nor arrived at by reasoning, a knowledge which, just because it is not abstract, cannot be communicated, but must arise in each for himself, which therefore finds *its real and adequate expression not in words, but only in deeds, in conduct, in the course of the life of man.* We who here seek the theory of virtue, and have therefore also to express abstractly the nature of the knowledge which lies at its foundation, will yet be unable to convey that knowledge itself in this expression. We can only give the concept of this knowledge, and thus always start from action in which alone it becomes visible, and refer to action as its only adequate expression.[4]

Because Conrad also believed that the altruistic impulse could be understood only by studying its expression in concrete action, the simplest way for us to grasp the strengths and weaknesses of a complex altruist is to examine his conduct.

Having little use for theories or abstract ideas, Emilia Gould acts intuitively, filling her daily life with small but compassionate gestures. At one moment, she works to save an old man's house from the path of a new railroad; while at another, she offers her arm to a weary patriot in a symbolic movement of support. Perhaps the best summary of her conduct comes from Doctor Monygham: "She thinks of me; of the wounded; of the miners; she always thinks of everybody who is poor and miserable." Yet such self-forgetfulness and human concern does not exist in a vacuum. By the close of the novel, after great personal disappointment, Mrs. Gould has learned the chief tenet of Conrad's mature altruism: that every human action takes place in an elaborate moral continuum, and that "for life to be large and full it must contain the care of the past and of the future in every passing moment of the present. Our daily work must be done to the glory of the dead, and for the good of those who come after." Such imagination—the ability to be "learned in the lessons of the past, concerned with the present, and earnest as to the future"—is denied to the typical egoist, and its presence is one of the identifying marks of the complex altruist in Conrad's fiction.

Still another sign is the sense of balance or moderation. Recognizing that his powers are limited, the hero tries to exercise his disinterested virtue in immediate personal relationships and not through institutional charity or in revolutionary movements that hope to reform the world. Dickens' Mrs. Jellyby with her natives from Borrioboola-Gha, as well as Conrad's own Peter Ivanovitch, are altruistic pretenders who are expressing a profound, if latent, egoism in the name of some higher philanthropy. This brand of humanitarianism is, to Conrad's mind, the diseased product of "crazy nerves or a morbid conscience."

Although self-forgetfulness is an attractive quality in a heroine like Mrs. Gould, it can obviously have serious drawbacks. Once, in a letter to a friend, Conrad explained the view that has since become familiar through such novels as *The Nigger of the "Narcissus"*: "Unfortunately . . . abnegation carried to an extreme . . . is not only profoundly immoral but dangerous, in that it sharpens the appetite for evil in the malevolent and develops (perhaps unconsciously) that latent human tendency towards hypocrisy in the . . . let us say, benevolent." As we shall see, the perils of altruism, as well as the virtues of egoism, were from the start among Conrad's essential subjects.

The strengths, then, of the complex altruist are constancy, courage, historical imagination, capacity for self-sacrifice, and a genuine concern for the welfare of other people. His defects are often docility, suffocating self-denial, and—worst of all—virtual defenselessness against the most aggressive forms of egoism. Mrs. Gould, remarkable for her loyalty, is perhaps even more memorable for her impotence and ultimate disillusionment. Although exasperated by the savagery of life in Costaguana, she can do little to relieve it; and she ends much like a "good-fairy, weary with a long career of well-doing, touched by the withering suspicion of the uselessness of her labours, the powerlessness of her magic."

A word should be said here about a less elaborate altruistic impulse that sometimes appears in one of Conrad's characters. In this instance, the sense of historical continuity is absent and a person instinctively performs an act of charity. Conrad is likely to express his admiration for the uncomplicated altruist, especially since he believes an act of genuine benevolence occurs infrequently enough. Yet, for reasons of development, he rarely makes such a figure the hero of one of his stories.*

THE EGOIST IN CONRAD'S EARLY NOVELS

The simplest way to see the difference between an adequate and an inadequate handling of the egoism-altruism theme is to compare *Almayer's Folly* and *An Outcast of the Islands* with *The Nigger of the "Narcissus."* In the two Malayan novels the subject is introduced in a fragmentary way, whereas in *The Nigger* it is given full treatment for the first time in Conrad's career. Although the comparison of novels in a study of the short stories may seem digressive, it will help to establish the exact nature of a major Conradian theme.

As a gallery of egoists, *Almayer's Folly* is impressive but incomplete; and although the image of egoism in the novel is often forceful, it is too restricted because many of the counterprinciples necessary for the full expression of Conrad's duality are not adequately developed. Virtually all the people in the novel are drawn from three classes of egoist and, with one or two exceptions, are treated in a repetitious and ultimately tiresome way. Almayer himself, lamentably drunk with self-pity and stranded in Sambir, has one dream and one dream only: a luminous vision of wealth and power in which he and his half-caste daughter will return to Europe rich and respected. In the singularity of his desire, he is a rapacious egoist whose enormous greed becomes the shaping idea of his life; but because he has an active and powerful imagination, he occasionally transforms himself into an obsessive egoist, a higher figure in Conrad's gloomy pantheon. When the novel opens, he is without genuine prospects and sunk in an atmosphere of squalid neglect,

---

* Simple-minded altruists who are revealed to be more comic than effectual appear from time to time in Conrad's fiction. See *Victory*, p. 20. I am aware that Conrad did not conceive of his characters according to the catagories I have described here. My "typing" is simply a convenient way to point up his preoccupation with a major theme and to make certain recurrent thematic strands clearer to the reader.

but he retains his limitless capacity for futile dreaming. Continually threatened with an absolute paralysis of will, "ruined and helpless under the close-meshed net of native intrigues," he always (until the last catastrophe) manages to conjure up at least one more compelling dream. Misguided, obviously; but in Conrad's eyes a man remarkable by "force of conviction and admirable consistency," an example of "that discord between the imagination in man and his ability to perform."

The best thing about Conrad's portrait of Almayer is the way in which the man is brought, inexorably, from a state of choked fury to his final condition of dreadful immobility and death. As his story comes to a close, a deadly cold creeps into his heart, and his face "seemed to know nothing of what went on within: like the blank wall of a prison enclosing sin, regrets, and pain, and wasted life, in the cold indifference of mortar and stones." Yet although the decline and fall of Almayer is memorable, it is not particularly sonorous; he drops from the curb into the gutter, whereas Conrad's most successful heroes are usually given more room in which to destroy themselves. The basic conflicts of his life are between different kinds of cupidity and blindness, between inadequate dreams and veiled though inescapable political realities. The complex forces that would have given his story more fullness are simply not present in his character or in his situation. He remains a stark but essentially limited study of the most familiar kind of human vulnerability.

The minor characters in *Almayer's Folly* are also greedy egoists, or in some instances merely simple-minded ones. Lakamba, Babalatchi, and Abdulla are refreshingly comic in their instinctive mixture of candor and cunning, and Mrs. Almayer is ghastly by token of her barbarous simplicity. Dain might have offered possibilities for greater development; yet he too remains a product of his heritage—reckless, savage, and simple. None of the natives emerges from the narrow world of "heavy work, fierce love, and general intrigue," and they never provide anything more than the most obvious kind of counterpoint. In the early activities of Lingard there are hints of a possible altruistic motif, but this is not worked out in the nov-

el; and as we learn from later works Lingard's charity is of a highly
problematical nature.

There is, however, one figure in *Almayer's Folly* whose development is clearly liberating for Conrad's art. Because she is torn by
conflicts that can be extended beyond the province of pure greed,
Nina Almayer, who resembles the heroes of Conrad's more famous
books, remains the only character in *Almayer's Folly* challenged
by problems of a complex kind. Before she had been sent to school
in Singapore and despite her mixed parentage, Nina was a typical
Malay girl, poised, self-contained, but with a "vague suggestion
of ferocity" in her impatient glances. On her return, however, people noticed that her intense, startled expression was "modified by
a thoughtful tinge inherited from her European ancestry." Just
as her years in Sambir brought out her native qualities, so her stay
in Singapore accentuated those traits derived from her father. Unhappily, Nina's education had been wholly inadequate, leaving her
torn between a shallow knowledge of Western culture and the powerful attraction of her Malay heritage. Whereas her mother had,
at least, the consolations of worshipping a piece of brass, Nina,
"brought up under the Protestant wing of the proper Mrs. Vinck,"
does not have even that; and at a desperate moment, the "narrow
mantle of civilized morality . . . fell away and left her shivering and
helpless." As the novel gets under way, Nina's Christian education,
which had permitted a few seductive glimpses of civilized life,
proves an unequal match for the atmosphere of Sambir, with its
"disgusting intrigues for lust and money."

After having been back in Sambir for three years, Nina can see
no difference between Christianity and barbarism, but only the
"same manifestations of love and hate and of sordid greed chasing
the uncertain dollar in all its multifarious and vanishing shapes."
Once "unskilfully permitted to glance at better things and then
thrown back in the hopeless quagmire of barbarism," she loses her
power to discriminate and, in fact, now prefers the savage sincerity
of her Malay kinsman to the effeminate, cultivated hypocrisy of the
white people she has met. Yet even after she has made her choice,

rejecting West for East, she cannot restore the shattered continuity of her life. Time and again, Conrad describes her predicament in terms of a struggle between her old existence and her new. The past, which she automatically equates with the hateful experience in the Singapore schools, is now a bed of cold ashes out of which her hopes for a happy present and splendid future can grow. Because of her love for Dain, "she threw away . . . her past with its sad thoughts, its bitter feelings and its faint affections, now withered and dead in contact with her fierce passion." And yet we know that, according to Conrad, no person—whether Malay or European—can afford to throw away his past, however ambiguous it may be.

Nina's fate, then, is unfortunate. Since she has not been trained well enough and lacks a usable tradition, she is pathetically isolated even in her escape with Dain. To be sure, the end of the novel is ambiguous: Is Nina supposed to live happily as a Rajah's wife, or is she destined eventually to be ill-treated as one of his concubines? Most likely the latter.* But however that may be, Nina was one of the first figures through whom Conrad could express some of his fundamental attitudes about life. Finally, though, her characterization is a disappointment; for after being the center of a struggle between Christian morality and native barbarism, she is reduced mid-way in the novel to a stock figure in a conventional love story. Occupied by Almayer's fate and Nina's romantic passion for Dain, Conrad let a major theme of the early part of the book remain undeveloped. There is still another sense, too, in which the handling of these materials is inchoate. In a later work like "Heart of Darkness," Conrad could use Kurtz and Marlow to represent two potential alternatives to the call of the wilderness; but in *Almayer's Folly* the theme is not viable because Nina's teachers —the representatives of Christian society—are unimpressive figures, and the unrestrained passions of the Malays win easily. Once Nina

* In an interesting essay, "Conrad's *Almayer's Folly*: Structure, Theme, and Critics" (*Nineteenth-Century Fiction*, June 1964), John Hicks argues the other side of the case. But the darkness of Nina's future is predicted by her mother and seems more in keeping with the closing mood of the book.

lapses into the savage mood, she is possessed by a force which "the genius of civilization working by the hand of Mrs. Vinck could never destroy."

It can be seen, then, that the major ethical struggles in *Almayer's Folly* are dramatized in the lives of two memorable yet restricted egoists, Almayer and Nina; and for this reason Conrad's remarkable first novel lacks range in precisely those areas where the works of his maturity are so successful. *An Outcast of the Islands* is (in this one respect at least) an advance on the earlier book, for here Conrad extends his range as a moralist. The conventional judgment of the second novel—that it is *Almayer's Folly* spilled into a bottle twice the size—is close enough to the truth to remain permanent. Little can be done to redeem the saga of the lamentable Willems, except perhaps as Carol Reed has done it, for the movies. If a reader wants Conrad in his early Malayan phase, *Almayer's Folly* offers adequate proportions of tangled vegetation and tormented castaways to satisfy a taste for the picturesque.

However, *An Outcast of the Islands* is an important novel in Conrad's development. Since 1950, several critics have argued persuasively that in choosing Almayer and Willems for heroes, Conrad was seduced by characters of minor importance and missed Tom Lingard, clearly a more fascinating subject. That Lingard is "the lost subject" of the Malayan trilogy (which ends with *The Rescue* twenty-three years later) is now well established. Yet it would be useful to look again at the backward progression of the three novels; for despite Conrad's failure to conceive of Lingard's character in a consistent or satisfactory way, the effort itself was not wholly without substantial benefits.

Just as Nina Almayer is a fragmentary version of several later heroes caught in the destructive contradictions of two cultures, so Tom Lingard is Conrad's first hesitant effort at what eventually was to become his finest creation—the romantic egoist obsessed with an ideal conception of his own fate. Unhappily, the process of development is slow to get started and then beset by difficulties and false leads. Not only does Conrad approach Lingard in a peculiarly oblique way (first at the end of his career in *Almayer's Folly*, then a few years younger in *An Outcast*, and finally as a vigorous young man in *The Rescue*); but in connecting the three portraits, Conrad's memory slips just often enough to make the character extremely difficult to interpret.

It seems clear that when Conrad described old Lingard in *Almayer's Folly*, he had only the vaguest idea of the dilemmas that would face the young captain in *The Rescue*. In his earliest appearance, Lingard is a major presence but a minor character, a retrospective hero whose feats of audacity are now legendary. Except for our sense of his importance in the action that led up to Almayer's present difficulties, we have little notion of Lingard's identity and, by the end of the novel, know only that his prospects are ruined. Without moving from the arena of Sambir, one can never get an altogether clear idea of his motives. To say, as one critic does, that in *Almayer's Folly* Lingard is "a sentimental egoist who derives a self-sustaining gratification from 'arranging' and 'improving' the lives of others," is to use knowledge that comes from another novel.

An Outcast of the Islands does give us a good deal more, which serves to make Lingard three-dimensional and increasingly difficult to understand; but since the captain is a secondary figure, he can only be approached indirectly. "The theme," Conrad once said of his second novel, "is the boundless, mad vanity of an ignorant man who has been successful but is without principle or any motive other than the satisfaction of his own vanity."[5] In the singularity of his ignorance and conceit, Peter Willems is the most unmistakable portrait of a rapacious egoist in Conrad's fiction. With nothing more than his own conscience and the doctrine of material success to guide him, he never acts from any motive other than personal expediency. His malice has force; his petty exploits variety; and his quest for physical satisfaction a certain ferocious energy. Yet, as the central character of a very long novel, Willems suffers from being static and predictable: No matter how fate treats him, he responds with sullen resentment, lack of judgment, and unwarranted confidence in his own superiority. Neither his relationship with Almayer nor his debilitating affair with Aissa allow much room for development, for all three participants have no genuine capacity for surprise. Conrad himself admitted that both Willems and Aissa are simple conceptions, "typical of mankind where every individual wishes to assert his power, woman by sentiment, man by achievement of some sort—mostly base." If, then, in reading *An Outcast of the Islands* we concentrate solely on Willems, or even on his protracted affair with Aissa, we are left after nearly 400 pages, with an image of the hero as bad example, a type that Conrad confessed was not very near to his heart.

There is a more absorbing subject in the relationship between Willems and Lingard. Contrary to his normal practice when dealing with complex figures, Conrad first introduces Lingard in a passage of such obvious criticism that one would think his heroic potential is permanently destroyed: "Tom Lingard was a master, a lover, a servant of the sea. The sea took him young, fashioned him body and soul; gave him his fierce aspect, his loud voice, his fearless eyes, his stupidly guileless heart. Generously it gave him his absurd faith in himself, his universal love of creation, his wide indulgence, his contemptuous severity, his straightforward simplicity of motive and honesty of aim."[6] And yet, as the most fabulous trader in the South Seas, Lingard remains a figure of considerable authority. Once he decides to rehabilitate the seventeen-year-old Willems, a conflict emerges that has a wider range of suggestiveness than almost any other in the novel. Lingard helps Willems twice: first, when he finds the half-starved young boy alone on a quay in Samarang and again, some years later, after Willems has been dismissed by his boss for petty theft. The first act of charity is whimsical, motivated more by instinctive pity for a stranded animal than by any complex sense of benevolence. The second act is more equivocal. Even the guileless old captain has had sufficient experience with Willems' devious ways to recognize his incorrigibility. Yet he offers the man still another chance for salvation, this time by sending him off to live in Sambir, possessed of the valuable secret of his trading source. Willems' violation of trust is only a matter of time; it had been inevitable from the start. In a curious way the two men turn out to be made for one another: Willems born to deceive; Lingard courting betrayal all his life.

The motives of Willems are always more than clear; those of Lingard, on the other hand, express some of the most subtle psychological intuitions of the novel. On the surface, Lingard seems little more than an officious man of good but dimly articulated intentions. Firmly convinced of his own rectitude, he has the "inclination to set right the lives of other people, just as he could hardly refrain—in defiance of nautical etiquette—from interfering with his chief officer when the crew was sending up a new topmast. . . ." Once we have watched Lingard in action, it takes little insight to interpret his charity as a desire to manipulate the lives of others; he is, like many thoughtless altruists, an unconscious Machiavellian. Unquestionably, he gets more satisfaction from his charity than the people who receive it, and few scenes in the novel match the smugness of Lingard patiently lecturing a captive audience on his own role as the savior of Sambir.

Yet Lingard would not be enigmatic if he were merely meddlesome. He makes a permanent claim to our attention by being the first figure whom Conrad uses to study the implications of a special blend of self-interest and compulsive benevolence. In the early meetings between Lingard and Willems there is a sense of mutual identification, of each man exercising an obscure appeal to the egoism of the other. At one point, Lingard admits "how he liked the man: his assurance, his push, his desire to get on, his conceited good-humor and his selfish eloquence. He had liked his very faults —those faults that had so many, to him, sympathetic sides." This attraction exists only in the flawed eye of the beholder, for Willems' appeal is not so much to Lingard's altruism as it is to his unacknowledged desire for self-destruction. That the kinship, once developed, has become mutually debilitating is no secret to anyone. Even Almayer has enough wit to accuse his benefactor:

Yes! Cat, dog, anything that can scratch or bite; as long as it is harmful enough and mangy enough. A sick tiger would make you *happy—of all things. A half-dead tiger that you could weep over and palm upon some poor devil in your power, to tend and nurse for you. Never mind the consequences—to the poor devil. Let him be mangled or eaten up, of course! You haven't any pity to spare for the victims of your infernal charity. Not you! Your tender heart bleeds only for what is poisonous and deadly. I curse the day when you set your benevolent eyes on him.*

Lingard gains stature by his confused, passionate idealization of his own altruism, both as a force for good and as a dangerous weapon for self-compromise. After the decisive treachery, he momentarily thinks of violent revenge; but then, typically, decides on "Justice only. It was his duty that justice should be done—and by his own hand." The cry for justice is just another instance of Lingard's weakness for abstract and grandiose notions. Yet excessive credulity —"the absurd softness of his heart"—masks a more pernicious flaw. Like Kurtz, Lingard has "something short, something wanting, something that would have given him a free hand in the work of retribution." And the "something," in this case, is his inability to recognize that behind the inarticulate benevolence lies a fatal attraction for damaging alliances. Thus his desire for justice is thwarted; his punishment of Willems leaves him dissatisfied; and his ruin is fascinating because it is so justly self-imposed.

Given all the hints that came before, the Captain Lingard who was supposed to be the hero of Conrad's third novel should have been a great creation. But, after three years of sporadic, notoriously slow work, Conrad abandoned the manuscript and did not go back to the story until much later in his career. For many readers the "riddle" of *The Rescue* (the reasons for the abandonment, the differences between the early manuscript and the published novel, etc.) is more interesting than the book itself. Of the many discussions of the problem, those by Thomas Moser are most relevant to our purpose. After comparing several versions of "The Rescuer" manuscript and the published novel, Moser concludes that the most important alteration is the oversimplification of Lingard's character. By cutting certain passages from the original manuscript,

Conrad obscured the most interesting facts of Lingard's psyche, the basic ambiguities of his romantic egoism—"the subtle difference between himself and other seamen; his egoistic longing for power; his lack of self-knowledge and his moral isolation. As a result, he has none of the vitality and intensity of Conrad's great self-destructive heroes. . . ."[7]

The essential question in the riddle of *The Rescue* will most likely remain unanswered. Many factors seem to have made the book impossible to finish in 1898–1899: Conrad had just married; he was involved in financial difficulties; his health was poor; at forty he still seemed uncertain about his future career; and so on. On another level, he had contradictory ideas about the novel's conception, not knowing whether it was to be a serious work or a potboiler designed to capture his share of an audience recently created by the stories of Stevenson and Kipling. Add to this Moser's theory that Conrad could not write satisfactorily about love, and you have a biographical and critical problem of considerable proportions. Although the final devitalization of Lingard does not occur until *The Rescue* in 1918, his importance for Conrad's work should be clear. He represents a preliminary stage in the evolution of Conrad's favorite hero: the romantic egoist whose faulty conception of self is tested in a situation in which the tensions between egoism and altruism are most fully developed.

This development can be seen for the first time in *The Nigger of the "Narcissus,"* a microcosm of a divided world which is also a microcosm of Conradian egoists. In this democracy of the sullen, the suspicious, and the thoroughly self-absorbed—where discipline is not "ceremonious" and "the sense of hierarchy is weak"—one can find every variety of egoist in Conrad's fiction.

The first to be introduced at length is old Singleton, sitting apart from the others, oblivious to the confusion of the forecastle, lost in the romantic exoticism of a popular Victorian novel. Singleton's egoism is admirable because it exists as an instinctive response to a fundamental challenge, and he carries a precious kind of loyalty into the action of the novel. Devoid both of fear and of weak-minded sentimentality, he refuses to worry about his own physical comfort and never gives "a thought to his mortal self." Because his egoism is so natural (and for the established order of the world, so necessary), it is heroic; and despite his comic insularity, he earns a profound measure of respect. There is even a sense in which Single-ton displays a touch of altruism, for he does devote himself to the well-being of others. Yet Conrad does not elaborate the point and is far more interested in the primitive force of his desire for self-preservation. That this desire is both admirable and almost mag-nanimous is a tribute to Conrad's ability to make the old sailor represent all those countless members of what W.H. Auden once called "The Invisible College of the Humble,/Who through the ages have accomplished everything essential." Perhaps this ac-counts, too, for the melancholy that marks Singleton's old age. Close to death, "a ready man with a vast empty past and with no future," his life's work is an achievement nearly anonymous.

Singleton's complement in the novel is the rapacious Donkin, the squalid agitator who cares for nothing *but* his mortal self. Torn, filthy, and repulsive, this "startling visitor from a world of night-mares . . . knows all about his rights but knows nothing of courage, of endurance, and of the unexpressed faith, of the unspoken loyalty that knots together a ship's company." His frenzied discontent is unsettling because he possesses a seductive eloquence that preys on the guilt and anxieties of normal men. Unlike Singleton, whose wisdom is unsparingly harsh, Donkin continually offers visions of luxuriant ease, a life of increasing rewards and decreasing obliga-tions. He appeals both to the greed and the sympathies of his fel-lows; and he is not only the "pet of philanthropists" but "of self-seeking landlubbers" as well.

Donkin's threat to the resolution of the ship's crew is matched and intensified by James Wait, another malingerer with a pas-sionate sense of his own importance. As a sequestered egoist refus-ing to participate in human society, Wait is certainly a puzzling figure. His entrance is so portentous, his subsequent behavior so disquieting, that he tempts readers to interpret his every move sym-bolically. Is he, as some people have insisted, the human unconscious, our capacity for blackness, the regressive instinct, Death, the secret sharer whom all men must finally know? There are enough faint leads to make some kind of a case for almost all of these; and yet, if we keep Conrad's admonition in mind the remarks of Ian Watt seem closer to the general implications of the story. In a foreword to the novel, written in 1914, Conrad insisted that Wait himself "is nothing; he is merely the centre of the ship's collective psychology and the pivot of the action." Watt reminds us that we can set this disclaimer aside only for the most imperative reasons, and he then goes on to argue "that the influence Wait exercises on the crew is an irrational projection of their own dangerous fears and weaknesses. . . . Order and disorder on the *Narcissus* are temporary, contingent, man-made; behind the mysterious and menacing authority of a St. Kitts' Negro there is only a common human predicament; Wait is a symbol, not of death but of the fear of death, and therefore, more widely, of the universal human reluctance to face those most universal agents of anticlimax, the facts; and the facts, as always, find him out."[8]

Two minor members of the crew complete the cast of egoists in the story. The Irishman Craik, fondly called Belfast, is a comic braggart, truculent, fiery, yet often soft-hearted, and like many of Conrad's simple-minded egoists is a descendant from Jonsonian comedy. As the crisis at sea approaches, Belfast refines his blustering arrogance and becomes increasingly more sensitive to human hardship. He adopts the dying Wait as his private charity patient and tends him with great devotion. Although some readers might mistake this devotion for genuine benevolence, Conrad reveals that it is based on self-satisfaction. Once having pulled Jimmy out of the submerged and toppled cabin during the storm, Belfast figuratively refuses to let his victim go:

He spent every moment of his spare time in Jimmy's cabin. He tended him, talked to him; was as gentle as a woman, as tenderly gay as an old philanthropist, as sentimentally careful of his nigger as a model slave-owner. But outside he was irritable, explosive as gunpowder, sombre, suspicious, and never more brutal than when most sorrowful. With him it was a tear and a blow: a tear for Jimmy, a blow for any one who did not seem to take a scrupulously orthodox view of Jimmy's case.[9]

When Jimmy dies, Belfast blames himself for not having stayed awake: "If I had sat up with him last night he would have kept alive for me." And Belfast's final lament for the lost object of his benevolence is the epitome of wounded self-esteem: "Who will miss him?" asks the sailmaker; "I do—I pulled him out," says Belfast.

Finally, the last example of invincible self-satisfaction is the cook, Podmore, a serious-minded man who goes to sleep reading the Bible and who attends church twice every Sunday when he is on shore. In his inability to say two words without reminding a listener of his religion, in the maniacal smugness of his hell-fire sermons, Podmore is the most typical obsessive egoist on board the Narcissus. "Beaming with the inward consciousness of his faith, like a conceited saint unable to forget his glorious reward," he constantly parades as God's special agent for saving the unholy lives of the crew:

Fundamentally he was right, no doubt; but he need not have been so offensively positive about it. . . . Had we been saved by his recklessness or his agility, we could have at length become reconciled to the fact; but to admit our obligation to anybody's virtue and holiness alone was as difficult for us as for any other handful of mankind. Like many benefactors of humanity, the cook took himself too seriously, and reaped the reward of irreverence. We were not ungrateful, however. He remained heroic. His saying—the saying of his life—became proverbial. . . . "As long as she swims I will cook!"[10]

Like Singleton, whose heroism is the product of his unthinking devotion, Podmore, also, has a capacity for heroism. As long as the ship does float he cooks, and at one of the most frightening moments of the storm he provides coffee for the beleagered crew. But the most obvious mixture of charity and self-righteousness comes in his splendid effort to convert the dying Jimmy. "His heart over-flowed with tenderness, with comprehension, with the desire to meddle, with anxiety for the soul of that black man, with the prize of possessed eternity, with the feeling of might." Yet at the height of his sublime vision, "a spark of human pity glimmered through the infernal fog of his supreme conceit."

These five men—Singleton, Donkin, Wait, Belfast, and Pod-more—(the only members of the actual crew itself who are in-dividualized) are the representative egoists in Conrad's fiction. It might be relevant at this point to answer the frequent complaint that the crew of the *Narcissus* is too numerous in the story. Once it is recognized that the only members who are described at any length are the five men just mentioned, the complaint loses much of its force.

The main threat to the morale of the crew comes from within its own ranks, and it is here that the first of several conflicts in the story is worked out. Although Donkin and Wait have qualities in common, they represent different aspects of the same menace. As an active malcontent, Donkin spreads his gospel of disunion by urg-ing specific gestures of insubordination; whereas Wait is less open, disrupting the daily order by lying around and making questionable demands on the loyalty of his shipmates. And yet, the distinction of *The Nigger of the "Narcissus"* rests not in the portraits of Don-kin and Wait (although both are stunning at first sight, they re-main shadowy figures in the novel) but rather in the gradually de-veloping portrait of the crew's psychological crisis.

When they first board the ship, most of the ordinary seamen are good-natured fellows, hiding an obvious naïveté and gentleness be-hind an external display of abusive high spirits. Despite the ag-gressive banter, one feels almost intuitively that they will be able to work together and to get the demanding job done. Yet when Wait starts to exercise his peculiar power, the narrator carefully estab-lishes the exact nature of the crew's vulnerability: "We were trying to be decent chaps, and found it jolly difficult; we oscillated be-tween the desire of virtue and the fear of ridicule; we wished to save ourselves from the pain of remorse, but did not want to be made contemptible dupes of our sentiment. Jimmy's hateful accomplice seemed to have blown with his impure breath undreamt of subtleties into our hearts."[11]

As the "undreamt of subtleties" become even more perplexing, basic certainties start slipping away and the men are caught in the grip of a servitude that saps their strength and resolution. At first, they fail to distinguish between the conflicting claims of duty and benevolence. For the moment, the demands of benevolence are singular; those of duty less clear and less immediate. The scantily clad Donkin needs something to wear; the crippled Wait requires a quiet place to rest and someone else to do his work. These needs are too obvious not to touch the common decency of the other men; but when the threat of dissension has become real, such decency is shown to be motivated by fear, ignorance, and self-interest. Put to the double test of the storm and the poisonous appeal of Jimmy Wait, the "vague and imperfect morality" of the crew is in great danger of collapsing. That it finally does hold up is due in part to luck and to the grace of the sea, but also to the actions of several benevolent men, whose conduct carries the essential morality of Conrad's story.

The crucial act of the middle section of the novel is Captain Allistoun's command restricting Jimmy Wait to quarters for the rest of the voyage. The captain's order, coming as it does shortly after the struggle to right the ship, causes the crew to stir toward mutiny. Lapsing back into their careless egoism, the sailors have just recently boasted of their splendid capacity for heroic labor and listened once again to Donkin's counterfeit speeches on the rights of man; now, when Jimmy—"the fit emblem of their aspirations"—is ordered to his cabin, they explode with indignation. At the point of the incipient mutiny, Allistoun emerges as the hero of the story. Refusing to be shaken by danger, he stands firm as Donkin heaves an iron pin at his head and then smashes Donkin's compulsive hold on the crew by handing the pin back and ordering it replaced.

Until this moment, Allistoun had been a minor figure in the action, a master mariner with all the traditional virtues of masculinity, self-discipline, and reserve. When he orders Wait to the cabin, the act seems at first to partake of that "latent egoism of tenderness toward suffering" which defines the crew's attitude toward the stricken Negro, and it certainly endangers the ship by nearly touching off a rebellion. But it soon becomes clear that Allistoun has a more complex sense of benevolence than any other man on the ship. He recognizes what only Singleton, and perhaps Mr. Baker, had suspected before: that Wait must be allowed to die at a natural speed for the good of the community; if he is allowed to work on deck, he might die too soon and become a martyr. The captain, acting from a realistic sense of discipline, knows that Wait must die; while the crew, acting from sentiment and fear, wants him to live. As events soon prove, Allistoun is the hero: "the little quiet man seemed to have found his taciturn serenity in the profound depths of a larger experience."

Although Allistoun is not developed with any fullness, he does convey the power of complex altruism in Conrad's world. A thoughtful, judicious man, with a keen sense of the past—of other crews and more frightening predicaments—he knows the difference between humane feeling and sentimental indulgence. It seems appropriate that the captain should have been named after Alfred Henry Alston, whose respected book on seamanship was one of Conrad's favorite possessions.

That Allistoun's victory over Donkin and the crew is not the final word in *The Nigger of the "Narcissus"* is a clue to the intricacy of Conrad's meaning. The crew must once again go through the baptism of fire by egoism. Although Donkin has been properly deflated, Wait continues to demoralize his shipmates, making them "highly humanised, tender, complex, excessively decadent . . . as though we had been overcivilized, and rotten, and without any knowledge of the meaning of life." For a short while after Jimmy's death, the crew is stunned by loss; but suddenly the fear of death evaporates, and they return to a measure of sanity again.

Marked as it has been by permanent scars and setbacks, the victory is tempered when one recognizes the fragility of the achievement. In his important essay on *The Nigger*, Albert Guerard has shown that the delicate sense of balance which the novel communicates is a product of Conrad's concern for structure:

The storm tests and brings out the solidarity, courage, and endurance of men banded together in a desperate cause. And the Negro James Wait tests and brings out their egoism, solitude, laziness, anarchy, fear. The structural obligation of the story is to see to it that the two tests do not, for the reader, cancel out.

. . . .

The problem was simply to avoid writing two distinct short novels, one optimistic and the other pessimistic. The two tests and two impressions of human nature must not be allowed to cancel out; we must forget neither the men's sentimentality and egoism nor their heroic endurance; at last, the dark knot of seamen must drift in the sunshine.[12]

There is one final way in which the lessons of complex altruism are used to control the pessimism of the novel. The narrator, who is identified as one of the crew, comes out at the end to speak in the first person, and he embodies the muted wisdom that Conrad feels is inherent in the action itself. His voice in the closing lines of the story reminds us of the meaning he and his shipmates have "wrung . . . from our sinful lives"; and his elegaic note conveys the sense of melancholy affirmation which, in the last analysis, is the major mood of the novel.

"YOUTH"

The full implications of Conrad's discovery of his essential subject can be seen in the major novels of 1900 and 1904. *Lord Jim* provides the classic investigation of the romantic egoist whose ideal conception of his own personality leads to disaster and an ambiguous redemption. The drama of Jim's crime is properly perceived only by Marlow and Stein, whose sense of human continuity makes them the most trustworthy observers of the situation. *Nostromo* offers the widest range of types in Conrad's fiction: the varied self-assertions of Charles Gould, Decoud, Captain Mitchell, Senor Hirsch, and Nostromo himself are judged in the context of the flawed yet complex altruism of Dr. Monygham and Emilia Gould. In much the same way, the short stories of this period draw their strength from Conrad's single-minded concentration on this basic theme. "Youth" is an attractive work with which to begin a discussion of Conrad's major period, for it allows an easy entrance into the complex world of "Heart of Darkness" and the longer novels. As a middle-aged recollection of a youthful adventure, the story remains an amusing song of innocence mingled with notes of sadness and loss, a mature man's reflections on the strengths and limitations of romantic illusion. As an analysis of character, it is unique among Conrad's stories, for it is the only extended study of the natural egoist.

The voice of the forty-two-year-old Marlow, heard for the first time in Conrad's fiction, controls our response to the events of twenty-two years before; and it is this voice rather than the specific events themselves that remains in our memory. Just as the anonymous narrator of *The Nigger* serves to convey a sense of mature wisdom, so Marlow (despite his sentimentality) gives the simple tale of catastrophe at sea whatever thoughtfulness it finally possesses. His main object is to modify certain conventional notions held by the four respectable men who listen to his story. Praising the glamour and beauty of youth, he regrets the tendency of older men to look with patronizing indulgence on their younger selves. To his mind, youth should not be patronized but respected, for it offers an important and unique opportunity; it is the only time when one can be boldly and wholesomely egotistical and still manage to get away with it. Because life has not yet become tentative and morally compromising, simple heroism is always possible; and because of this singularity, youth—the years of power and illusion—is the "best time" of one's life.

Young Marlow's charm is a product of his thoughtless audacity and optimism. With a romantic gift for seeing enchantment in every common event, an inability to conceive of failure, and a willingness to play the heroic fool, he maintains his vitality when more experienced men are bent by the cruelties of circumstance. One useful clue to his personality can be found in the books he reads while waiting for the *Judea* to be repaired at Tyne. In describing two selections, Carlyle's *Sartor Resartus* and Burnaby's *Ride to Khiva*, he expresses a dogmatic preference for the work of the soldier to that of the philosopher. One glance at the memoir explains the choice. Burnaby, an active traveler, was legendary for his feats of physical strength and for an arduous 300-mile ride across central Asia to Khiva in the winter of 1875–76. His narrative of the event, which went through many editions in the late 1870s, would have been an agreeable bit of reading for young Conrad to take aboard the *Palestine* in the autumn of 1881. Burnaby seems to have been a courageous but somewhat ludicrous figure, several of whose most famous escapades were marked by comic failure. Like many of his type, he seems often to have blundered through a dangerous journey simply to see if it could be done. The preference of the twenty-four-year-old Conrad (or the twenty-year-old Marlow) for the extravagant adventurer rather than the dyspeptic philosopher is, for such an egoist, natural enough.

The limitations of enthusiasm are as obvious as its virtues. For the natural egoist, success is usually dependent on good fortune and on certain necessary conditions of the test itself. Although the physical challenge is formidable and even at times squalid, it can never be insurmountable and must contain the seeds of glamour. Then, too, there should be something inherent in the situation that the hero can call magical, that he can transform into an emblematic trial of life. If, in fact, the test should prove more exacting, if it should demand moral as well as physical resiliency, then the natural egoist is apt to be inadequate and eventually compromised by his own limitations. But this does not happen in "Youth." Conrad does not betray his hero; he simply holds his actions up to sympathetic laughter, and the way in which this is done reveals the modesty of Conrad's aims in the story.

The dominant feature of Marlow's narration is the careful alternation between realism and romance, a movement that eventually establishes the delicate and distinctive tone of the story. Both an ode and an elegy, "Youth" is a celebration of adolescent strength and enthusiasm tempered by a clear recognition of its shortcomings and its transitory nature. Many of the most effective touches in "Youth" call attention to young Marlow's idea of heroic endeavor only to contrast it with the comic realities of his situation:

We tried everything. We even made an attempt to dig down to the fire. No good, of course. No man could remain more than a minute below. Mahon, who went first, fainted there, and the man who went to fetch him out did likewise. We lugged them out on deck. Then I leaped down to show how easily it could be done. They had learned wisdom by that time, and contented themselves by fishing for me with a chain-hook tied to a broom-handle, I believe. I did not offer to go and fetch up my shovel, which was left down below.[13]

Obviously, the beauty is less in the situation than in Marlow's romantic imagination, and yet Conrad keeps Marlow's rhetoric under control by forcing him again and again to return to the mundane present—five middle-aged men drinking together around a table. By having Marlow continually ask for another drink, Conrad is, as Murray Krieger has noted, "jarring the reader—as he is jarring Marlow's listeners and even Marlow himself—out of the beckoning, tempting grasp of romance. What is being told us, we are forcibly reminded, is past, irrevocably behind us, faded and done with, despite the teasing and deceptive vividness of narration. For always the vividness is accompanied by Marlow's conversational rhetoric that establishes the perspective of time and of a sad, aging wisdom."[14]

This gentle contrast is also supported by the way Conrad handles the relationship between natural egoism and an altruism based on long life and experience. Although most of the story is a tribute to natural egoism, Conrad does from time to time reflect on the ironies that accompany its expression in any social context. Because of his proud independence, the natural egoist seems to be an archetype of unaccommodated man; for he continually scorns the protection of those insitutions that have been designed to make his trials easier, and part of his appeal comes from his refusal to be restricted by the institutions that traditionally tie men down. And yet, on the *Judea*, the young Marlow is continually reminded of his dependence on the good will of other people. The Captain's wife mends his shirts, his shipmates pull him back up from the burning hold, and so on. Although the egoist's debt to the instinctive benevolence of ordinary people is implicit in the action of the story, Conrad is careful to point out that only the older Marlow understands the full implications of human dependence. Natural egoism is seductive because it is so forceful; but its true qualities—its defects and virtues—can only be understood by a man whose judgment has been conditioned by knowledge not available to youth.

The importance, then, of Marlow's shifting tone of voice is clear enough. At one moment, he is the bard of youthful self-reliance, and at another, the measured spokesman for experience, aware of tradition, the continuity of craft, and the facts of growing old. In the delicate interplay of these two tones the major distinction of the story rests.

But *why* Conrad should have felt the need to invent Marlow in the first place is a more puzzling critical question. Of all the answers Conrad's own is the least helpful:

One would think that I am the proper person to throw a light on the matter; but in truth I find that it isn't so easy. It is pleasant to remember that nobody had charged him with fraudulent purposes or looked down on him as a charlatan; but apart from that he was supposed to be all sorts of things: a clever screen, a mere device, a 'personator,' a familiar spirit, a whispering 'daemon.' I myself have been suspected of a meditated plan for his capture. That is not so. I made no plans. The man Marlow and I came together in the casual manner of those health-resort acquaintanceships which sometimes ripen into friendships.[15]

Other commentators have tried to trace Marlow to specific Polish or English literary conventions. Zdzislaw Najder cites several famous Polish tales in which soldiers, friars, or travelers are used as carefully manipulated surrogates of the author.[16] And Walter Allen evokes the power of *Maga* to explain Conrad's choice: "To gather together a number of men of the world round a dinner table . . . is one of the oldest and now one of the stalest, contrivances in English fiction, and perhaps it is especially associated with *Blackwood's Magazine*. Conrad early wrote for that periodical . . . and it may be that at first he was merely conforming to a way of story-telling traditional to *Blackwood's*."[17] This last point is most likely untrue, since in the ten-year period from 1889 to 1899 (when Conrad was in a position to read *Blackwood's*) there were no stories of this kind at all. In much earlier times such stories did appear, but it is unlikely that Conrad read copies of *Maga* before 1880.

Recent critics, such as Albert Guerard, have tried to suggest that Conrad's use of Marlow was more a matter of aesthetic necessity than convention. After the varied narrative experiments in *Tales of Unrest and The Nigger*, Conrad seems to have moved quite naturally to the development of a *persona*. At this moment in his career, none of his earlier methods of narration were entirely adequate. Drama at first hand, with its demands for accurate dialogue, eluded him, as did the interior drama of the mind. He found it unsatisfactory to view the world purely as spectacle, and he was rarely successful in commenting directly on the course of life's action. A narrator who might observe events and later interpret what he saw must have seemed to Conrad a satisfactory solution to the problem of achieving a workable distance from his materials.

There are thematic as well as technical advantages to be gained by using Marlow. Since the conflict between egoism and altruism was becoming paramount in his fiction, Conrad needed some way to embody the counterprinciples necessary to give the dualism its full power. By allowing a gap of twenty years and having the older man tell his own story, Conrad was able to establish the simple yet effective contrast on which the story is based. As one studies Marlow's role in "Heart of Darkness" and *Lord Jim*, it becomes clear that he is being used in an increasingly involved way to express the lessons of complex altruism under the formidable attack of different kinds of egoism. But this point must wait for demonstration.

Writing "Youth" for *Blackwood's* probably had little influence on the conception of Marlow, but it certainly had some effect on what he had to say. In addition to the convivial, conversational style (which takes for granted that the listener is a member of the same select middle-class society), there are passages in the story which suggest that Conrad may have been deliberately catering to the patriotic ultraconservative point of view for which *Blackwood's* was so famous. On the first page, he calls the lawyer "a fine crusted Tory, High Churchman, the best of old fellows, the soul of honour"; and then later Marlow wonders why his mates were so loyal to the *Judea*:

> It wasn't a sense of duty; they all knew well enough how to shirk, and laze, and dodge—when they had a mind to it—and mostly they had. Was it the two pounds ten a-month that sent them there? They didn't think their pay half good enough. No; it was something in them, something inborn and subtle and everlasting. I don't say positively that the crew of a French or German merchantman wouldn't have done it, but I doubt whether it would have been done in the same way. There was a completeness in it, something solid like a principle, and masterful like an instinct—a disclosure of something secret—of that hidden something, that gift of good or evil that makes racial difference, that shapes the fate of nations.[18]

There is a similar passage written before Conrad worked for *Maga* that offers a revealing comparison because it seems more balanced and a good deal less jingoistic. The *Narcissus*, coming proudly home, sees the coast of England, which "resembled the high side of an indestructible craft riding motionless upon the immortal and un-resting sea."

> The dark land lay alone in the midst of waters, like a mighty ship bestarred with vigilant lights—a ship carrying the burden of millions of lives—a ship freighted with dross and jewels, with gold and with steel. She towered up immense and strong, guarding priceless tradi-

tions and untold suffering, sheltering glorious memories and base forgetfulness, ignoble virtues and splendid transgressions. A great ship! For ages had the ocean battered in vain her enduring sides; she was there when the world was vaster and darker, when the sea was great and mysterious, and ready to surrender the prize of fame to audacious men. A ship mother of fleets and nations! The great flagship of the race; stronger than the storms! And anchored in the open sea.[19]

There is grand rhetoric here, but not flag-waving; the passage is more like John of Gaunt's celebration of England than the typical laureate's ode. The selection from "Youth" closely resembles a later paragraph in "Heart of Darkness" in which Marlow speaks of the vast amount of British red on a wall map of Africa, where "some real work" is being done.[20] In both instances Conrad seems to be straining to find something public to praise.

"HEART OF DARKNESS"

The true value of "Youth" was recognized from its first appearance, and within a few years it began appearing regularly on lists of the world's best ten or twenty or fifty short stories. But when readers picked up the spring issues of *Blackwood's* in 1899, they found the serial called "The Heart of Darkness" something of a puzzle. It was not so much a matter of narrative, or even of baffling public meaning. After all, despite a blurred time sequence and certain *fin de siècle* hyperboles, the plot was relatively easy to follow; and from first to last the text was filled with unmistakable attacks on colonial barbarism. It seems rather to have been the alien personal vision, the unrelieved desolation of the grove of death, the dubious psychic horrors of the dying Kurtz, that sounded the harsh note; and since the tale proved both offensive and unsettling, many people agreed with the reviewer who dismissed it as "quite extravagant according to the canons of art."[21] Even those who admired the work often gave praise for the wrong reasons, singling out the attack on Belgian brutality or saying (as the *Bookman* did) that it was "a symbolic picture of the inborn antagonism of two races, the white and the black."[22]

Today, of course, the situation has changed. Most literate people know that by probing into the heart of the jungle Conrad was trying to convey an impression about the heart of man, and his tale is universally read as one of the first symbolic masterpieces of English prose. Psychologists, Marxists, and mid-western Buddhists have provided readings of "Heart of Darkness" as an adventure story, a black travelogue, a political exposé, a descent into Hades (with or without return), a quest for the grail, Conrad's search for his father, and a prototypical night journey or exploration of the hidden self. Along with these general interpretive pieces, there have been a large number of essays singling out persistent clusters of imagery—images of brightness, gloom, isolation, madness, disease, sterility, physical decomposition, diabolism, and violent death. After sixty-five years, Conrad's story is at last being read attentively (if, at moments, too wildly), and its historic role in the development of the modern novel has been commemorated many times. Even those critics to whom it is "an immemorial cliché of the craft of fiction" recognize its undeniable power and originality, admtting that, for most novelists, "after 'Heart of Darkness,' the recorded moment— the word—was irrevocably symbol."[23] Yet despite all this attention, "Heart of Darkness" remains, like one of its characters, an enchanted princess in a fabulous castle: seen, admired, but even now still just beyond reach.[24]

For instance, only recently have readers understood the importance of the elaborate frame in which Marlow tells his adventure to four listeners, a lawyer, an accountant, a company director, and the unnamed narrator of the entire tale.[25] Although concentrating on his own education, Conrad's mariner tries to get his listeners to recognize their own complicity with all the forces of destruction described in the story. Twice, he makes lengthy interruptions in his narrative. The first occurs when Marlow speaks disparagingly of his companions as fellows performing tricks on a tightrope for "half-a-crown a tumble"; the second occurs some time later, just after he has described the frenzied attack on the steamer and his sense of lonely desolation at the possibility of never meeting Kurtz. The comment about the tightrope walkers is challenged by a growl, "Try to be civil, Marlow," and the second speech is stopped by the contemptuous word, "absurd!" Both these breaks are important. The first proves that the group is still attentive, while the second so unnerves Marlow that it sets off an astonishing single paragraph, five page outburst, in which he summarizes (not through moralizing but through breathless narration) nearly every major theme in "Heart of Darkness": the nature of the protective lie; the relationship between innocence and experience and the need to live with an active knowledge of evil—to breathe dead hippo and to find places to bury the stuff in—; the role of women in a criminal society; the flirtation of Kurtz with the devils of darkness, his egoism, his ivory, his station, his rites, his river, his report, and his appeal for Marlow; the necessity of testing one's innate loyalty, not to one's self but to "an obscure, back-breaking business"; the heroism of Kurtz, of Marlow, of the Intended, and of the second-rate helmsman who steered; the criticism of Marlow's audience for sinking into the soporific security of middle-class life; the guilt of Europe for the making of Kurtz; and finally the contemptuous assault on "the dust-bin of progress" and all "the dead cats of civilization." To borrow Marlow's reaction to Kurtz's report: "a beautiful piece of writing."

Just as T. S. Eliot introduces the figure of Tiresias at almost the exact middle of "The Waste Land"—at line 218 of a 434 line poem —so Conrad places the two narrative breaks equidistant from the beginning and the end of the story, forty-nine pages from the opening and forty-eight pages from the close. Whether this was conscious is unimportant (almost certainly it was not); what matters is the effect. At the first break, Marlow had reached the high point of his narrative, starting up the river toward the inner station, admitting that "the reality fades. The inner truth is hidden—luckily, luckily." There is, in this section of the story, a continuing and compulsive play on the word *inner*. Marlow is going up a river where the inner truth is hidden, toward his nemesis at the inner station, where his innate strength will be finally tested. The double interruption and the digression that follows serve several purposes. Neatly varying the mood of morbid introspection, they emphasize Marlow's present neurasthenia, his inability even now to tell his story in a straightforward way; and at the same time, they reveal the incomprehension of three of the four men to whom the story is being told.

This point about the frame and two seemingly minor narrative interruptions may seem insignificant. But when added to the large number of other typically Conradian stratagems, it is a dramatic reminder of Conrad's care in manipulating the emotional effects of his narration. The intricate system of moral reflectors developed logically from Conrad's intense concern for the cognitive value of experience; so that the echoing frame, used simply in "Karain" and more elaborately in "Youth," becomes the fundamental method for conveying a complex set of impressions in "Heart of Darkness." As Conrad reminds us in the famous author's note: "That sombre theme had to be given a sinister resonance, a tonality of its own, a continued vibration that, I hoped, would hang in the air and dwell on the ear after the last note had been struck."[26] Readers who complain about the artificiality or clumsiness of Conrad's method have failed to respond to the vibration, to a vital stage in Marlow's personal drama of discovery. Having been told early in the story that Marlow did not represent his class, we can see, at the close, that the whole point of his telling the Congo adventure to a director, a lawyer, and an accountant is to test their ability to "breathe dead hippo, so to speak, and not be contaminated." Just as the manager of the central station was impressive because he inspired uneasiness, so Marlow's function within the frame of "Heart of Darkness" is to inspire uneasiness among his friends, the representative figures of London—that other darkness. The fact that only the unnamed narrator recognizes this and responds in any significant way is a blunt commentary on the imaginative failure of those men who by their titles are obvious representatives of the ruling class of modern commercial society.

Recent criticism has made readers look more attentively at the way in which the frame of "Heart of Darkness" is pieced together.

Since the progress of Marlow is the main subject of the story, the importance of "presentation" as such is obvious, and "Heart of Darkness" is only partially understood if one fails to consider its remarkable narrative mode. However, there are other problems about the handling of theme and character in the story that have to be approached in a more old-fashioned way. Although the difference between showing and telling can explain certain things about Conrad's art, a more traditional question can be just as helpful in coming to an understanding of this difficult story: What kind of man was Marlow before, during, and after the Congo experience?

In "Youth," forty-two-year-old Marlow reminisces about himself at twenty; in "Heart of Darkness" the subject for contemplation is now closer to thirty, and the passage of nearly a decade has made all the difference. In the first story, the older man contrasts naïveté and experience; in the second, he describes the critical moment when the innocent went stumbling across the shadow line. We first glimpse the older Marlow on deck of the *Nellie*, where he sits in his familiar pose of gloomy meditation. His portentous opening, "and this also has been one of the dark places of the earth," is followed by a warning from the anonymous narrator that the pallid figure about to speak does not resemble the ordinary seaman. Unlike most sailors, who are as a rule sedentary and unreflective, Marlow is a wanderer with a long history of cheerless introspection, who now tells stories of a vaguely evocative kind. When Marlow resumes the narration, his skeptical remarks about history and heroism reveal not only his contemplative nature and the range of his reading but his complex understanding of the relationship between past and present. The main point of his opening comments on Roman Britain—the difference between an informed and an uninformed egoism—is one that only a man of some experience can recognize. Thus, despite his melancholy, Marlow is accepted immediately as an authoritative guide to the events that follow; later he will emerge as the spokesman for the positive values of the story.

The important fact about Marlow's dark wisdom is that it hardly existed before the trip to the Congo. The young man who saw a map of Africa in a London shop front and decided to follow his childhood dream is, at the start, an instinctive egoist, motivated by little more than an impatient desire for adventure. At first, he moves briskly through the company offices in Brussels, his exuberance checked only by a slowly developing suspicion of the lunacy of his employers. This suspicion, awakened by an encounter with the startling grotesques who staff the company offices, remains mild for the moment. Despite the two knitting phantoms, the witch-like secretary "full of desolation and sympathy," the clerk who quotes Plato while hinting at cabalistic knowledge, and the maniacal doctor who painstakingly measures the heads of the damned, Marlow leaves the building uneasy but still confident. In a final interview with his aunt, he good-naturedly jests at her solicitude and naïveté, and manfully boasts of his own sensitivity to the economic foundations of reality.

Once the African journey gets under way, however, disquietude quickly replaces confidence as Marlow is instructed in the absurdity of his situation. Shocked by knowledge of widespread mismanagement and folly, he forsakes the mild jokes about the profit motive and turns to desperate irony at the criminality of these "high and just proceedings." From the day he left Europe until he had reached the outer station along the Congo River, Marlow's sense of Africa had been negative but abstract; for he never stopped long enough to get a particularized impression. Now, however, at the first station, he learns something concrete about man's role in the squalid drama of exploitation. His first teacher is the company's chief accountant, a man so devoted to correct ledger entries and to keeping up appearances that he is a lesson in the fortitude of ignorance and a living proof that vacuousness can have its wondrous side. In a landscape so dismal and a moral climate so corrupt, the accountant at least puts up a show; and Marlow reluctantly confesses that this mannikin earns a certain measure of amused respect, for his starched collars and elegant shirtfronts were unquestionably "achievements of character." Although stuffed with sawdust, the accountant and people like him nevertheless provide factitious support for the entire European effort in the Congo. It begins to dawn on Marlow that one source of power for an imperial operation comes from a direct and simple-minded vanity. The other, more compulsive source of energy behind the African experiment is pure greed, a human quality about which Marlow learns a great deal in the Congo. Most of the officials who work at the various outposts of progress are, like the members of the Eldorado Exploring Expedition, "reckless without hardihood, greedy without audacity, and cruel without courage." Once in their midst, Marlow is forced to abandon his earlier notions about how money works in society. In a previous conversation with his aunt, when he had "ventured to hint that the company was run for profit," he assumed an air of tolerant superiority. Now, he realizes how shallow and inadequate his earlier ideas had been; for not only is the company "run for a profit," it is run, without the slightest decency, for profit without limit; and the men who run it emerge not as simple businessmen but as predatory adventurers, as "sordid buccaneers."

Although Marlow's indictment mounts with impressive force throughout the story, it is finally a secondary element in Conrad's overall conception. As is perfectly obvious, the main burden of meaning and interest in "Heart of Darkness" is carried by Kurtz and Marlow, who in some fatal and obscure way are meant for one another. When Marlow first came to the coast of Africa, he had been a natural egoist who desired only to prove himself in an arduous situation. Although his intelligence and good nature were not nearly so obvious as his high spirits, he was undeniably quick witted, compassionate, and hard to fool. Once he begins to sail up the river, he learns his lesson immediately, recognizing that the jungle is a force of darkly ambiguous appeal and that the European enterprise —supported by fools and fortune hunters—is a criminal fiasco of the most scandalous kind.

No wonder, then, that he should respond favorably to the promise of meeting Kurtz. Conrad's teasing introduction of his demonic hero is justly famous: After an abrupt series of brief but tantalizing remarks, Marlow is ready to swear eternal loyalty to a man he has never seen. One close look at the portrait of Kurtz that emerges from these scraps of information will reveal why Marlow is so quickly seduced. In addition to his more obvious gifts of intelligence and creativity, Kurtz has two qualities that would immediately attract the younger man. Not only is he self-reliant and self-absorbed; he is a romantic idealist with a grandiose mission, "an emissary of pity, and science, and progress and devil knows what else." To Marlow's mind, Kurtz is his superior both in courage and in noble idealism, the two virtues that he himself values most highly.

In the days before his arrival at the inner station, Marlow thinks of Kurtz in two ways, first as the figure in a startling visual tableau and then as a disembodied voice, the tableau an emblem of Kurtz's natural egoism and the voice representative of his seemingly articulate idealism:

As to me, I seemed to see Kurtz for the first time. It was a distinct glimpse: the dugout, four paddling savages, and the lone white man turning his back suddenly on the headquarters, on relief, on thoughts of home—perhaps; setting his face towards the depths of the wilderness, towards his empty and desolate station. I did not know the motive. Perhaps he was just simply a fine fellow who stuck to his work for its own sake.[27]

The man presented himself as a voice. Not of course that I did not connect him with some sort of action. Hadn't I been told in all the tones of jealousy and admiration that he had collected, bartered, swindled, or stolen more ivory than all the other agents together? That was not the point. The point was in his being a gifted creature, and that of all his gifts the one that stood out preeminently, that carried with it a sense of real presence, was his ability to talk, his words—the gift of expression, the bewildering, the illuminating, the most exalted and the most contemptible, the pulsating stream of light, or the deceitful flow from the heart of an impenetrable darkness.[28]

Marlow's initial response to Kurtz is based, then, on the two most obvious qualities in his own makeup. Yet each time he discovers something new about his nemesis, his allegiance becomes that much more paradoxical. Admittedly, Conrad's presentation of Kurtz is not notable for its clarity, and a reader is never quite sure how much of the mystery surrounding him is the product of art and how much of evasion. Nevertheless, the source of Kurtz's spectacular appeal can be traced back to his obsessive egoism. Although Marlow never denies that Kurtz's moral idealism has become moral barbarism, that his admirable self-sufficiency has degenerated into an overwhelming pride in "my Intended, my station, my career, my ideas," he insists that Kurtz is remarkable for having the true courage of his hallucination: "He won't be forgotten. Whatever he was, he was not common. He had the power to charm or frighten rudimentary souls into an aggravated witch-dance in his honour; he could also fill the small souls of the pilgrims with bitter misgivings: he had one devoted friend at least; and he had conquered one soul in the world that was neither rudimentary nor tainted with self-seeking."[29]

This passage offers an important clue to the riddle of Kurtz's charismatic attraction. In a world filled with rudimentary and greedy egoists, Kurtz—despite his charlatanism—at least has the imagination to conceive of greatness and the single-mindedness to carry his dream to its inevitable, terrifying conclusion. On one hand, he can write an eloquent report that appeals to "every altruistic sentiment" and, on the other, is demoniacal enough to end it with the postscript, "exterminate all the brutes." One day he will seem, in a "weirdly voracious aspect," to "swallow all the air, all the earth, all the men before him," but on another will accept the implications of his moral extravagance and judge life as "the horror, the horror."

In one respect, Kurtz resembles a familiar type in the literature of the past two hundred years—the presumptive outlaw who gains a degree of admiration by crossing the boundaries of conventional morality and exploring the possibilities of living on the other side. But this is not the final image that Conrad wishes us to take away from the story. Kurtz is less an inspiration than a warning. For all its audacity, his life is a chilling demonstration of the destructive extremities of pure ego and the price one pays for trying to live outside civilization: "I had to deal with a being to whom I could not appeal in the name of anything high or low. I had, even like the niggers, to invoke him—himself—his own exalted and incredible degradation. There was nothing either above or below him, and I knew it. He had kicked himself loose of the earth."[30] This total isolation comes to Kurtz only after he has passed through nearly all the familiar stages of Conradian egoism. Starting as a venturesome natural egoist, he talks himself into an obsessive concern with civilizing the natives, becomes torn by his desire for wealth and power, and is finally driven to sequester himself as the most voracious divinity of the land. As such, Kurtz is the first of Conrad's characters to embody nearly all the egoistical compulsions that keep reappearing in the novels and stories, and to attach them to an idea which, in conception at least, appears to be altruistic. Although Kurtz's initial idealism is eventually shown to have been shallow all along, he never quite loses his fatal charisma; and despite Marlow's recognition that the "gorgeous eloquence" was without substance, Kurtz can never be wholly repudiated.

Much of Kurtz's forcefulness comes from his representative nature, for Conrad uses him to say as much as he could at this point in his life about the claims and consequences of human egoism. It is also this exemplary quality that makes Kurtz so shadowy as a human being. As a rule, when Conrad describes an obsessive or a sequestered egoist, he sacrifices the verisimilitude of conventional character portrayal and concentrates on making the man a convincing emblem of some broad pattern of human conduct. Many of the details about Kurtz describe his actions in an obviously symbolic way and are more closely related to the meaning of his Satanic quest than to his specific characteristics as a human being. After reading "Heart of Darkness" one is more apt to remember the savage decline and fall of European idealism than the fate of a particular individual. Even such exceptionally vivid concrete details as Kurtz's luminous bald head and his fantastically long body seem chosen to make an ironical larger point; the baldness of his head corresponds to the ivory he so crassly covets, while his height belies the Germanic origins of his name. Then, too, Kurtz is disembodied for another reason. Since one of the major themes of "Heart of Darkness" is the hollowness and yet the enchanting power of public rhetoric, Conrad presents Kurtz more often "draped nobly in the folds of a gorgeous eloquence" than in the traditional garments of an ordinary human being.

But whether Kurtz is emblem or individual, he has a decisive impact on Marlow's life. No one would argue anymore that Marlow's education rather than Kurtz's adventure is the center of interest in Conrad's story. Having begun as a self-confident young adventurer, Marlow is painstakingly instructed in different kinds of evil, banal and otherwise, learns things about himself that he hardly suspected, and comes home in a state of complete shock. Yet despite the psychic scars and the blasted imagination, Marlow does emerge as wise in the lessons of complex altruism; and since these are the most positive values in Conrad's universe, they require extended definition.

The delicate balance between sympathy and revulsion in Marlow's response to Kurtz—his ability to see him as both an inspiration and a warning—is the product of a view of life notable for its intelligence. Marlow's refusal to follow Kurtz to the last stages of his dark exploration is based not so much on the conventional man's cowardice as on his refined sense of human paradox. The experience that Marlow undergoes in the Congo is marked by an almost unbearable doubleness: every vice has its seductive virtue; every virtue its unsuspected, heartbreaking vice. Yet despite Marlow's attraction for Kurtz's peculiar kind of blackness, he finally accepts, however cautiously, the price to be paid for civilization. This acceptance is hard won and not without its own high cost. Just as all Europe contributed to the making of Kurtz, so in another sense did it contribute to the making of Marlow, the man who comes to the wilderness protected by certain defenses against the darkness. These defenses—courage, loyalty, and pragmatism—are tested and shown to be artificial props against a force that is clearly more natural. But Marlow accepts them as necessary and certainly preferable to no defenses at all. They are preferable because his commitment to civilization—to the past, present, and future of the race

—proves to be stronger than his commitment to certain forms of the truth. His lie to Kurtz's fiancée is in this sense an admission that civilization (and particularly simple altruists) must be protected from the truth about itself. Not always, but occasionally; for the fact that Marlow tells an accurate version of the story to the four men on the *Nellie* suggests that there are moments when the truth can be told.

The ultimate vision of the complex altruist is undeniably austere. Admitting the attraction of diabolism, he must nevertheless, from a sense of balance and continuity, reject extremes of human behavior; and yet by so doing he denies the possibility of those forms of heroism achieved only by the romantic egoist. Theatrical self-assertion, unchecked individualism, obsessive egoism—these are the paths to glory and self-destruction in a typical Conrad story. With his skeptical self-awareness and rejection of fanaticism, Marlow seems pale and anonymous in comparison with Kurtz. His survival leaves him with very little to cheer about.

"Heart of Darkness," then, is the second work in which Conrad treats the theme of egoism and altruism in a complex and memorable way. In *The Nigger of the "Narcissus"* the crew represents the full spectrum of egoistical possibility, while Captain Allistoun and to a lesser extent Mr. Baker speak for mature altruism. In the later work, Kurtz's hallucinatory egoism is in itself a composite of nearly all the patterns usually found in Conrad's work, while the pragmatic wisdom of Marlow provides the antithetical principles needed to make the dualism work. The melancholy affirmation of *The Nigger* becomes even harsher and more problematical in "Heart of Darkness." The essential conflict, however, is the same.

TYPHOON AND OTHER STORIES

After finishing "Heart of Darkness" Conrad did not immediately begin work on "The End of the Tether," the third of the pieces in *Youth, a Narrative, and Two Other Stories,* for which he was under contract to William Blackwood. He decided instead to make good on an old promise to William Heinemann for a volume of four stories; and after completing *Lord Jim* "with a steady drag of twenty-one hours," he wrote "Typhoon," "Falk," "Amy Foster," and "Tomorrow" (as well as his share of *Romance*) in quick succession between early September 1900 and January 1902. This raised a delicate problem, for he had previously promised *Blackwood's* first refusal of his short stories and had many times expressed a desire to publish nowhere else. The four stories in question could not be printed in *Maga* because of an unwritten rule that anything appearing in the magazine must be published by the firm in book form. At first, Conrad felt a bit guilty at the desertion and justified himself in a note to Meldrum: "Do you think Mr. B'wood is in any way offended or annoyed. He need not be. One does what one can. . . ."[31] But Conrad's devotion to *Maga* had not been without its moments of doubt. As early as the summer of 1899 he had told Meldrum, "it is I suppose understood that I have a free hand in placing my stories elsewhere too than in Maga," and asked, "don't you think?—there may be too much of Conrad in *Maga* by and by."[32]

The desire to please Heinemann was not the only reason for Conrad's interest in serializing his work outside Edinburgh. In 1900 he faced still another financial crisis and desperately hoped to get more money for his stories. In the autumn of that year, he accepted J. B. Pinker's services as his literary agent, an arrangement that brought about an important change in Conrad's business life. At first, Pinker had no exact sense of where Conrad's stories were to be placed; but after several rejections, he managed to get "Typhoon" accepted by the *Pall Mall Magazine* and "Amy Foster" by the *Illustrated London News*. "Falk" proved impossible to serialize. "Typhoon" and "Amy Foster" were sold *after* they were written; while "Tomorrow," which later appeared in *Pall Mall*, may have been composed with that magazine in mind. On the whole, Conrad was satisfied with Pinker's early efforts and admitted that "Typhoon" and "Amy Foster" brought higher price than he had ever received for short stories. Pinker's checks of £4 per 1,000 words of manuscript were larger than the customary fees from *Blackwood's*, which had been £2/10 per 1,000 for such works as "Youth" and "Heart of Darkness."*

For the first time in his career, Conrad no longer played a direct role in selling his fiction. He continued to indicate preferences, but most often Pinker was guided by the amount of the fee and not by the quality of the magazine. As Pinker began to place stories for satisfactory prices, Conrad took less and less direct interest in the magazine publication of his work; and after he stopped writing for *Blackwood's*, his fiction generally appeared in magazines of high circulation and low quality. But although he often boasted of his obedience to artistic rather than financial compulsions, Conrad could never become wholly indifferent to the restrictive pressures and appeals of periodical publishing. Happily, his novels suffered less than his stories, for he thought of them as more serious projects and was less inclined to compromise for a magazine audience. When he did—as was the case with *The Secret Agent*—he sometimes tried to restore the excised passages in the book version of the novel. He took less care with his stories and let them stand for the most part as they first appeared.

It is, however, difficult to generalize about the conceptual differences between a Conrad novel and a story. For all his thoughtfulness, Conrad seems rarely to have known whether a new work was to be long or short. In fact, his normal habit was to begin every work as a short story; and with the exception of *Almayer's Folly*, each of his thirteen novels and all his tales were begun in this way. Once the work had been started and Conrad had become totally involved in his material, he could decide which subject allowed for imaginative extension and which did not. Then, if luck and circumstance allowed, he could choose to write a story or a novel. *Lord Jim* is a classic example of a process that occurred throughout Conrad's career. It began as a short story about the pilgrim ship; but when

---

* Conrad said he received £100 for "Typhoon," £60 for "Falk," and £40 for "Amy Foster." *Pall Mall Magazine* generally paid £5 per 1,000 words for short fiction. For an account of Conrad's finances at this time see William Blackburn's introduction to *Joseph Conrad: Letters to William Blackwood*.

Conrad came to realize that the most fascinating element was Jim's psychology, he developed the original tale into a novel.

For Conrad the course of a creative work was thoroughly unpredictable, depending not only on the vagaries of inspiration, but on poor health, a low bank account, and taxing relations with editors. To be able to plan on an uninterrupted period of six months or a year to write a novel was an emotional and financial luxury he almost never enjoyed. For this reason, he had little control over the length of his work and was more obviously harassed by outside influences than most writers.

After Conrad's agent assumed the responsibility for selling his stories, the influence of periodical publishing on his work became less direct and is increasingly difficult to analyze. Conrad's relations with the *Pall Mall Magazine* is an instructive case in point, for that journal is typical of those in which he published his stories between 1905 and 1910. *Pall Mall* had been founded by the American millionaire William Waldorf Astor in the belief that a large section of the reading public would welcome and support "a periodical that aimed at securing and maintaining a high standard of literary and artistic taste." Although the editors hoped to maintain a nourishing balance between "a lighter form of literary food" and "more solid material to suit other tastes," the articles that did appear were mostly of light and general interest. Nearly all the early pieces reflected a current mood of virile optimism and were concerned with the active man in a dangerous but fascinating natural landscape. "Pygmies and Ape-Like Men of Uganda Borderland," "The Most Difficult Climbs in Britain," "Grouse Shooting in Yorkshire," and "The Centenary of Alexandre Dumas" are representative titles; and Meredith, Harte, Kipling, Haggard, and Hardy published some of their worst fiction in the *Pall Mall*. By the time Conrad appeared in the magazine its mood had become more mellow. Beerbohm was sketching the great and near great; and male supremacy was giving way to "My Domestic Pets and What Became of Them" and some tales for children. The tone in literary studies was set by a long series on Bacon and Shakespeare that treated the cipher theory at great length. When the editors wished to know what serious writers thought about matters of current interest they sent questionnaires to Israel Zangwill, Hall Caine, Ian Maclaren, and Rider Haggard.

In May 1914 Albert Kinross celebrated the twenty-first birthday of the *Pall Mall* by writing its history in a short article. Buoyant about the past and happily confident for the future, he serves as an adequate representative of the kind of reader for whom the magazine was written. In a discussion of a Kipling story, Kinross calls the Boy Scout movement "certainly the most hopeful thing of this century,"[33] and goes on to praise *Pall Mall*'s editors for their vigor and good conscience. He cites the past twenty years as the great age of the short story and mentions Harte, Kipling, W. W. Jacobs, and Henry James as its finest exponents. Then, in a revealing aside, he remarks that fiction of the future must move quickly to match the temper of the age; modern man does not have time to waste on expansive story-telling. At first, Kinross is critical of his contemporaries, claiming that the accelerated pace of modern living has led to "a pathetic demand for optimism and assurance that everything will come out right." "Failure, nowadays, is so cruel a business that few people have the courage to occupy their minds with it outside office hours. They see and dwell enough upon it there, and the popular writer has to make for romance and a happy ending, as never he had to make before."[34] But Kinross' regret is only temporary. He firmly believes that the audience, *not* the writer, should dictate what goes into a popular magazine; and he agrees with the editors, who elsewhere in the same issue reaffirm their belief that "The first business of a magazine is to entertain, and to do that it must deal truthfully with many different phases of life; in other words, it must be artistic in the best sense of the word."[35]

There can be little question that the editors of *Pall Mall* were guided by the desires of their audience. When the magazine was hardly a year old, two enormously successful novels helped to standardize certain conventions of popular fiction and to set the tone for the kind of stories published in *Pall Mall Magazine*. Anthony Hope's *The Prisoner of Zenda* (1894), a new kind of rococo romance, set in the imaginary kingdom of Ruritania, provided brilliant costumes, generous sword play, midnight meetings, and thrills on every page; while George du Maurier's *Trilby* (1894), a sentimental rather than a rococo romance, gave the reader a highly idealized version of student life in the Latin Quarter, and a heartrending story of little Trilby and Svengali, her wicked exploiter. Both books were instantaneous successes (*Trilby* sold 80,000 copies in three months) and are sometimes considered the inspiration for Sienkiewicz's *Quo Vadis* (1896), S. Weir Mitchell's *The Adventures of François* (1899), and Charles Major's *When Knighthood Was in Flower* (1898)—the best-selling novels of the decade.

Although the subject matter of each of these works was different, they shared a common aim: to offer a momentary escape from life's problems by providing vicarious adventure. They seemed to have been written as proof of Conrad's belief that "the feeling of the romantic . . . lies principally in the glamour memory throws over the past and arises from the contact with a different race and a different temperament."[36] The fiction that entertained the readers of *Pall Mall* conformed to the successful stereotype. Adventure stories like "The Lost Rearguard" and "The Silver Skull" and the exotic tales of Sir Gilbert Parker often dealt with courtly rogues in colorful surroundings; and the romances like "Bird's Love" or "The Skirts of Chance" celebrated the good and the beautiful by never deviating from an established sentimental ethic. "Behari's Masterpiece," by D. Beames and Edgar Jepson (March 1899), describes an Indian servant who imaginatively robs rich men without being caught. During his most audacious theft, he stops to knock out several women and tie their hair together because, as he thoughtfully remarks, "It pleased me." The narrator comments, "I recognized the artist and knew that the curious craving for the grotesque, to our Western taste the bane of the artists of the East, had come upon him."[37] The second group can be represented by a tale such as "The Consumptive," by C. J. Cutliffe Hyne. A man named Tennant, dying of consumption in the Canary Islands, reveals to his closest friend that he had feigned a sordid love affair in order to break an engagement with the girl he was to marry. The motivation, of course, is noble; he felt that he had no right to bring the spectre of death to the wedding. The friend, however, thinks differently, and notifies the girl, who runs to her lover's side. A doctor turns up to reverse the diagnosis and the story concludes, "The girl linked her fingers over his arm, and looked up wistfully into his worn face, and murmured, 'Life! Isn't it wonderful, wonderful?' "[38]

Conrad admired George Roland Halkett, who edited *Pall Mall* for many years, and Maurice Greiffenhagen, who provided attractive illustrations for "Typhoon" and "The Inn of Two Witches," but he seems to have had little direct contact with the people at the magazine. The stories that he published in its pages are among his most optimistic and least demanding works: "Typhoon," "Tomorrow," "Gaspar Ruiz," "The Duel," "The Inn of Two Witches"— for the most part simple pieces of no narrative complexity and (with the exception of "Tomorrow") either good-humored or violent. "Typhoon," the first to appear in *Pall Mall*, is the only successful story in the group and it had originally been conceived with *Blackwood's* in mind.

"TYPHOON"

The idea of writing a short story about a steamship carrying a crowd of Chinese coolies through a severe storm had occurred to Conrad as early as February 1899, when he mentioned it as a projected fiction called "Equitable Division," and again in January 1900, by which time the title of the unwritten story had been changed to "Skittish Cargo."[39] Since he had not yet decided to furnish Heinemann with four stories, Conrad spoke of the new work as destined for *Maga*. It was started sometime in the early part of September 1900, and comments about its progress appear regularly in his letters of the period: "I've not yet finished the *Typhoon* which is to prolong my wretched existence. That infernal story does not seem to come off somehow."[40] Then, two months later, "The typhoon is still blowing. I find it extremely difficult to express the simplest idea clearly."[41] And finally, in December, "the Typhoon is all but finished and pleases me now so that I am sorry it isn't for *Maga*."[42]

Ever since its first appearance, "Typhoon" has been praised as a masterpiece of clarity and good sense. Unlike most of Conrad's

best stories, it is without mystifying elements and has never pro-
voked the kind of interpretive arguments that have characterized
critical discussions of *Lord Jim* or even *The Secret Agent*. This
simplicity is a result of its deliberately limited subject and the
obvious directness of its language and point of view. Like "Youth,"
it is a straightforward treatment of a familiar Conradian situation:
a blunt, unimaginative captain teaches a more intelligent younger
man a few lessons about the heroic possibilities of simple-minded
egoism. Yet what makes "Typhoon" so memorable is less a matter
of subject or theme than of style and narrative manner.

Those works for which Conrad is most admired today—*The Nigger of the "Narcissus,"* "Heart of Darkness," and *Nostromo*—are
densely metaphorical, with the major stress on the atmospheric,
evocative quality of a situation or experience. At almost every turn,
Conrad uses metaphors that are generally centrifugal: they start
from a sharply observed fact and then tend to move toward something larger, more abstract, less clearly defined. At one point in
Lord Jim, for instance, Marlow, trying to convey the difficulty of
evaluating Jim's story, speaks of the elusive "language of facts, that
are so often more enigmatic than the craftiest arrangement of
words." Basic reality is, of course, subjective in *Lord Jim*; the voyage
toward discovery is full of uncertainties and shifting contours. But
in "Typhoon" Conrad is not at all concerned with the elliptical
nature of truth. On the contrary, he is interested primarily in the
comic triumph of a naïve, unimaginative hero; and in this story,
reality is concrete, open to empirical analysis. "Facts," the narrator
tells us, "can speak for themselves with overwhelming precision."

Although the physical descriptions in "Typhoon" are especially
forceful, there is a precise, almost prosaic, quality about the writing
(if "prosaic" can ever be applied to a language so richly figurative
as Conrad's). This may be explained, in part, by Conrad's insistent
use of specific detail and of simile rather than metaphor to reinforce
the crucial thematic contrast of the story. This contrast is established in the first few pages when Captain MacWhirr and his first-
mate Jukes are set side by side as foils. MacWhirr is an absolute
literalist, a self-assured man, invulnerable to doubt, almost totally

devoid of a metaphorical imagination. Worshipping at the altar of common fact, he continually "expostulates against the use of images in speech," and writes letters about the weather that are so "prosy, so completely uninteresting," that his wife fears that he may someday come home for good. Jukes, on the other hand, sets a premium on understanding the meaning of his experience; an energetic, reasonably imaginative man, he is alternately awed, amused, and distressed by the monumental dullness of his captain.

The early sections of "Typhoon" consist of a series of vignettes that dramatizes the struggle between fact and fancy, with fancy invariably coming off second best. Jukes thinks it queer for an Englishman to sail under a Siamese flag; but MacWhirr, the literalist, unable to grasp the mate's meaning, checks the flag book and returns to observe, "There's nothing amiss with that flag. . . . Length twice the breadth and the elephant exactly in the middle." Jukes stammers, fumbles, and walks away. The paradigm is completed when MacWhirr and Jukes face the typhoon. This storm has none of the metaphysical overtones of natural catastrophes in Conrad's other work, for it is repeatedly compared to a raging human being: "a furious gale attacks . . . like a personal enemy. . . . Its howls and shrieks seemed to take on . . . something of the human character, of human rage and pain—being not vast but infinitely poignant."[43] MacWhirr, of course, deals with the storm in precisely the way he would deal with any other concrete fact of existence; he is calm, undramatic, bent simply on getting the disagreeable job done, whereas Jukes is imaginative enough to be terrified by the holocaust. But MacWhirr saves the day. "Faithful to facts," he knows for certain that the China seas are "full of everyday, eloquent facts, such as islands, sand-banks, reefs, swift and changeable currents—tangled facts that nevertheless speak to a seaman in clear and definite language."[44]

Conrad's clear and definite language in "Typhoon" is perfectly chosen to describe what is, after all, an overwhelmingly physical experience. At the worst moment of Jukes' misery and despair, he stumbles into his captain in the dark storm on deck and the two embracing men courageously stand their ground. It is the actual *fact* of MacWhirr's strong right arm that helps Jukes regain his balance on more than one occasion. The need for tenacity in the face of severe outward obstacles is reinforced by many strands of imagery in "Typhoon" that are often mechanistic and have a kind of surface, metallic hardness. Engines are described with prolonged affection: "there was the prudent sagacity of wisdom and the deliberation of enormous strength in their movements"; and men are often praised for functioning with the vigor of machines. Time and again, Conrad calls attention to the things of the real, surface world, and the storm scenes are brilliantly evocative because of his obsessive interest in detail, in what it was like to be there:

The motion of the ship was extravagant. Her lurches had an appalling helplessness: she pitched as if taking a header into a void, and seemed to find a wall to hit every time. When she rolled she fell on her side headlong, and she would be righted back by such a demolishing blow that Jukes felt her reeling as a clubbed man reels before he collapses. The gale howled and scuffled about gigantically in the darkness, as though the entire world were one black gully. At certain moments the air streamed against the ship as if sucked through a tunnel with a concentrated solid force of impact that seemed to lift her clean out of the water and keep her up for an instant with only a quiver running through her from end to end. And then she would begin her tumbling again as if dropped back into a boiling cauldron. Jukes tried hard to compose his mind and judge things coolly.[45]

Five of the seven sentences in this paragraph have similes that move away from ambiguity toward greater and greater specificity. The ship seems headed into a void, but hits a wall instead; it reels like a clubbed man, quivers as if it is lifted high out of the water, and then tumbles as if dropped into a boiling cauldron. These images—and there are literally scores more like them—are especially effective because of their immediate link with the world of direct sensation.

There are one or two other illustrations of how Conrad carefully uses a prosaic structural device in order to strengthen the unity of effect in his story. Whenever he wishes to sketch a minor character in only a few strokes, he invariably falls back on simile: the helmsman's passive face is "like a stone head fixed to look one way from a column"; the second mate growls "like an industrious gorilla"; and the Chinese coolies moan "like baying hounds" and look "like bees on a branch." The majority of these similes are visual, and reinforce Conrad's reputation as a pictorial writer; but, because much of the story takes place in total darkness, many of the images are aural as well.

Then, too, Conrad tells part of "Typhoon" in the form of letters from the three chief characters to people back home, and this device is perfect for a story in which facts speak so insistently for themselves. MacWhirr's letters are tiresome, full of common names; the engineer's are somewhat livelier, but trifling; and Jukes's are intelligent and sensitive to the external world. One of the most damning things that Conrad can say about anyone in the tale is directed against the malicious second mate, who "never wrote any letters," lives in a world of "casual connection," and does "not seem to hope for news from anywhere."

"Typhoon," then, gains part of its unity from Conrad's manipulation of pure fact. In his famous strictures on Conrad, E. M. Forster has remarked, "If he had lived only in his experiences, never lifting his eyes to what lies beyond them: or if, having seen what lies beyond, he would subordinate his experience to it—then in either case he would be easier to read. But he is in neither case."[46] This charge has been repeated in a more elaborate form by Marvin Mudrick, who sarcastically refers to Conrad's exaggerated reputation as a "poet in fiction" and objects to the "unctuous thrilling rhetoric," the "colorful irrelevance of metaphor" in *The Nigger of the "Narcissus."* Some of the liveliest skirmishes among recent writers on Conrad have been fought on the grounds of his grandiloquence and symbolism.[47] But "Typhoon" rarely figures in this critical quarreling because its precision makes it one of Conrad's least problematical works. It remains one of the few Conrad stories that everyone likes, which is the one way of saying that it is more art-ful or unified but obviously less ambitious and profound than, say, *The Nigger* or *Lord Jim*.

"FALK"

Two weeks after finishing "Typhoon" Conrad went to work on "Falk," one of the most curious and least known of his important stories. Of the four works in the volume *Typhoon*, "it was . . . for 'Falk' that Conrad had the softest spot."[48] Disappointed at Pinker's inability to get it accepted for serial publication, he complained to Blackwood that "no one seems anxious to gather [it] in," and went on: "Probably on account of his size, because his behavior, if can-nibalistic, is extremely nice throughout—or at any rate perfectly straightforward. I think so well of the story that if it hadn't been for very shame after the avalanche of *Jim* I would have sent it North to try its luck with you. But it was impossible, and moreover it must go for Mr. Heinemann's volume."[49] Only two months later, how-ever, Conrad changed his mind, and asked George Blackwood if he might take "Falk" after all: "The story is good; its size alone (24000 w) is against the speedy placing of it, and placed serially it must be because I had an advance on it from Pinker."[50] Blackwood's ultimate refusal to take the tale did not dampen Conrad's enthus-iasm for it. He wrote Cunninghame Graham in the following year: "*je me berce dans l'illusion* that 'Falk' is *le clou* of that little show."[51]

"Falk" is narrated by a young captain who has just received a command in the Dutch East Indies. While engaged in clearing up the confusion left by his eccentric predecessor, he spends time visiting another ship in the same port, the *Diana* of Bremen, com-manded by a dour Teutonic captain named Hermann. On board the *Diana* are Hermann's wife, four children, and niece, a lovely, taciturn girl who attracts the attention of Falk, owner of the only tugboat in the area. The captain cannot move his ship without the assistance of a tug, but Falk, thinking him a rival for the girl, refuses to do the job. At one point, he actually abducts the *Diana* for a short time in an effort to keep the girl away from the captain. After a series of misunderstandings, the narrator makes it clear that he has no interest in the girl, and agrees to speak for Falk if the tug owner will help move his ship. Falk provides still another complication by insisting that a grim fact about his past be aired before marriage. Years earlier he murdered a man and committed cannibalism on a stranded steamer. Hermann, outraged at first, finally recovers and gives permission for his niece to marry.

In the Author's Note to "Falk" (written nearly twenty years after the story) Conrad insisted that his primary interest was "not on the events but on their effect upon the persons in the tale,"[52] and it is clear from the full title, "Falk: A Reminiscence," that the piece is about something lived through and remembered. It tells in essence how a young, inexperienced captain learns that there are critical moments in life when the codes of society are useless against the elemental pressures of instinctive egoism.

"Falk" begins in much the same way as "Heart of Darkness." Several men, all of whom are connected in one way or another with the sea, are dining in a small hotel. The mood at the start is not the forbidding gloom that hovers over the *Nellie* but a note of faint, musty decay. The room, the service, and even the food itself recall ancient times, ". . . the night of ages when the primeval man, evolving the first rudiments of cookery from his dim consciousness, scorched lumps of flesh at a fire of sticks in the company of other good fellows; then, gorged and happy, sat him back among the gnawed bones to tell his artless tales of experience—the tales of hunger and hunt—and of women, perhaps!" These modern men, too, tell artless tales, and one of the group starts talking about "an absurd episode in his life."[53]

His story begins at the moment of initiation. The new captain, only thirty, feels unfit for command and keeps retreating for relief to the *Diana*, whose homely deck reminded him of a cottage in the country, and whose "venerable innocence apparently put a restraint on the roaring lusts of the sea." The *Diana* is "world-proof," and knows nothing about the brutality of instinct. But in the end, a ruthless disclosure is "left for a man to make; a man strong and elemental enough and driven to unveil some secrets of the sea by the power of a simple and elemental desire."

For a while, though, life aboard the *Diana* is tempered by calm domesticity. The two women sit knitting, much like the weavers of fate in "Heart of Darkness," surrounded not by black wool but by "billows of white stuff." When the family wash is stretched on the poop deck "trunks without heads waved at you arms without hands; legs without feet kicked fantastically with collapsible flourishes. . . ." Although these details suggest frightful things to come, the mood at the moment is lazy well-being. Stressing the whiteness of the ship's wood and the pastoral green of its ironwork, the narrator continually evokes images of "guileless peace, of arcadian felicity." When Hermann's untidy little girl carries her soiled doll on deck, it is called a disgrace to the ship's purity, "an abominably real blot on that ideal state." Of the seven people on board, only the niece possesses qualities that are raw and still vital, and she is constantly being likened to an allegorical statue of the Earth—simple, pagan, olympian, "constructed . . . with regal lavishness."

The idyllic life of Hermann's family is contrasted sharply with the shabby, deceitful atmosphere in Schomberg's shore hotel where everyone speaks ill of everyone else. Yet clearly life in either place is incomplete. The *Diana*, except for the girl's opulence, is scrubbed and unreal; while Schomberg's hotel has malice enough to sink the spirit. The narrator-captain is surrounded by pettiness and by lives lived at half speed, for he spends most of his time on deck of the *Diana* or eating at the restaurant in Schomberg's hotel. His dissatisfaction follows him to the privacy of his own cabin where he is engaged in sorting out muddled records and unpaid bills left by his notorious predecessor, who had spent most of *his* time writing obscene verse, playing the fiddle, and sleeping with a harlot on shore.

The atmosphere of fustiness and decay with which "Falk" opens is extended carefully through the first half of the story. There are implicit criticisms of conventional people whose insignificant lives are bound by habit and who have few, if any, elemental responses. Finally, Falk bursts into this semi-Eden. Strong and inarticulate, always associated with his tug, he reminds the captain of a centaur —not a man-horse, but a man-boat, seen always from the waist up on deck. At the start of the action, he is a disagreeable, miserly, anti-social extortionist—and the captain's nemesis—but his masculine force is undeniable. When he seizes the *Diana*, the simple towing operation has all the suggestiveness of "abduction, of rape."

Falk's single-minded behavior disconcerts everyone around him. Hermann rages against his cupidity, his truculence and bad manners; Schomberg is bitter at his refusal to eat the hotel's meat, as any decent white man should; and even the captain is appalled by the ruthless way in which Falk goes after what he wants, seemingly unrestrained by morality or even common decency. But as the story unfolds, the captain identifies with Falk against the others, just as Marlow comes to be loyal to the particular nightmare of his choice. He is fascinated by the appeal of a man who never practices duplicity, whose arrogant conduct resembles the candid force of a natural phenomenon. Gradually, Falk's ingenuousness draws the captain away from the shabby egoism of Schomberg and Hermann, and there is a striking contrast established between the exuberance of Falk and the sterile atmosphere of human pettiness that surrounds life in the port, where the air is thick with misapprehension, half-truth, and malicious innuendo. Worn down by fighting against "false fate" and baseless gossip, the captain is drawn to Falk because he was "a ruthless lover of the five senses," whose chief concern was,

Not selfishness, but mere self-preservation. Selfishness presupposes consciousness, choice, the presence of other men; but his instinct acted as though he were the last of mankind nursing that law like the only spark of a sacred fire. I don't mean to say that living naked in a cavern would have satisfied him. Obviously he was the creature of the conditions to which he was born. No doubt self-preservation meant also the preservation of these conditions. But essentially it meant something much more simple, natural, and powerful. How *shall I express it? It meant the preservation of the five senses of his body—let us say—taking it in its narrowest as well as in its widest meaning.*[54]

Until this moment, the captain had missed the basic reality of the situation because his perceptions were blurred by a mass of irrelevant detail. The shock comes when he realizes that Falk is a truly classic hero whose endurance, cunning, and superb strength represent the "absolute truth of primitive passion." And finally, when Falk marries the girl, the captain is delighted at the match of this "complete couple," this bearded god and his nameless goddess.

Most notable in "Falk" is Conrad's manipulation of his materials to make a compelling point about a formidable social taboo. There is never any real question of morality in Falk's cannibalism; it is seen not as criminal barbarism but as an act of simple necessity, the admirable egoism of self-preservation. Falk's guilt is caused by his fear of what society would do to him if his secret came to light, not by any doubts in his own mind that the deed was justified. His confession is prompted by a need to clear the air, to make himself understood. By comparison, the representatives of society appear far more devious in their sentimental refusal to admit the virtues of a ruthless but wholly natural egoism.

Recognizing that his subject might be considered offensive, Conrad deliberately arranged the sequence of events to make Falk's cannibalism seem inevitable and trivially unimportant compared with the maliciousness of Schomberg and the stupidity of Hermann. But by postponing the climax and filling the middle of the story with cautious moralizing, Conrad weakened a work that in conception at least seemed destined for greater interest. Because of this circumspection, Falk himself never emerges as a very convincing character. Obviously, he should stand in the same relation to the inexperienced young captain as Kurtz did to Marlow—an unnerving figure who establishes mutual loyalty by the power of his primitive appeal. But despite the clarity of design, the drama of the relationship is never fully realized. Whereas Kurtz and Marlow wrestle in the jungle for the highest possible stakes, the captain and Falk have their long-awaited confrontation during a feigned card game in Schomberg's hotel, a disappointing anticlimax that gives Conrad an excuse to wrap up the story with a mild joke.

There is evidence to suggest that deliberate caution and strained humor were only two of several methods Conrad used to soften the shock value of "Falk." An early version of the story, existing in manuscript at Yale, includes several paragraphs that were later cut from the printed text. These deletions are mostly of two kinds: specific details about the sexual promiscuity of the captain's predecessor ("on the 5th given to Mathilde 5. 10s," etc.) and passages describing the psychological dilemma of the captain himself. By paring down such elements, Conrad was trying to make his story less objectionable and less analytical, more suitable for the audience of a popular magazine.* But by failing to develop the character of the narrator, he weakened the story in one of its vital places. Even though Falk exists "in a sort of mental twilight," he does convey the physical presence of natural egoism; but without intelligence and a rich inner life, the young captain never emerges as a fit antagonist to respond to Falk's appeal. A Marlovian figure, the narrator lacks Marlow's quickness and substantiality. Since "Falk" is without an articulate spokesman for the values of complex altruism (or even a different kind of egoism), it lacks the suggestiveness of stories like "Heart of Darkness" or "The Shadow-Line" with which it has so much in common.

"AMY FOSTER"

"Amy Foster," the third of Conrad's four stories for Heinemann, has an uncertain genesis. Written quickly in June 1901 immediately after the completion of "Falk," it was inspired in part by Ford's *Cinque Ports* (1900), which describes the hostile reception of a German castaway stranded in England. Years later, Ford claimed that Conrad "had simply taken 'Amy Foster' from the writer, with no particular apology and had just rewritten it—introducing Amy

* Bruce Johnson provides a more detailed study of the two versions in "Conrad's 'Falk': Manuscript and Meaning," *Modern Language Quarterly*, XXVI, 2 (June 1966), 267–284.

herself, who had not existed in the writer's draft."[55] Jessie Conrad questioned the truth of this assertion and added that Amy was based on the character of a maid who had worked for the family for many years and who inspired Conrad by her "animal-like capacity for sheer uncomplaining endurance. . . ."[56] Recently, Richard Herndon has reexamined the problem in great detail and, after tracing Conrad's debt to Ford, to Flaubert, and to local topography, admits that the origins of the tale are "complex and somewhat baffling."[57] Conrad seems to have borrowed the basic idea and some details from Ford (for instance, the castaway in *Cinque Ports* is called "Mad Jack" while in "Amy Foster" he is "Yanko," and both are hounded into pig pens), but he also drew on his own experience and invention.

The quest for the sources of "Amy Foster" has now been joined to the investigation of biographical parallels in its action. Because the story describes the hostile reception of a central European exile in England, it is often treated as a fictional projection of Conrad's sense of personal estrangement. His isolation, his frequent ill-health, and his difficult marriage are generally thought to be reflected in the melancholy relationship of Yanko Goorall and his stolid English wife. Although discussion of such parallels is undeniably interesting, it sometimes obscures the fact that "Amy Foster" has a relevance beyond the reach of biography. It is one of Conrad's finest short stories and its treatment of the power and deficiencies of both natural egoism and instinctive altruism is closely related to the thematic developments of his major fiction.

The story has a familiar narrative frame. Kennedy, the village doctor at Colebrook, tells a visiting friend about the marriage of a neighborhood girl to the lone survivor of a historic shipwreck. In sketching Yanko's early history, Kennedy likens him to an animal or an object growing freely in a natural landscape, a woodland creature or a tree coming to full strength. Having had the misfortune to be cast ashore in a foreign place, Yanko tried to establish his right to live simply as a member of the community, but was thwarted by the suspicions of the townspeople, who failed to see the decency beneath his eccentric manner. After nearly everyone else had beaten him with stones and umbrellas, Amy Foster approached with a few pieces of bread and by this "act of impulsive pity" brought him "back again within the pale of human relations." Despite her oppressive dullness, Amy did at least have enough imagination to fall in love, "to discover her ideal in an unfamiliar shape." As a physical being, she suffered from "a curious want of definiteness"; but she achieved moral identity by the force of her instinct for charity. However, as the story unfolds, Kennedy reveals that Amy's altruism was flawed by its narrowness and inflexibility. Able to deal only with the simple or the mildly eccentric, she quickly lost her nerve when faced with acts of incomprehensible violence:

She had never been heard to express a dislike for a single human being, and she was tender to every living creature. She was devoted to Mrs. Smith, to Mr. Smith, to their dogs, cats, canaries; and as to Mrs. Smith's gray parrot, its peculiarities exercised upon her a positive fascination. Nevertheless, when that outlandish bird, attacked by the cat, shrieked for help in human accents, she ran out into the yard stopping her ears, and did not prevent the crime.[58]

Amy's frantic inability to help the parrot is the first hint of the fatal weakness that later caused her to abandon her husband.

As the drama of the Goorall marriage moves toward its melancholy climax, Dr. Kennedy's purpose in telling the story to his friend becomes clearer. His original wish had been to illustrate a modern tragedy, different from the Greek, "less scandalous and of a subtler poignancy, arising from irreconcilable differences and from that fear of the Incomprehensible that hangs over all our heads. . . ." But once the evidence is revealed, another more specific tragic pattern emerges. "Amy Foster" reflects the typical Conradian struggle between the contradictory claims of different human impulses. Yanko's natural egoism—his desire to express his peculiar individuality in an unfamiliar setting—is shown to be sadly deficient because it is too easily the prey of an indiscriminate charity. Tossed between the brutal antagonism of the villagers and the mindless generosity of Amy, Yanko quite sensibly chooses the latter; but this only makes him vulnerable to a new and more insidious set of destructive conflicts.

After the marriage, Yanko tries to maintain his eccentric spontaneity, teaching his son native folk songs and hoping to reconstruct the continuity between his past and present life. But Amy's failure to comprehend his basic needs is frustrating and finally destructive. When he feverishly cries out for water in an incomprehensible language, she runs terror struck from the house, leaving him to die. But Yanko is the victim not only of her misunderstanding but of his own as well, for he has failed to recognize the ambiguous nature of his debt to his wife. At one point in the story, Dr. Kennedy wonders if the more powerful force shaping Yanko's conduct was his memory of Amy's compassion or his own instinctive love of life, and he finally admits, "perhaps he was seduced by the divine quality of her pity." Despite the increasing restrictiveness of his life, Yanko insists that Amy is "not hard, not fierce, open to compassion, charitable to the poor." Refusing to admit that a good heart is not enough, he is victimized (like so many of Conrad's other heroes) by the latent egoism of tenderness to suffering.

One theme, then, of "Amy Foster" is the inability of simpleminded altruism to calm the basic fear of the unfamiliar or to heal the rift arising from irreconcilable differences between people. If such divisive threats are to be adequately met, a more complex defense is needed, and such a defense is offered by Dr. Kennedy. Because Yanko hardly speaks English and Amy is inarticulate, the meaning of their lives must be interpreted by a reflective observer. As is obvious from the structural defects of "The Idiots," Conrad could not dramatize the "obscure trials of ignorant hearts" without a detached narrator. An altruist by profession, Kennedy has both the intelligence and wide range of experience to place the tale in a larger context. He provides both the intimate details which only an attending physician would know and the sense of scientific detachment which establishes the moral significance of the action. Unfortunately, since he was more an observer than a participant, his elaborate classical allusions and solemn moralizing are sometimes strained and unconvincing. He is never able to speak with the authority of Marlow, who could afford rhetoric because he at least suffered for it. Kennedy may have been a thematic and structural necessity for Conrad, but he is a mixed blessing for the reader.

So, for that matter, is the title. When Conrad began "Amy Foster," he called it "A Husband" and then later "A Castaway," which places the emphasis where it should be, on Yanko rather than Amy. But Conrad wished to sell the story to a popular magazine and must have felt the chance of doing so would have been better if Amy were the center of interest. Ironically enough, Pinker sold "Amy Foster" to the *Illustrated London News*, where it was serialized in three parts during December 1901. Just as it does today, the *News* celebrated empire and royalty with oppressively artless drawings and an absolute minimum of printed text. Conrad's bitter story of a crazed foreigner destroyed by the cruelty of English townspeople could hardly have been more out of place. But an obliging artist provided two prominent illustrations of Amy, one of which shows her helping her mother feed the family, an event that has little relevance to the main action of the tale. Then, too, the editors surrounded "Amy Foster" with gay sketches of Christmas festivities, and the printed text was so fine that only an especially devoted admirer would risk serious eye strain to read it. More than one reader must have found the Princess of Wales and her household staff (including the Equerry in Waiting and various Ladies of the Bedchamber) more suitable holiday fare than the pathetic Amy Foster.

"TO-MORROW"

The last of the four works that eventually made up *Typhoon and Other Stories* was obviously meant as a companion piece to "Amy Foster." Just as that story had been first called "The Husband," so the work now known as "To-morrow" was originally titled "The Son." But aside from this preliminary title and the date of completion (January 1902), very little is known about its origins. Conrad once told Ford that the character of the son is "*All your* suggestion and *absolutely my* conception. It's most interesting and funny to see."[59] And again in 1904, Ford helped turn the story into a one-act play by extracting all the dialogue from the original manuscript. But it is impossible at this date to determine the exact role he played in the original composition of the story.

"To-morrow" describes the obsession of old Captain Hagberd, who has come to Colebrook (the village in which "Amy Foster" takes place) with the idea that his long-lost son will turn up "in one day more." He buys two houses, rents one to a young girl and her blind father, and settles down to wait for his son. As his fantasy takes on more complex shape, he implicates Bessie Carvil, the girl next door, by promising that his son will marry her. Self-effacing and unable to resist the captain's compulsion, Bessie forgets her initial misgivings and romantically shares his hope. Their savage dislocation is unquestionable: Hagberd is deranged; old Carvil poses as a domestic tyrant, exploiting his infirmity to keep Bessie as his nurse; and the girl herself is so frustrated that she conceives of the unknown Harry as her lover. Finally, the son does arrive, drawn to Colebrook by an advertisement and a chance to pick up some easy money. But when the old man fails to recognize him and wildly reveals the marriage scheme, Harry draws back. Raging against this attempt to shut him up like a "tame rabbit in a cage," he borrows a half-sovereign from Bessie, kisses her with great pomp, and runs off to resume his life as a thoughtless adventurer. While old Hagberd stands shouting about his "trust in an everlasting tomorrow," Bessie is left stricken with humiliation and despair.

Although "To-morrow" is not worth very much as a short story, it has an important, if negative, place in Conrad's career. It is the first of many short stories wholly ruined by Conrad's refusal to follow up the possibilities inherent in its subject matter. Captain Hagberd, Harry, and Bessie Carvil form a triangle different in kind from any Conrad had presented in fiction before, and one which in conception at least is suggestive. At first glance, the basic situation in "To-morrow" resembles that of "Falk" and "Amy Foster." The lives of several people suffering from illusion, diseased imagination, or repressed desire are dramatically affected by the sudden appearance of a figure from a different, less restrictive society. Falk defies Hermann and the young captain; Yanko challenges Amy and the townspeople; and Harry Hagberd defeats his father and Bessie Carvil.

"Every mental state," Conrad says at one point in "To-morrow," "even madness, has its equilibrium based on self-esteem." In this light, Captain Hagberd's lunacy can be seen as the disease of an obsessive egoist, whose entire view of the world rests on the return of his son and the receipt of filial affection. Bessie is also a recognizable type, the good-hearted but simple altruist who has sacrificed her life because of a failure of nerve. Acting most often from two compulsions, pity and hope, she is victimized by a "madness that had entered her life through the kind impulse of her heart." Harry, the young son, is a natural egoist in the tradition of Falk. Comparing himself to the Mexican *gambusinos*, he insists that

these [adventurers] wandered alone. They knew that country before anybody had ever heard of it. They had a sort of gift for prospecting, and the fever of it was on them, too; and they did not seem to want the gold very much. . . . They were too restless. . . . It was not for the gold they cared; it was the wandering about looking for it in the stony country that got into them and wouldn't let them rest.[60]

In outline, then, "To-morrow" has all the ingredients of a typical Conrad story: an obsessive egoist and a simple-minded altruist fail to contain a man who acts from aggressive self-interest. But it clearly fails because only one of the characters, young Harry, comes close to carrying off his role. Since Captain Hagberd's obsession is so obviously a product of a deranged mind, and not based on an ideal conception of self, he is easily dismissed as a special case. He has none of the universality of Conrad's obsessive heroes (Kurtz, Jim, or Charles Gould), and his neurosis remains a private rather than a public catastrophe. Bessie, too, is a failure, for she is another of those mute and soulful women Conrad could not bring alive on the page. Described as profound, sensitive, and compassionate, she says nothing in the story to live up to her advance notices. In fact, she usually expresses emotion by catching her breath or crying with dry, noiseless sobs. As the story unfolds, she is steadily reduced to a position of helpless desperation, but her dilemma is never made meaningful because she lacks the most basic power to communicate it. The final pages of "To-morrow," in which Conrad tries to convince the reader of her misery, are among the most discomforting examples of his "adjectival insistence": "She heard him at last, and, as if overcome by fate, began to totter silently back towards her stuffy little inferno of a cottage. It had no lofty portal, no terrific inscription of forfeited hopes—she did not understand wherein she had sinned."[61] Just as Dr. Kennedy does not quite convince us that Amy Foster is a diminished version of Antigone, so Conrad fails to make Bessie a twentieth-century descendent of Dante's lost souls. Harry Hagberd may not be a triumph of characterization, but he is more persuasive than his feeble adversaries and does at least convey the doubleness of natural egoism, its harshness and innocence, its brutality and dramatic appeal.

The developmental failure that weakens "To-morrow" was to some degree a result of Conrad's desire to sell the story to a periodical. His original intention was to write a more comprehensive treatment of the main theme, and an early version of the tale has revealing material that does not appear in the printed text. For instance, the following passage suggests that Conrad had hoped to give "To-morrow" a wider frame of reference, as he did with "Amy Foster":

Strangers pressing through the little seaport would remember perhaps that strange and striking figure; American tourists would exclaim in the streets—for Brenzett had had a history in its time and had known a prosperity for whose return it sat waiting on the identical grounds of Captain Hagberd's expectations as to his son. It had been there once and therefore it would return. Only Brenzett was not mad, at least not outwardly.[62]

The deletion of the reference to the American tourists and to the complicity of the villagers may have been made from a desire to avoid offense and analysis, the twin devils of magazine fiction.

"To-morrow" is not only the weakest of Conrad's early stories, but perhaps the first work wholly wrecked by being compromised for an audience. No story written before is quite so simple in technique or subject matter, and each of the early works has at least liveliness or daring. "To-morrow" has few of the virtues of Conrad's best work and shares many of the faults of his later stories which obviously were aimed at a popular market. Written after he had begun to appear in the *Pall Mall Magazine* and during the composition of *Romance*, it is, by his own admission, "Conrad adapted down to the needs of a magazine," but "by no means a pot-boiler." In this instance, the confession is more persuasive than the defense.[63]

Finally, there is an amusing irony about the first appearance of "To-morrow" in print. The editors of *Pall Mall* had the rare gift of being able to make everything in their magazine blend neatly with everything else. The last paragraph of "To-morrow" appears on page 547 of the issue for August 1902 and its closing sentences about "hopeful madness," terror, heartbreak, and the insanity of "trust in an everlasting tomorrow," are followed immediately by this poem:

SUNSHINE AND SHADOW
Florence Prime

To-day the sun is warm and bright,
  The sky is soft and blue,
The flowers are smiling in the light:
  But darling, where are you?

To-morrow I shall see your face,
  Shall I hold your hand in mine,
And, though the sky be black with clouds,
  For me the sun will shine.

In vain for me the thrushes sing,
  In vain the sunbeams play;
The world seems empty, dull, and cold,
  For you are far away
  To-day, my love, to-day.

> *The rain may fall, the wind may blow,*
> *The tempests roar to-morrow;*
> *But I shall be with you, my own,*
> *And there's an end to sorrow:*
> *To-morrow, love—to-morrow.*

A few years later, Conrad turned "To-morrow" into a play, a genre he hated for robbing fiction of any possible suggestiveness. In this instance very little was lost.*

"THE END OF THE TETHER"

The commercial qualities of "To-morrow" stand out even more vividly in comparison with Conrad's next story, "The End of the Tether," written between March and October 1902. Although the promise to Heinemann had been fulfilled, Conrad still had one debt outstanding. He owed *Maga* a story to complete *Youth, a Narrative*, which was scheduled for publication in the fall. But since he was back in the secure company of old friends, he felt delight rather than anxiety and told George Blackwood:

I am ready now, thank God! To take in hand the completion of the Youth volume of stories. I say: thank God, because it is an unspeakable relief to write for Maga instead of for "the market"—confound it and all its snippetty works. To open one of their Magazines is like opening your tailor's book of patterns for trouserings—only the book of patterns would be the more genuine production of the two.[64]

The relief, however, was not to last very long. At the start, the story proved difficult to write; then, when it was finished, a lamp on Conrad's table suddenly exploded and a good part of the manu-

---

* Eric Bentley's choice of *One Day More* for his recent anthology, *The Modern Theatre*, is an act of piety. The play is worse than the story. In her first volume of reminiscences, Jessie Conrad groups "To-morrow" with "those stories Conrad could never find a good word for." Two others were "The Black Mate" and "The Inn of the Two Witches." (*Joseph Conrad as I Knew Him*, p. 119.)

script was burned past recognition. The crisis was severe, for *Blackwood's* had already started the serialization and was nervously waiting for the next installment. Describing his state of mind as "frenetic idiocy," Conrad sat down to rewrite what had been destroyed and managed by enormous effort to finish just in time.

The circumstances surrounding the composition of the story show what working for *Maga* meant to Conrad. Although "The End of the Tether" is Conrad's longest short story, it moves at a pace that in no way mirrors the stress under which it was written. Conrad received constant encouragement in letters from Edinburgh, and when the first installment reached the editorial offices, Blackwood wrote: "I have the pleasure of enclosing your cheque £19 in acknowledgement of the September installment of "The End of the Tether," which I think continues to make good progress. The interest seems to me to steadily increase, and the story has now reached a stage which holds the attention of the reader."[65] When the piece was finished, the publisher wrote once again: "It seems to me that you have been very successful with the working out of the story, and the end is most effective. I am sorry for the delay in the publication of the book, but you could not have done justice to the story in less space."[66]

Conrad spoke of being "heartened greatly" by the encouragement and felt confident that he could hold his audience.[67] He extended his analysis far beyond the length of what other magazines would normally accept; and since he need not worry about having the work rejected, he could use more subtle techniques than he employed in the *Typhoon* volume. It is easy to understand why, years later, Conrad told Garnett that "the *Maga* public was . . . the one to catch on best to my stuff."[68]

Yet a close look at "The End of the Tether" reveals that *Blackwood's* influence on Conrad's writings was by no means wholly beneficial. The two obvious weaknesses of the story—excessive length and uncertainty of tone—can be traced to the conditions under which Conrad worked for the Edinburgh magazine. As early as June 1901, ten months before he began to write the story, Conrad had a strict sense of his commission for *Maga,* since the editor had told him:

> With regard to your inquiry about "Youth" and "Heart of Darkness," I find that these two stories together make 182 pages of the volume. They are already stereotyped so the rest will have to be set uniform.
>
> I do not think the volume could be made less than 300 pages, and as there are about 300 words in the page, that leaves forty thousand words to be supplied. If you think the story you thought of writing should run to twenty thousand words or so, just keep it at that, and write another one, and send them both to me for Maga. This will more than extinguish your debt, and be satisfactory to both of us.[69]

Conrad had no other story at hand to add to the volume so "The End of the Tether" had to fit these specifications. In later discussions between author and editor, the figure kept shifting back and forth from 30,000 to 40,000; but in any case the order was for a very long short story.

That "The End of the Tether" is stretched out far beyond the interest of its materials has been a critical commonplace for nearly sixty-five years. But its second flaw—the uncertainty of tone—has not been widely recognized. Recent readings of the story have established that Conrad intended his protagonist to be a vulnerable hero, humiliated and destroyed by his own moral failures as well as by the crush of circumstance. Since 1958, new evidence has been published which proves conclusively that in intention at least Conrad meant to convey exactly this impression. Yet two puzzling questions remain: Why have most readers held the opposite opinion so passionately and for so many years? and is there something in the fabric of Conrad's story that has added in part to the confusion?

The early reviewers, for instance, went wrong at once. Stirred by the "vivid, deeply moving" quality of Whalley's dilemma, they found the old man himself poignant, heroic, and genuinely inspirational. Conrad, at the first sight of the reviews, rushed off an exasperated letter to Edward Garnett with this memorable comment: "Touching, tender, noble, moving . . . Let us spit!"[70] Yet in 1913, when he was in a position to correct Richard Curle's critical monograph, Conrad let the offending words stand; and from that moment on, "beautiful," "touching," "tender," and "moving" became inextricably linked with the fate of Captain Whalley. Curle's remarks, not Conrad's, set the standards for the many interpretations that followed.[71] Whalley was established as the victim of circumstance, more sinned against than sinning, whose courageous struggle against fate demonstrated his fundamental grandeur of spirit. Yet such a reading is obviously not the one Conrad intended, nor is it justified by the closing section of the story itself. In a letter written to his publisher's assistant David Meldrum, which was first printed in 1958, Conrad makes this unmistakably clear.

The Elliot episode [in which Whalley meets an old colleague] has a fundamental significance insofar that it exhibits the first weakening of old Whalley's character before the assault of poverty. As you notice he says nothing of his position but goes off and takes advantage of the information. At the same time it gives me the opportunity to introduce Massy from way back without the formal narrative paragraphs. But the episode is mainly the first sign of that fate we carry within us. A character like Whalley's cannot cease to be frank with impunity. He is not frank with his old friend—such as the old friend is. For, if Elliot had been a genuine sort of man Whalley's secrecy would have been that of an intolerable fool. The pathos for me is in this that the concealment of his extremity is as it were forced upon him. Nevertheless it is weakness—it is deterioration. Next he conveys a sort of false impression to Massy—on justifiable grounds. I indicate the progress of deterioration the shaking the character receives and make it possible thus to by and by present the man as concealing the oncoming of blindness—and so on; till at last he conceals the criminal wrecking of his ship by committing suicide. And always there is just that shadow, that ghost of justification which should secure the sympathy of the reader.[72]

Turning that "ghost of justification" into something far more substantial, many critics have insisted that Captain Whalley is one of Conrad's heroic creations. Yet it is beyond doubt that Conrad was interested not in Whalley's fortitude or his bad luck, but in the flaw that motivated his life, the weakness that led so inexorably to his criminal act. The crucial contrast between the old man's physical stature and his moral makeup is essentially ironic: in appearance Whally is of heroic mould—a pilgrim with a great white beard, a "blinded Sampson," a "presumptuous Titan"—and yet in perception he is very much life size. He fails to recognize that his kind of romantic idealism is no longer relevant to the modern age; that, in a sense, his final pilgrimage is in a remote land, among a strange, unpredictable breed of men. He is only vaguely aware that his life represents "an archaic curiosity . . . a screed traced in obsolete words—in a half forgotten language." Vulnerable because of paternal pride, the overwhelming love for his daughter, he enters into the disastrous covenant with Massy; and his religious point of view proves too ingenuous, too idyllic, for the evil that finally engulfs him. Man, according to Captain Whalley, might be "silly, wrongheaded, unhappy; but naturally evil—no."

One of Conrad's important themes in "The End of the Tether" is that physical prowess is simply no substitute for a failure of moral response. Whalley may deserve our admiration for his tenacity, and our pity for his miserable predicament; but that in no way excuses his lapse into duplicity and cowardice, even if such deception had been originally prompted by love. For Conrad, the old man's single failure was more provocative than all of his earlier successes (which are merely reported and never dramatized) because it provided an opportunity to expose frailty and the weaknesses of an unarmed view of life based on illusion and simple-minded piety. The greater part of "The End of the Tether" deals sympathetically with Whalley's "spotless life" and his gradual breakdown; but the last twenty pages of the story are a relentless attack on his hollowness, stupidity, and failure of nerve. The "spotless life had fallen into the abyss," and "in the steadily darkening universe a sinister clearness fell upon his ideas. In the illuminating moments of suffering he saw life, men, all things, the whole earth with all her burden of created nature, as he had never seen them before."[73] And yet he decides to "cling to his deception with a fierce determination to carry it out to the end. . . ." It is here, in Whalley's refusal to accept the implications of his newly gained knowledge, that Conrad places his ultimate and crushing failure.

Those readers who see Whalley's end as heroic are simply ignoring the last part of the story, for the full extent of Conrad's condemnation can be understood only if the closing pages (in which the planter, Van Wyck, and Whalley's daughter receive the news of his death) are given their proper stress. Like "Heart of Darkness," "The End of the Tether" concludes on a sharp note of irony: Whalley, like Kurtz, sees the horror of his life and has his memory perpetuated by an enormous lie. Yet the ending of "Tether" is even more desperate than that of "Heart of Darkness." Kurtz, at least, has a final vision of the truth and dies; Whalley has a vision and stubbornly denies its validity. Marlow, at least, comes away with the truth about Kurtz; but no one ever learns the truth about Whalley, except perhaps the malicious first mate, who is aware that the death was not accidental. Conrad's point here is that everyone is deceived; the authorities, the skeptical Van Wyck, and the captain's daughter (who resembles Kurtz's fiancée)—all innocently share an image of Whalley that is woefully incomplete. And then, too, the final line of the story: "she had loved him, she felt she had loved him after all" seems in context undeniably charged with irony.

Part of the critical confusion about "The End of the Tether" is based on a failure to give the ending its due. Yet some of the blame must also rest with Conrad himself, for he spent far too much energy building up Whalley as an heroic figure and not nearly enough establishing his culpability and justifying his punishment in dramatic terms. The old captain's strength, courage, and honorable intentions are celebrated for more than one hundred pages; but his flaws of simplicity and moral flabbiness are given much less attention and may, for some readers, seem quite minor in comparison with his virtues. Whalley's weaknesses are simply not given enough play in the story to evoke a profound response, and Conrad's persistent attempt to sound the grand note is finally unconvincing. Whalley is caught on the way down, when he is already facing ruin; one calamity after another falls on his head; and then we are asked to judge him harshly for moral insufficiency. There is a sense in which it all happens too late, that Whalley is, as Van Wyck puts it, already "beyond good and evil." And this is why some readers come away from "the End of the Tether" with the unhappy feeling that the poor man is helpless to defend himself—a victim and, because of his dumb, instinctual stoicism, a kind of hero.

The striking imbalance between sympathy and judgment which has caused so many people to misread the story may have been a result of Conrad's desire to please his editors in Edinburgh. Just before he began "The End of the Tether," Conrad confessed to Ford: "I haven't a single notion in my head. The 'Wonderfulness' you have suggested is nowhere for the moment. Blackness is the impression of life—past and future; and though it is no doubt true and correct one can hardly fabricate 'Maga' stuff out of it. 'Tis too subtle. 'Taint raw enough."[74]

It seems likely that Conrad began with the intention of keeping the "blackness" of things from being the major note of his story, but was caught up by it in the end. This would explain in some measure the incompatibility between his initial high praise of Whalley as a hero and the final uncompromising attack on him at the close. The severity of the ending and of Whalley's ignominious defeat may well have been unconscious, for in later years Conrad spoke of his character with obvious warmth, and in his final remark on the subject, took his leave of Captain Whalley in terms of "affectionate silence."[75]

* * *

Six of the seven works discussed in this chapter are among Conrad's most impressive stories. With the exception of "To-morrow" (which may well be the only deliberate potboiler in the group), each work examines an important aspect of human life with force and originality, and each is an experiment in narrative different from anything that came before. From 1896 to 1903, Conrad's short stories are all of a piece; the seven works discussed in this chapter grew logically out of the six earlier ones both in theme and technique. And it is significant, too, that the period of Conrad's greatest development in the short story form coincided with his favorable publishing arrangement with *Blackwood's* and Heinemann.

In July 1896 Fisher Unwin suggested a collection of five stories of which Conrad had already written two, "The Idiots" and "An Outpost of Progress." From this point on, his next eleven stories were written with the idea of volume publication in mind. Unwin's suggestion materialized as *Tales of Unrest* (1898). Then, after "Youth" appeared, Blackwood offered to publish a volume of three stories which later became *Youth, a Narrative* (1902). Finally Conrad promised Heinemann a book of four tales which was published in 1903 under the title of *Typhoon and Other Stories*. After 1904 Conrad's short stories were usually written one at a time without any clear idea of future publication. Of course, he *always* planned to sell single stories to periodicals, but the later pieces (after 1904) were written almost exclusively with magazine publication in mind. The fortunate arrangement with *Blackwood's*, and to a lesser extent with Heinemann, gave Conrad a freedom that he would not have for at least another decade.

One index to his satisfaction can be found in the similarity between the magazine versions and the stories as they appeared in book form. As two scholarly studies have shown, the great majority of changes were verbal and decidedly minor.[76] "James Price" in *Cosmopolis* becomes "Henry Price" in the book version of "An Outpost of Progress"; the revisions in "Heart of Darkness" were for the most part grammatical; and so on. In the words of George Whiting, "The conclusions are obvious. . . . The fact that few changes were required proves Conrad's concern that his serial text should be reasonably perfect."[77] Later in his career, Conrad's attitude toward the magazines became more patronizing, and he often gave a periodical a rough version of a work that he planned to reshape for book publication.

Thus, the end of Conrad's association with *Blackwood's* and

Heinemann was a turning point in his career. Having found no new hospitable market for his serious work and still laboring under a great need for money, he finally decided to concentrate on the long novel, where he could exercise more freedom and perhaps make a more substantial claim to popular success. Conrad's novels were by no stretch of the imagination commercial successes, but they did at least outsell his volumes of stories. *Almayer's Folly* (1895) went into a second edition in 1896 and a third in 1902; *An Outcast of the Islands* (1896) reached a second edition in 1907; *The Nigger of the "Narcissus"* (1898) was reprinted in the year of its publication; and *Lord Jim* (1900) had a second printing in 1900, a third in 1904, and a fourth in 1905. *Romance*, which Conrad admitted was "dans le genre fort en vogue avec le public en ce moment-ci," went into a second edition a month after publication, setting a faster pace than any book he had published before. Admittedly, these were very small editions—an average first printing ran to about 2,000 to 3,000 copies, and the third and fourth of *Lord Jim* were only 525 copies each—but this still marked an improvement on the sales of *Tales of Unrest* (1898), which took eleven years to reach a second edition, and *Typhoon* (1903), which never required a regular second edition at all. The only book of stories whose sale matched the novels was *Youth, a Narrative* (1902), which had two printings totaling 4,200 copies and appeared in a third edition in 1909.*

Conrad turned his full attention from short stories to the novel for two reasons. He felt the inadequacy of the short story as a vehicle for expressing his more complicated ideas about society, politics, and individual moral dilemmas; and he thought that his chances of being a popular success were better in the longer form. (In the early 1900s, as today, once a writer was fairly well established his novels were considered more valuable commercial properties than volumes of short stories.) After 1903, a clear pattern emerges in Conrad's career. From 1903 to 1913, he wrote successful

---

* Speaking of this volume in 1899, Conrad said, "If only five thousand copies . . . could be sold! If only! But why dream of the wealth of the Indies?" (Jean-Aubry, I, 283).

novels and bad short stories; then from 1914 to 1924 (after he became a best-selling author), he wrote virtually no stories at all but mainly a series of inferior novels, which magnified the flaws of his potboiling tales. Obviously, he eventually wrote short stories only when he had to; when wealth ended the necessity, he stopped writing them. In 1905, however, the need was still great, and Conrad wrote to H. G. Wells, "I've been writing silly short stories, in which there's no pleasure and no permanent profit. But for temporary purposes they come in handy."[78] The history of Conrad's short story career from 1905 to 1916 is a history of work being done for temporary purposes. With the notable exceptions of "The Secret Sharer" and "The Shadow-Line," the later tales are not central to his achievement. One of the differences between Conrad's early and late work is the difference between a man writing what he wants to write and writing what he thinks someone else is anxious to read.

4
Stories During
the Years
of the Great Novels

Before 1904, the majority of Conrad's stories and novels were moral dramas of isolated individuals tested by the unfamiliar menace of a primitive world. With *Nostromo*, however, Conrad moved in a different direction. Conceiving this novel as "an intense creative effort on what, I suppose, will always remain my largest canvas,"[1] he wrote the first of several long works depicting not only the disasters of individuals but of whole segments of society as well. Once this choice had been made, Conrad was preoccupied by more public drama, and the short story form—concerned with individual human episodes—was too narrow to meet his needs. He wrote no stories at all while he worked for two years on *Nostromo*, and only an actual request for a serial from the *Strand* magazine gave him enough incentive to return to the form again. The short story had by this time become an instrument for raising money quickly, and Conrad admitted to Algernon Methuen that *A Set of Six* (1908) had a less serious intention than any of his previous story collections:

All the stories are stories of incident—action—not of analysis. All are dramatic in a measure but by no means of a gloomy sort. All, but two, draw their significance from the love interest—though of course they are not love stories in the conventional meaning. They are not studies—they touch no problem. They are just stories in which I've tried my best to be simply entertaining.[2]

A SET OF SIX

On the surface, A *Set of Six* does not seem very different from Conrad's other work. The stories all deal with the familiar themes of heroism, betrayal, guilt, and illusion; and there is enough brutality and madness to match the somber moods of earlier collections. Even the title page strikes an authentic Conradian note, commenting ironically on man's state in the world:

> *Les petites marionettes*
> *Font, font, font,*
> *Trois petits tours*
> *Et puis s'en vont.*
>   Nursery Rhyme[3]

But on closer examination, the stories can be seen to have many more features in common with conventional magazine fiction than with Conrad's serious work.

Most of the pieces in A *Set of Six* are not based on personal experience. In the past Conrad's best stories were all drawn from events in which he had participated, which he had witnessed at first hand, or of which he had heard from someone else; and usually these works were far more convincing than the stories he invented. Moreover, the elaborate narrative structure based on memory and reflection, which had given shape to his best fiction, is drastically simplified in A *Set of Six*. Although narrators are still used, they are different from the controlling voices of "Youth," or even "Falk." Then, too, the conflict between varieties of egoism and altruism, central to his finest stories, now becomes peripheral or almost nonexistent. Finally, a new emphasis is placed on love and humor, two elements that Conrad seemed to think were indispensable in popular fiction.

His opinions on these last two subjects are well known. In early letters Conrad often complained that his pessimistic subject matter foreordained his unpopularity; and in the year before *Chance* appeared, he boasted that "the girl novel" would bring him luck with the public. Throughout his career he was exceptionally sensitive to being called "a gloomy writer" and, as early as 1898, took pains to reassure William Blackwood that a narrative called "The Heart of Darkness" was not particularly bleak.[4] As late as 1922, when Richard Curle was preparing a critical article, Conrad revised the manuscript and told its author, "I struck out the phrase in which the word *tragedian* occurs. It is a repetition, but you have no idea with what force it comes to the ordinary reader! . . . Don't forget, my dear, that as a *selling* author my position is by no means assured in the U.S. yet; and the average mind shrinks from tragic issues."[5]

A *Set of Six* is the first book in which Conrad is primarily concerned with exploiting the conventions of popular fiction, and each of the stories can be read as an experiment in handling a time-honored formula: "Gaspar Ruiz" rests on sheer force and exaggerated sentiment; "The Brute" on grim sensationalism and sardonic humor; "The Anarchist" on melodrama and murder; "The Informer" on political intrigue of the cops-and-robbers sort; "The Duel" on valor and romantic history; and "Il Conde" on simple and sudden violence. That these formulae fail tells us something important about the qualities of Conrad's major fiction.

"GASPAR RUIZ"

When the *Strand* asked for a story in the fall of 1904, Conrad responded with the first section of "Gaspar Ruiz" and an outline for the rest. But after the editors decided not to use it, he put the manuscript aside until November of the following year. During the winter, Pinker managed to find interested readers at *Pall Mall*; yet even here the editors hesitated, hunted for a new title, and finally buried the piece in the back of the magazine. On its appearance in July–October 1906, it carried a subtitle ("The Story of a Guerrilla Chief") and four section headings ("The Bars of the Prison," "The Closed Door," "The Piece of Ordonnance," and "A Strong Man's End"), none of which appears in the final book version.

Based on actual events, the story takes place in Chile during the revolution of the 1830s.[6] Gaspar Ruiz, a Republican soldier, is captured by the Royalists and forced to fight on their side. During a furious attack, he is recaptured by the Republicans and ordered shot as a deserter; but after miraculously surviving the firing squad, he escapes into hiding. A simple peasant, with a mind "hardly active enough to take a discriminating view of the advantages or perils of treachery,"[7] he is at the mercy of his passions rather than his ideas. When he is protected by an aristocratic family, his loyalties shift once again, and he falls in love with their daughter, Erminia. Even after he has been restored to favor among the rebels, Gaspar wishes to marry her. Unhappily, the girl's fierce Royalist sympathies compel the civil governor to object to the marriage, forcing the enraged Ruiz to murder him and to flee once again. After several more involved turnabouts, Gaspar marries Erminia and becomes a leader of an army against his old friends, the Republicans. Some time later, Erminia gives birth to a daughter and both fall into the hands of Gaspar's enemies. In his effort to free them from a fortress, Gaspar has a dismantled cannon mounted on his back and fired at the huge walls. When the recoil smashes his spine, Erminia—who at first had seen him less as a lover than as an instrument of revenge—confesses her passion and commits suicide.

"Gaspar Ruiz" is the most overextended short story Conrad had written up to this time, and its weaknesses are particularly instructive for this study. I have tried to show at some length in earlier chapters how Conrad's normal narrative method involves the use of memory as a moral instrument. After the events of a typical story are interpreted by a sensitive observer, they are given their full significance by the quality of his response. Even when Conrad started to write for the popular magazine audience, he did not drop this method entirely, but simplified it; and most of the resulting stories are shallow and unevocative. As a revealing instance of the deterioration of Conrad's method, "Gaspar Ruiz" is worth studying in some detail.

An omniscient narrator begins with a series of statements about the effect of revolution on individual fame. Some people, he claims, are raised out of obscurity by their heroic actions but are soon forgotten; while others, especially leaders, are immortalized by writers

and live in books. One such is General Santierra, who at the time
of the Chilean revolution, was a lieutenant in the Republican army.
The narrator then drops Santierra to speak of Gaspar Ruiz, only to
have the general reappear ten pages later in the role of a second narrator. Santierra tells several dinner guests about his contact with
Ruiz in the early years of the revolution; and from this point on,
the story has alternate narrators. Every time Santierra is at a loss
for information, the first observer picks up the thread of the story.
Only at the very end is he revealed to be a dinner guest at the general's house.

The clumsiness may seem to be a trifling weakness; given Conrad's intention, however, it suggests a disturbing confusion in technique. In the author's note to *A Set of Six*, written in 1920, Conrad explains his choice of narrator:

*The manner for the most part is that of General Santierra, and that
old warrior, I note with satisfaction, is very true to himself all
through. Looking now dispassionately at the various ways in which
this story could have been presented I can't honestly think the General superfluous. It is he, an old man talking of the days of his youth,
who characterizes the whole narrative and gives it an air of actuality
which I doubt whether I could have achieved without his help. In
the mere writing his existence of course was of no help at all, because
the whole thing had to be carefully kept within the frame of his
simple mind.*[8]

Obviously, Santierra is supposed to be Conrad's moral spokesman.
Yet the question remains: How trustworthy is the old man's response? At the end of the story, he describes Erminia's death:

"I cannot describe to you the sudden and abject fear that came
over me at that dreadful sight. It was a dread of the abyss, the dread
of the crags which seemed to nod upon me. My head swam. I pressed
the child to my side and sat my horse as still as a statue. I was speech-
less and cold all over. . . . My heart stood still, and from the depths
of the precipice the stones rattling in the bed of the furious stream
made me almost insane with their sound. . . ."

General Santierra ceased and got up from the table. *"And that is all, señores,"* he concluded, *with a courteous glance at his rising guests.*

"But what became of the child, General?" we asked.

"Ah, the child, the child."

He walked to one of the windows opening on his beautiful garden, the refuge of his old days. Its fame was great in the land. Keeping us back with a raised arm, he called out, "Erminia, Erminia!" and waited.[9]

The girl, or rather, the woman appears. She has lived as the general's housekeeper for some thirty years, and Santierra ends the story with her praise:

"Good, patient, devoted to the old man. A simple soul. But I would not advise any of you to ask for her hand, for if she took yours into hers it would be only to crush your bones. Ah! She does not jest on that subject. And she is the own daughter of her father, the strong man who perished through his own strength: the strength of his body, of his simplicity—of his love."[10]

For the first time since "An Outpost of Progress," Conrad uses something like the surprise ending of Maupassant. The result, however, is not sudden, or shocking, or in any way revelatory, but only crudely sentimental. Instead of providing his story with "a sting in its tail," Conrad ends with a gentle touch of benevolence, asking the reader to believe that Gaspar's great force lives in the simple yet awesome presence of his daughter.

Another serious weakness in "Gaspar Ruiz" can be traced to Conrad's reliance on his nostalgic and simple-minded general. The only way in which such a narrator could be used to achieve the typical Conradian effect would be to have the first observer act as a sophisticated foil; but nothing of this sort happens. For sixty pages Santierra is too overbearing, constantly using bombast to force tragic responses on situations that are only violent and circumstantial. Describing the death of Ruiz, he tells his audience: "He lay there before me on his breast under the darkly glittering bronze of his monstrous burden, such as no love or strength of man had ever had to bear in the lamentable history of the world. His arms were spread out, and he resembled a prostrate penitent on the moonlit ground."[11] Nothing in the blundering life of Ruiz has prepared us for such rhetoric, and there is nothing in the story to counteract its transparent theatricality.

Here, then, are two of the most familiar features of conventional magazine fiction: on one hand, contrived and overwrought emotion (strong feelings of pity and horror are said to have occurred but are not demonstrated); and on the other, exaggerated delicacy and compassion (virile characters are suddenly shown to have acted from motives of great tenderness, and we are asked to believe in their magnanimity and good nature).

The other flaws in "Gaspar Ruiz" are also symptomatic of Conrad's work after *Nostromo*. There is a preoccupation with such complex themes as political duplicity and the debasement of genuine social ideas when put into action; but these themes, so memorably handled in full-length novels, are too heavy for the delicate frame of the short story and tend to be either oversimplified or imperfectly conveyed. The familiar conflict between egoism and altruism, also evident here, is superficially treated. Ruiz's egoism—the reflexive self-assertion of an "acquiescent soul"—and Santierra's altruism— sentimental to the point of senility—are both simple-minded. The only interesting character is Erminia, driven by a desire for revenge. Never given an adversary worthy of her obsession, however, she remains a dim figure.

Obviously, Conrad recognized the company that "Gaspar Ruiz" should keep. When a reviewer compared it with Turgenev's "Lear of the Steppes," Conrad exploded in a letter to Garnett: *"The Lear*!!!! that infernal magazine fake with the *Lear of the Steppes*!!!! It is enough to make one wonder whether the man understands the words he writes—whether he has sense and judgment enough to come in when it rains."[12] In 1920 he turned the original tale into a movie script called "The Strong Man" (which was never filmed) and wrote to Richard Curle, "I am ashamed to tell you this—but one must live. . . . The Movie is just a silly stunt for silly people. . . ."[13] Such an end for "Gaspar Ruiz" is odd yet fitting, for it has many of the characteristics of a class B film: a fast-moving plot, a group of uncomplicated characters motivated by love and revenge, a stolid hero who performs a superhuman feat of bravery, and a deathbed scene in which the heroine confesses her undying love as a baby sleeps tenderly at her breast. Such a combination of force and sentiment made "Gaspar Ruiz" a perfect choice for *Pall Mall Magazine*, which—if it had been founded twenty-five years later—would have been a rich source of nourishment for Hollywood script writers.[14]

"THE BRUTE"

Of the three works that immediately followed "Gaspar Ruiz" ("The Brute," "An Anarchist," and "The Informer"—all written between November 1905 and January 1906), "The Brute" is the least substantial. The only facts known about its genesis were revealed by Conrad in the author's note to *A Set of Six*:

The first I heard of [the ship's] homicidal habits was from the late Captain Blake, commanding a London Ship in which I served in 1884 [actually 1885] as Second Officer. . . . The existence of the brute was a fact. The end of the brute as related in the story . . . really happened to another ship. I have unscrupulously adapted it to the needs of my story thinking that I had there something in the nature of poetical justice.*

"The Brute" begins when the narrator drops by a neighborhood pub to hear a stranger tell the story of *The Apse Family*, a huge, fabulously built ship with the savage distinction of having killed

---

* As he often did, Conrad mingled facts from his own career with the fictional materials. Several details in "The Brute" are borrowed from "Youth": Jermyn, the morose North Sea pilot, appears for a second time; and Colchester, Beard's home in "Youth," becomes the name of a captain in "The Brute." To reinforce the similarity, Conrad gives both captains "iron-grey hair."

a person on every trip it made.* After describing some of its adventures and mentioning its victims (one of whom had been his brother's fiancée), the stranger ends with an account of how "the brute" was wrecked because its careless Captain Wilmot spent his time watching a seductive governess instead of the ship's compass. In an offhand way he notes that Wilmot, broken as a seaman, is reduced to driving a wagon in Australia; and when somebody asks, "Anybody lost?" he replies, "No one unless that fellow, Wilmot . . . and his case was worse than drowning for a man."

Since "The Brute" never rises above the anecdotal, Conrad's relaxed attempt to imply something about unrestrained malevolence never assumes any real coherence. None of the ship's victims is given personal identity, and the sequence of events remains gratuitous, without the unsettling force that senseless violence can so often have. But the story could have been effective, even as a slight anecdote, if it were not for its complete confusion of tone—its bewildering mixture of indignation, sarcasm, and false heartiness. Many of the serious statements are undercut by a casual cheerfulness, an attempt at sly humor; and several of these jests are irrelevant to the story of the ship and its victims.

Never before did Conrad seem to have so much trouble getting in and out of a story. The first narrator begins: "Dodging in from the rain-swept street, I exchanged a smile and a glance with Miss Blank in the bar of the Three Crows. This exchange was effected with extreme propriety. It is a shock to think that, if still alive, Miss Blank must be over sixty now. How time passes!"[15] And he ends with the same coyness: "On going out I exchanged a glance and a smile (strictly proper) with the respectable Miss Blank, barmaid of the Three Crows."[16] But Miss Blank plays no other role in the story, and the narrator himself is hardly less a cipher.

Other attempts at forced liveliness follow, and they too fail to come off. Described as wearing comfortable tweeds, the second narrator punctuates the story of the destructive ship with homely

---

* The name of the ship, *The Apse Family*, may have been based on *The Bates Family*, a ship destroyed near Singapore in mid-September 1880, at the same time the *Jeddah* and the *Cutty Sark* were experiencing the notoriety exploited by Conrad in *Lord Jim* and "The Secret Sharer."

comments about his being "the baby of the family" and being hen-pecked by his wife. Conrad may have been trying to set up a con-trast between the domesticity of the stranger and the outrageous violence of the Brute; but if so, he was unsuccessful, since these embarrassed comments work against any serious effect the story might have had.

Whenever Conrad tries in fiction to strike up a friendship with the reader, it is a clear sign of trouble. Once, in a revealing comment to Richard Curle, he described how his method, "perfectly devoid of familiarity as between author and reader, aimed essentially at the intimacy of a personal communication."[17] "The Brute" is a useful example of the method when it has broken down, for many of the narrator's remarks are designed to establish the kind of fa-miliarity between author and reader that never suited Conrad, whose temperament was unfit for hearty backslapping. Conrad's mature method allows him to achieve intimacy while still keeping his distance—a balance never maintained in "The Brute."

Conrad's original intention must have been fairly serious, for he subtitled the story "A Piece of Invective"; and when it appeared in *A Set of Six*, he described it as "An Indignant Tale." But the sharp-ness is so vitiated by the strained humor that this tale, aimed at a wide audience, seems to have had little impact. Rejected by *Black-wood's* as being both uninteresting and derivative,[18] it was finally sold by Pinker to the London *Daily Chronicle*, becoming the first of Conrad's stories to appear in a daily newspaper. "The Brute" has one other bleak distinction: it is the only Conrad story in which a physical object is more important than any human being.

The qualities that brand "The Brute" and "Gaspar Ruiz" as potboilers are all on the surface. In the South American tale, emo-tion is contrived, language inorganic, and the final effect crudely sentimental; in the story of *The Apse Family*, a tone of awkward conviviality spoils what might have been a forceful, if minor, anecdote. The weaknesses in Conrad's next two works are less seri-ous. Both "An Anarchist" and "The Informer" are controlled and reasonably convincing stories; and if in the final analysis they seem insignificant, it is not because of any basic falseness, but because they were insufficiently developed, minor variations on a theme that receives definitive treatment in *The Secret Agent* and *Under Western Eyes.*

The immediate impulse behind the writing of the two terrorist stories is unclear. Ford Madox Ford must have been responsible for some of the material, since he had contacts with extremists and, at the time of the peasant uprisings, spoke seriously of going to Russia "to see the revolution from within."[19] But aside from Conrad's admission that "the pedigree of these tales is hopelessly complicated," few revealing facts about the stories have come to light.

"AN ANARCHIST"

"An Anarchist" is narrated by a lepidopterist who becomes interested in the history of a solitary workman named Paul on a South American cattle estate. Some years earlier, while living in Paris and minding his own affairs, Paul became carelessly drunk, shouted "Vive l'anarchie," and landed in jail. An ambitious socialist lawyer, hoping to create a martyr for the revolutionary cause, inflamed the court and got Paul a maximum sentence. Once free, the bewildered man kept being rejected by employers as a dangerous risk and eventually wandered back among anarchists, for whom he had no particular feeling. Pressed by his new associates, he became involved in a bank robbery, was double-crossed, arrested again, and sent to the island fortress of St. Joseph's. During a violent prison break, he managed to get free in a small boat with two of his old confederates who were responsible for his arrest. At gun point, he forced them to row toward the coast of South America; but when, sighting a ship, they shouted, "Vive la liberté," he murdered them and tossed the bodies into the sea. After he had reached the cattle estate, he was enslaved by the ruthless manager. He now rejects the narrator's suggestion to escape, deciding, "I shall die here . . . away from *them.*" The narrator concludes, "On the whole, my idea is that he was much more of an anarchist than he confessed to me or to himself; and that, the special features of his case apart, he was very much like many other anarchists. Warm heart and weak head—that is the word of the riddle. . . ."[20]

A simple story with a steady line of action and little analysis, "An Anarchist" is not—as some readers have suggested—a "savage" piece of work. It might have been, if Conrad had used the irony of *The Secret Agent*, or magnified the absurdity of the victim's position or the homicidal intentions of his tormentors (as he did in "Amy Foster"). Instead, he makes the anarchist's plight merely pathetic, not nearly as engrossing as the truly savage predicaments of Winnie Verloc or Yanko Goorall. The major tone of "An Anarchist" is conveyed by an image that appears twice in the tale. When the narrator first meets Paul, he remarks: "He did not like to lie awake in the dark, he confessed. He complained that sleep fled from him. '*Le sommeil me fuit*,' he declared, with his habitual air of subdued stoicism, which made him sympathetic and touching." And in the last lines he repeats the image: "Sometimes I think of him lying open-eyed on his horseman's gear in the low shed full of tools and scraps of iron—the anarchist slave of the Maranon estate, waiting with resignation for that sleep which 'fled' from him, as he used to say, in such an unaccountable manner."[21] Although this image of lost sleep reinforces the theme of guilt and recognition, the force of such recognition is deliberately muted ("subdued stoicism" sets the note), and the story fails to achieve any cumulative power.

But the main trouble with "An Anarchist" is its thinness. The story is purely circumstantial; no coherent view of conspiracy and sedition can be sifted from its pages; the anarchists themselves hardly appear, and their victim is merely a lonely man with rotten luck and no particular self-awareness. The narrator's insistence that Paul is "more of an anarchist than he confessed to me or to himself" appears forced, since not all blunderers are anarchists, and Paul never displays any consciousness of ideology: "the principal truth discoverable," in his views, "was that a little thing may bring about the undoing of a man."[22] Although Paul's final rejection of society is a painful gesture, it has little public or even private significance. His situation is passive and he himself indifferent; we learn what was done to him by others, but get little sense of what he did to himself or how his ideas about life are changed by his experience.

Once again, as in "The Brute," Conrad tried to lighten the gloom with humor. The opening paragraphs are filled with jokes about modern advertising and catching butterflies, and there is a crude caricature of the estate manager who keeps asking the narrator,

"How's the deadly sport going today?" Conrad may have been trying to set up another ironical contrast between the catcher of butterflies and the victimized, virtually impaled, workman; but this connection is never very clear and is not even mentioned in the last two-thirds of the story. This particular collector of butterflies has none of the earnestness or intelligence of his more celebrated colleague, Herr Stein, in *Lord Jim*.

Despite Conrad's efforts to seize on the comic element in the story of the hapless anarchist, the humor is always beside the point. The natural affinities between melodrama and sinister farce is Conrad's subject in *The Secret Agent*; but in "An Anarchist" such a connection hardly exists.

"An Anarchist" was the first Conrad story to be printed in *Harper's Magazine*, where he was later to publish "The Informer," "The Secret Sharer," and "The Partner." Early in 1903, Colonel George Harvey, president of Harper and Brothers, agreed to buy *Nostromo* sight unseen, and Conrad said "the terms are the best I've ever had."[23] During the next ten years, Harper's became Conrad's main American publisher and with its two periodicals, *Harper's Weekly* and *Harper's Magazine*, published five books (including *Nostromo*, *The Secret Agent*, and *Under Western Eyes*), four stories, and a handful of autobiographical sketches.

At first, Conrad had hoped for a steady, uncomplicated relationship with one publisher, and Colonel Harvey seemed ideal. Not only was he president of a book firm and two magazines, but he independently edited the *North American Review*. Conrad had always favored publishers with magazine connections and told Harvey: "I of course don't know how far you desire me to be 'your' author—and of course also I am not asking that question. My feeling is that I would not like to see my future work scattered amongst various publishing houses—as it has been in the past."[24]

In the following year, Conrad accepted an offer from Methuen and Company to publish his next three novels in England, and for the moment his tangled publishing affairs seemed to be straightening out. Despite some unfinished business with Heinemann and Blackwood, Conrad was to stay with Harper's from 1906 to 1912 and with Methuen from 1906 to 1915.

It soon became clear, however, that both Harper's and Methuen considered Conrad to be just one moderately successful author on their long and noteworthy lists, and he began to chaff from lack of attention. But since he was bound to Methuen by contract and to Harper's by large fees, Conrad suffered in relative silence, telling Pinker in 1905, "Harper's is not perfection but I think we ought to keep with them."[25] As his financial situation became increasingly more bleak, Conrad grew restive and spoke often of switching allegiances to firms that would advertise his works more actively. His letters during this period contain references to Harvey and "his henchmen," Methuen and "his shop." In April 1909, when a Harper's executive stopped him on the street asking to have Harper's handle his next book, Conrad could hardly contain his astonishment. With undisguised irony, he told the man "he wasn't aware of his relationship with Harper's being interrupted."[26]

Although the history of Conrad's relationships with Methuen and Harper's is impossible to reconstruct fully at this date, it seems as if he stayed with Methuen because he had signed a contract and with Harper's because they paid well. In 1911 he told Pinker, "I don't like my position with Methuen. . . . It is not as if Methuen were a firm owning an old established magazine from whom one could expect some advantages in the way of serial publication. A very important point which we have secured to a certain extent with Harper's, whatever their shortcomings as a publishing house may be."[27] And a year later he was more specific: "Even now Harper's pay me 100gn for a short story (9,000 words) and they will take three every year if I like to send them."[28]

During 1912, when *Chance* began to appear in the *New York Herald*, Conrad took advantage of his increased popularity and accepted an offer from Doubleday and Page to publish his books in America. In March 1913 he signed with J. M. Dent in England. During the last eleven years of Conrad's life, Doubleday and Dent were his major publishers.

When Conrad first appeared in *Harper's Magazine* in 1906, the journal had just celebrated its fiftieth anniversary; and in a birthday article, the editor made this revealing comparison:

There are really only two types of magazine, excluding, of course, those devoted to some distinct specialty. Blackwood is the original of one type, Harper of the other. . . . The distinction is not that of an illustrated from an unillustrated magazine. Harper is not Blackwood plus suitable illustrations. Some things—for example, the best kind of fiction—might be common to both, but there would always be this difference, that Blackwood would by choice appeal to a limited class of highly cultivated readers, proposing to meet special demands of that class, while Harper would be addressed to all readers of average intelligence, having for its purpose their entertainment and illumination, meeting in a general way the varied claims of their human intellect and sensibility. . . . Blackwood would begin on the highest level of special literary excellence. . . . Harper, starting from the lowest level to which Blackwood could properly fall, would, with always the most ready accommodation to popular interest, steadily ascend.[29]

Ten years later, again in a reminiscent mood, the editor remarked that one of the most noteworthy features of the years from 1900 to 1910 was the growth of the short story, which had driven the serial novel (once a great favorite) into partial obscurity. The new policy at *Harper's* was to allow only one serial at a time to run in the magazine, whereas "every number . . . contains seven or eight short stories of exceptional and varied interest."[30] By the early years of the century the short story had become the dominant magazine form, and the dangers of dominance were soon obvious.

The majority of the nine hundred stories that appeared in *Harper's* during this ten-year period were romances, most of which were written by ladies with three names: Mary Shipman Andrews, Elizabeth Stuart Phelps, Harriet Prescott Spoffard, Grace Ellery Channing, Lily A. Long, Emma Bell Miles, Mary Wilkins Freeman, Madeline Yale Wynne, Sarah Barnwell Elliott, and Abby Mequire Roach. Most followed the pattern of boy meets girl, with the setting—not the plot—varying occasionally. Boy met girl in bohemian New York, old Virginia, rural New England, southern France, the ruins of Rome, or the drawing rooms of northern Ohio. If the central motif was not romantic, it would most likely be something worse: a bathetic tale about insufferably cute children, variously titled "Petticoat Push," "Little-Girl-Afraid-of Dog," and "Flyaway Flittermouse." The patron saint of these writers was George du Maurier, whose *Trilby* brought *Harper's* great acclaim when it was serialized in 1893.

Every so often a memorable work would break into the magazine. Hardy's *Jude the Obscure* appeared there under the title *Heart's Insurgent* in the middle nineties, and Twain's "The Man that Corrupted Hadleyburg" was published in December 1899. Generally, however, when a notable writer appeared in *Harper's* it was with his least interesting work. Howells published one-act plays and less than his best fiction, James wrote travel sketches, and Twain was likely to provide "A Horse's Tale," in which Buffalo Bill's horse is the narrator.

The most remarkable thing about *Harper's* fiction was its uniform size. Of eighty-four short stories that appeared between September 1905 and August 1906, not one was more than 8,500 words in length, and the great majority were between 7,000 and 8,000 words long. Even Henry James in his late manner could not break the rule: "Julia's Bride" was printed in two parts, each of about 8,000 words. Obviously, if a writer wanted a story to appear in *Harper's*, he had to use a rather exact yardstick to measure its length.

Was it a coincidence that Conrad's "An Anarchist" was 8,000 words, "The Informer" 8,500, and "The Secret Sharer" (printed in two issues) 16,000 words long? It is impossible to know for certain, since Pinker may have tallied the words and then sent the pieces off to *Harper's*. But the reverse would have been more likely, for Conrad used to speak about Harper's 9,000-word short stories[31] and frequently received requests for new work from H. M. Alden, the editor.

Although the subject matter of "An Anarchist" and "The Informer" was not suited to *Harper's*, the severity of both tales is deliberately undercut by a curious strain of self-conscious humor. To make his work even more palatable, Conrad sometimes provided passages for the magazine audience that would be cut from the book

version when it appeared. The following example shows Conrad
trying to ease his way into the reader's confidence with the kind of
chatter that was a trademark of F. Marion Crawford. It appeared
only in the magazine text of "An Anarchist."

*What makes [the story] interesting is its imbecility. In that it is not
singular. The whole of the public and private records of humanity,
history and story alike, are made interesting precisely by that price-
less defect, under which we all labor—to our everlasting discom-
fiture, but to each other's entertainment and edification. The story
contains all the elements of pathos and fun, of tragedy and comedy,
of sensation and surprise—whereas from rational conduct there is
nothing to be expected of a touching, instructive, and amusing nature. I am sure to be misunderstood, but I disdain to labor a point
which to me seems absolutely self-evident. I will only remark that
the whole body of fiction bears me out. Its main theme, I believe,
is love. But it has never entered any writer's head to take rational
love for a subject. We should yawn. Only the complicated absurdi-
ties of that psycho-physiological state can arouse our interest and
sympathy. However, there is nothing loving or lovable in what I am
going to relate.*[32]

While working for *Blackwood's*, Conrad was able to write virtually without restriction; while working for *Harper's* he seemed to
meditate more often than was helpful on the demands of the
audience. *Harper's* had no interest in length or psychological complexity; for a writer who often needed 10,000 words just to get under
way, this was a severe handicap. Since Conrad's two main outlets
for short fiction between 1904 and 1912 were *Pall Mall* and *Harper's*, it is not surprising that his stories became less substantial than
the work of his earlier years.

"THE INFORMER"

"The Informer" is another tale in which an adequate main idea is
not sufficiently developed. Like "The Brute," it is based on a rather
plain external contrast; but in this instance the contrast is at least

relevant to the meaning of the central action, instead of being tacked onto it. A collector of fine porcelain learns from a friend that Mr. X, a notorious pamphleteer and the greatest rebel of modern times, is also a connoisseur of exquisite china and would like to pay him a visit. The two men meet and are oddly attracted to one another. The anarchist, fastidious, impeccably dressed—more like a count than a rebel—fascinates the narrator with his insistence that "there's no amendment to be got out of mankind except by terror and violence";[33] whereas the narrator, with a whole way of life based upon "a suave and delicate discrimination of social and artistic values,"[34] appeals to the anarchist's love of fine living. During their talk, Mr. X viciously attacks the idle classes as "amateurs of emotion," who feed their vanity by buying his subversive writings and supporting his cause, without realizing that they are contributing to their own destruction. When the simple-minded narrator says such absurd things never happen in England, Mr. X proceeds to tell a story to prove his point.

A rich girl with a neurotic desire to assert her individuality "had acquired all the appropriate gestures of revolutionary convictions— the gestures of pity, of anger, of indignation against the anti-humanitarian vices of the social class to which she belonged herself."[35] Having decided to let the anarchists use her house in Hermione Street as a safe front for printing seditious leaflets, she completes her commitment by falling in love with a romantic revolutionary named Sevrin. Mr. X, then an important figure in the Brussels underworld, is troubled by the fact that all the plans prepared in Hermione Street invariably failed. Convinced a police informer was masquerading among the anarchists, he plans a fake raid in the hope that the informer would tip his hand to men he thought were police officers. At the moment of crisis, Sevrin reveals himself as the spy in order to save the girl, but she scorns him as a traitor. After their quarrel, he commits suicide and she enters a convent. Mr. X concludes, "What does it matter? Gestures! Gestures! Mere gestures of her class." Some time later, the narrator, told by his old friend that Mr. X "likes to have his little joke sometimes," comments, "I fail to understand the connection of this last remark. I have been utterly unable to discover where in all this the joke comes in."[36]

Although Conrad's evocation of the duplicity that surrounds anarchist activities has an impressive credibility, the story never generates much power because the girl and Sevrin are pasteboard figures manipulated to make a point. Even the personality of Mr. X is not clearly conveyed. A fascinating scoundrel, defiantly outwitting his associates both in and out of the social order, he is never engaged by an equal adversary. The girl and Sevrin are blinded by their absorption in false convictions, and the collector is simply too inexperienced in the ways of the world to understand the grim comedy. Mr. X's dilemma of being an anarchist spoiled by success is one of the fine ironic touches of the story, but the actual drama inherent in this predicament is not exploited. Whatever drama does exist in "The Informer" comes from a stock theatrical device and not from the clash of character or belief.

Perhaps Conrad intended this to happen, for he had enormous contempt for the blind brutality of revolutionary intrigue, and saw idiocy rather than subtle drama in such senseless activities. He subtitled the story "An Ironic Tale"; and by keeping his distance and creating two narrators (both of whom are deliberately made unsympathetic), he managed to give the entire story absurd overtones and to condemn the anarchist world by placing it entirely outside our sympathy. Yet because of Conrad's inimical intention, "The Informer" remains more interesting as a piece of invective than as a short story.

"IL CONDE"

"Il Conde," which followed at the end of the year, is free from the obvious faults that mar the other works in *A Set of Six*. It is, in fact, an excellent example of how Conrad's newest preoccupations with direct plotting and narrative simplicity were finally wedded to an idea that demanded just such treatment. He wrote the tale in only ten days, admitting, "I am rather proud of that little trick";[37] and fifteen years later, in the author's note to his collected works, he explained:

Il Conde (misspelt by-the-by) is an almost verbatim transcript of the tale told me by a very charming old gentleman whom I met in Italy [an acquaintance, Count Szembek]. I don't mean to say that it is only that. Anybody can see that it is something more than a verbatim report, but where he left off and where I began must be left to the acute discrimination of the reader who may be interested in the problem.[38]

The story begins with the narrator's description of the count, a kindly man of quiet urbanity, whose ordered existence has been free from unconventional events. On returning to Naples from a visit, the narrator learns that his old acquaintance had been held up at knife point by an aristocratic young bandit and forced to surrender a small amount of money and a worthless watch. Sometime later, while catching his breath in a cafe, he had been accosted a second time and viciously insulted for having held back a twenty-franc piece. Terribly shaken, "his belief in the respectable placidity of life having received this rude shock," the old count now feels that "anything might happen."[39] Although certain that his health could not survive another journey, he decides to leave Naples, not from fear but because "his delicate conception of his dignity was defiled by a degrading experience."[40] The narrator remarks at the close that such a trip amounts to suicide.

"Il Conde" is most interesting for the straightforward way in which Conrad creates sympathy for the old man and yet leaves no doubt that he is an accessory in the unsettling crisis of his old age. A life-long advocate of moderation, the count is driven to self-destruction by excessive delicacy. On the surface, his plight seems imposed from the outside, a gratuitous assault on decorum; but as the significance of his acts becomes clear, his complicity is undeniable. Through the careful juxtaposition of ironic detail, Conrad is able to provide the kind of substantial character portrayal absent from his short fiction since the days of "Typhoon" and "Amy Foster." Although its success is modest, "Il Conde" retains a currency not shared by its neighbors in *A Set of Six.*

The sympathy comes first. In the opening pages the narrator describes the old man's cloak of refinement as attractive though mildly precious; then in the second part he reveals how delicacy can turn sour and self-destructive. The refinement is mainly a matter of social decorum, of knowing the right cloth or the precise word. Like Prufrock, the count is "Deferential, glad to be of use / Politic, cautious, and meticulous"; and as the details of his life accumulate, he becomes the image of defenseless decency.

When he describes his "abominable adventure," the count unconsciously confesses his extravagance and irrationality, and the narrator uses these admissions to accentuate the fundamental ironies of the old man's situation. When he first mentions his mishap, the count cries out, "It is very serious. Very serious," and yet asks permission to delay his narrative until both men had finished dinner. This blatant instance of false delicacy is matched a few minutes later when the count explains that he failed to scream out for help because he feared the bandit might claim *he* was the aggressor. The absurdity of this response has bothered several critics who have written on "Il Conde." John Howard Wills, whose "Adam, Axel, and 'Il Conde' " is a remarkable instance of undisciplined ingenuity,[41] claims that the count is silent because he recognizes his secret sharer; and even John V. Hagopian, whose essay is the best thing in print on the tale, seems to see some truth in the argument.[42] But surely the count's own explanation, though less theatrical, is more convincing. He failed to call for help because he was frightened of creating a scene: "it was in his character to shrink from scandal, much more than from mere death."[43] Again, the motive is false delicacy, not the sudden discovery of his own criminal potentiality.

Once the count's imagination is inflamed, he searches for explanations that will soften the shock. First, he insists that the "young man was perhaps merely an infuriated lunatic," and that no one's self-esteem "need be affected by what a madman may choose to do. . . ." For a short time, these defenses work, allowing him "to argue himself into comparative equanimity." But the second crushing insolence destroys his balance and he flees from Naples. The narrator sums up: "*Vedi Napoli e poi mori*. It is a saying of excessive vanity, and everything excessive was abhorrent to the nice moderation of the poor Count. Yet, as I was seeing him off at the railway station, I thought he was behaving with singular fidelity to its conceited spirit. . . ."[44]

Although "Il Conde" is a straightforward piece of work, a number of critics have seen it as symbolic, either of the expulsion from Eden (Wills) or "the violence that was to overtake Europe in 1914" (Frederick Karl[45]). The origins of these interpretations can be found in certain stray details of the story. But as John Hagopian has proven in his useful corrective essay, the details are never developed; and the story is too frail to bear the implications of myth and symbol. In fact the distinction of "Il Conde" is of an entirely different order. Although it does have some teasing and suggestive details, it is a work that constantly backs away from complexity and exploits some of the most familiar conventions of magazine fiction: direct narrative, a suspenseful plot, a simple hero, and an undifferentiated villain. Some of the characteristic Conradian devices are present, but only in skeletal form. The narrator has Marlow's irony but none of his analytical power; leitmotifs occur but are remarkable for being monotonic; tell-tale phrases point the way too clearly; and so on. "Il Conde" remains one of the most artful of Conrad's pot-boilers; that is all the weight it can safely carry.

"THE DUEL"

About six weeks after finishing "Il Conde," Conrad announced to Pinker a new story called "The Duel" and added, "my modesty prevents me saying that I think the story good. Action sensational. The ending happy."[46] Set in France during the Napoleonic wars, "The Duel" follows the careers of two officers who for sixteen years fight duels to settle small points of honor. Feraud, from Gascony, is the typical southerner—hot-tempered, boastful, quick to reach for a sword; whereas D'Hubert, from Picardy, exemplifies the modest, reflective qualities of the man from the north. Although

Feraud is always the aggressor, D'Hubert is ceremonious enough never to refuse a challenge and soon finds that their quarrel orders his life during the difficult years of war. Finally, after outwitting Feraud, D'Hubert spares his life for a promise never to fight again. Unknown to the defeated man, his rival sends money for support because "it's extraordinary how in one way or another this man has managed to fasten himself on my deeper feelings."

As DeLancey Ferguson has shown, Conrad based his story on an actual rivalry made legendary in journals throughout the nineteenth century.[47] The 1858 version that Ferguson uncovered from *Harper's* includes many details later to appear in "The Duel." Whether Conrad knew this version or some other is unclear; but whatever the source, the original proved so absorbing that he could scarcely bother to conceal his borrowings. Originally Fournier and Dupont, Feraud and D'Hubert follow the same sequence of mutual maiming in the story that their counterparts did in real life; and similar motives, situations, and snatches of dialogue appear both in the source and its re-creation.

If Conrad had been content to retell a striking anecdote, "The Duel" might have made a brisk, light-hearted companion to "Il Conde." But instead, he decided to use the fragile story as support for his reflections on the spirit of the Napoleonic age, about which he had read widely for many years. Planning to call the tale "The Masters of Europe," Conrad wished to make the exuberant singularity of Feraud and D'Hubert exemplary of the "childlike exaltation of sentiment," the naïve heroism, so characteristic of early nineteenth century France. Putting aside the question of whether such feelings were actually a major element in the *Zeitgeist*, one can still fault Conrad for his banal treatment of the theme and for his failure to develop the more promising of his two subjects.

The "secret sharer" motif, handled here with an attempt at comedy, is potentially more interesting than the grandiose "spirit of the age," especially in a writer whose analytical gifts were primarily moral and psychological. Almost gratuitously chosen by Feraud, D'Hubert comes to feel both an "irreconcilable antagonism" and an "irrational tenderness" toward his adversary, admitting that their conflict has put "special excitement into the delightful, gay intervals between the campaigns." The repetition of the phrase "irreconcilable antagonism"—used by Conrad six years before to define the conflict between egoism and altruism—is a clue to a genuine source of interest in the relationship between Feraud and D'Hubert. Unable to reconcile the facts of daily life with the passionate state of his own feelings, Feraud turns his tumult into an abstract idea, noisily defending the illusion of wounded honor half-way across Europe. D'Hubert, despite an instinctive desire for kindly action, lacks the assertive intelligence to keep his life from being directed by the egotistical claims of his adversary.

Instead of analyzing the obsessive psychology of the two officers, Conrad keeps pointing to the absurd fatality of their predicament and its relation to the spectacular passions of the age. Skimming past the animosities of Feraud and the peculiar acquiescence of D'Hubert, he settles on familiar generalizations about military gossip and the racial distinctions between north and south. The more repetitive the plot becomes, the more apt is Conrad to insist on its grand and glamorous scale; and the characters are soon reduced to ludicrous figures in opéra bouffe. D'Hubert overhears his reputation slandered in a cafe conversation and experiences the "horror of a somnambulist who wakes up from a complacent dream of activity to find himself walking on a quagmire"; while Feraud, learning of his assignment to a small town, responds with "a fierce rolling of the eye and savage grinding of the teeth," sinking under "the leaden weight of an irremediable idleness."[48]

Despite the story's tiresome length and rhetoric, Conrad's large intentions led several of his friends to mistake the will for the deed. Edward Garnett went so far as to see a fusion of the two main strands in Conrad's temperament: the warm, affectionate, essentially feminine character of his maternal ancestors, the Bobrowskis; and the cold, sardonic, essentially masculine traits of the Korzeniowskis. Yet despite such enthusiasm, "The Duel" proved a difficult story to market, and Conrad wryly mentioned that "It has been waved away by more than one editor I believe—and the Pall

Mall Magazine (which favors me generally as witness *Typhoon, G. Ruiz*) accepted it with some hesitation I am told. A complimentary phrase to the address of the P.M.M. would be a reward of moral courage and some insight."[49]

* * *

From 1905 to 1907, when Conrad wrote the commercial stories in *A Set of Six*, he was also working on *The Secret Agent, Chance,* and *Under Western Eyes*. Convinced that only novels had any serious effect on his reputation and fortune, he concentrated most of his fading energy on long works. Or, to be more exact, he would start every work of fiction as a short story, and then—if it seemed to have possibilities for development—would turn it into a novel. The three famous books mentioned above began as stories called "Verloc," "Dynamite," and "Razumov."

Although the complete sales figures for Conrad's books are no longer available, the few remaining records are proof enough of his lack of readers. Harper and Brothers has provided the American sales figures, given in the table on p. 148, for five of the six volumes that Conrad published between 1904 and 1911;[50] the records of English sales available from Methuen are different in format, but tell the same story.[51]

On reflection, Conrad liked to think that money problems had no effect on the actual writing of a story; he once told Pinker, "While I am writing I am not thinking of money. I couldn't if I would. The thing once written I admit that I want to see it bring in as much money as possible and to have as much *effect* as possible."[52] But in other letters of the same period, there are remarks that contradict this. In January 1908, while working on the first version of *Under Western Eyes*, he wrote Galsworthy:

And perhaps no magazine will touch it. Blackwood's, since the Old Man has retired, do not care too much to have my work. I think of trying the Fortnightly. Ah! my dear, you don't know what an inspiration-killing anxiety it is to think: "Is it salable?" There's nothing more cruel than to be caught between one's impulse, one's act,

AMERICAN RECORDS (Year, First Printing, Sales)			BRITISH RECORDS (Edition, Year, Printing)		
Nostromo			*The Mirror of the Sea*		
1904	3,000	NA	First	1906	1,511
1905		NA	Second	1913	506
1906		68	Third	1915	508
1907		90	*The Secret Agent*		
1908		38	First	1907	2,511
1909		38	Second	1914	2,531
The Mirror of the Sea			Third	1916	1,001
1906	3,000	1,654	*A Set of Six*		
1907		488	First	1908	2,524
1908		55	Second	1920	1,016
1909		54	*Under Western Eyes*		
1910		54	First	1911	3,000
The Secret Agent					
1907	4,000	2,676			
1908		138			
1909		21			
1910		21			
1911		40			
1912		73			
Under Western Eyes					
1911	4,000	1,976			
1912		737			
1913		154			
1914		188			
1915		234			
A Personal Record					
1912	2,500	1,345			
1913		134			
1914		127			
1915		153			
1916		225			

and that question, which for me simply is a question of life and death. There are moments when the mere fear sweeps my head clean of every thought. It is agonizing,—no less. And,—you know, —that pressure grows from day to day instead of getting less.[53]

Despite this discouragement, Conrad remained dedicated to the writing of long novels; and once when Pinker asked for something short, he answered, "No, decidedly, I mus'nt interrupt my work for a Short-Story. And generally I must go on finishing the commenced books Chance—Rescue etc. It's the big novels that *tell*."[54]

"THE SECRET SHARER"

In 1903–1904, while working on *Nostromo*, Conrad had gone two years without writing a short story, and only a request from the *Strand* magazine brought him back to the form. In 1909 a similar situation developed. Except for the revision of his first story, "The Black Mate," he had not written a short work since the spring of 1907. Then, without warning, he received a visit from Captain C. M. Marris, recently back from the Malay Seas. As Conrad explained to Pinker:

It was like the raising of a lot of dead—dead to me, because most of them live out there and even read my books and wonder who the devil has been around taking notes. My visitor told me that Joshua Lingard made the guess: "It must have been the fellow who was mate in the Vidar with Craig." That's me right enough. And the best of it is that all these men of 22 years ago feel kindly to the Chronicler of their lives and adventures. They shall have some more of the stories they like.[55]

This liberating stroke forced Conrad to write about personal experience (or at least personal memories) for the first time since "The End of the Tether." The three stories inspired by the visit of Marris ("The Secret Sharer," "A Smile of Fortune," and "Freya of the Seven Isles") are notable because they blend qualities drawn from both periods of Conrad's working life. They are based on first-hand experience (his most reliable source) and they explore substantial themes; but they are also full of the conventional devices of bad magazine fiction. Since they draw from the best and the worst of Conrad, it is possible to account for their peculiar strengths and weaknesses only by recognizing their divided nature.

The supreme case in point is "The Secret Sharer," widely acclaimed as a psychological masterpiece, and the subject of more fanciful interpretations than any of Conrad's other stories. Yet no one who has written on this problematical tale has given a wholly reliable sense of its peculiar distinction. Polemical and highly selective, the average reading of "The Secret Sharer" is easily open to charges of partiality or distortion .

Take, for instance, the argument about Leggatt's representative status. Because there is ample evidence to suggest his symbolic nature, critics have been trying for years to explain what he stands for. In the 1940s R. W. Stallman insisted that Leggatt represents both the captain's moral consciousness and the world that lies below the surface of our conscious lives. But, as J. L. Simmons and others have pointed out, Leggatt can hardly be both at the same time. Moreover, when Stallman follows this contradiction with a third, aesthetic allegory, his essay sinks under its own extravagance. Albert Guerard, in several influential discussions of the story, then tried to establish Leggatt as the embodiment of the criminal impulse in the narrator's personality. According to Guerard, Conrad's story dramatizes the act of sympathetic identification with an outlaw and the achievement of self-mastery when the secret self is exorcised. But, lately, this interpretation has been convincingly undermined by several writers, the most thorough of whom is Daniel Curley. In his essay, "Leggatt of the Ideal," Curley has brought together all the evidence against Leggatt's putative viciousness. First, Conrad recast the *Cutty Sark* source material to make Leggatt more agreeable; if he had wished to create a character in some ways disreputable, he need not have made any changes at all. Second, there are many details in the story itself to counter the argument that Leggatt is lawless. And third, Conrad protested vigorously when he read a review calling the mate a "murderous ruffian,—or something of the sort."[56]

But, as if unable to leave well enough alone, Curley and others have argued that Leggatt represents not a lower but a higher self, the captain's image of the ideal. Yet, just as there is adequate evidence to deny Leggatt's villainy, so there is proof to smudge his status as an ideal figure. As I shall suggest later, the captain does not want to model himself on Leggatt; he wants to be able to show some of his traits of manliness in a time of crisis. One thing can be said with certainty about Leggatt: he is neither higher nor lower, only different.

Similar assertions, either mutually exclusive or self-contradictory, have been made about other teasing elements in the story. Is the floppy hat a symbol of the human personality or of the captain's compassion or is it merely a floppy hat? And why does the captain bring the ship so dangerously close to shore? According to several recent critics, he shaves the coast because (1) he wants to make Leggatt's departure as safe as possible; (2) he considers it a matter of conscience to prove to Leggatt that he understands his predicament; (3) he wishes to pay Leggatt for his self-knowledge; (4) he needs an exceptionally forceful gesture to "change the nature of his relationship to his crew"; (5) he must symbolically reenact an extreme situation resembling Leggatt's crisis on the *Sephora*; (6) he hopes to lay the ghost of his secret sharer, as Marlow laid the ghost of Kurtz. Remarkable motivation for a character who rarely thinks deeply about his own situation!

In reaction to such strenuous analysis, some critics—most notably Frederick Karl and Jocelyn Baines—have argued that on the psychological and moral level "The Secret Sharer" is rather slight: "the surface in this case *is* the story."[57] Although this is more persuasive than the so-called alchemical readings, it is not wholly satisfactory either. To say that "The Secret Sharer" is a straightforward tale implies that the mysterious symbolism is not there, a fact belied by quotation and the experience of the common reader. Usually, in the face of a work improperly understood, critics blame one another; but in this case the work itself is at fault. Although "The Secret

Sharer" is a fascinating and provocative story, its details are at times so vaguely portentous that readers are seduced into hunting for a complex symbolic consistency which the work does not possess.

None of the famous interpretations (like Guerard's night journey or Stallman's aesthetic allegory) can be supported without tampering with the text, either by omitting relevant material or by bending it out of recognizable shape. Because the darkness, the headless figure, the sleeping suit, and the idea of a secret self all have persuasive connections with the unconscious, Guerard's reading has, at first, a genuine appeal. But in addition to the dubious argument about Leggatt's criminality, there is nothing in the story to support Guerard's belief that the captain gains self-control by coming to terms with the dark side of his nature. On the contrary, Leggatt's attractiveness is based less on some sinister appeal than on an obvious self-possession and strength. Seeing him as a man of action who saved his ship by courageously setting the foresail, the captain dismisses the killing as a trifling accident: "it was all very simple. The same strungup force which had given twenty-four men a chance, at least, for their lives, had, in a sort of recoil, crushed an unworthy mutinous existence." By the end, the captain has learned nothing about his own capacity for evil; he has learned only to assume confident command of his ship.

True enough, the identification between the captain and Leggatt is conveyed with such overwhelming insistence (the words "double," "other self," "secret sharer" occur nearly forty times) that an interpretation resting on the singular appeal of manliness appears to rob the story of its celebrated allusiveness. However, on close examination, much of that allusiveness will not bear looking into. Instead of developing the complex psychological implications of the events, Conrad frequently makes tantalizing rhetorical promises that he later fails to keep. Because it touches on some of the characteristic subject matter of modern literature, "The Secret Sharer" has often been praised as profound. But despite an intensely dramatic plot, the story is a flawed piece of work, psychologically static, and symbolically consistent only on a rather obvious level. As Ian Watt has argued in another connection, Conrad's symbolism is not a matter of obscure and esoteric secrets but only of extending and generalizing the implications of his "things, events and people."[58] The best way to appreciate the quality of "The Secret Sharer" is to establish which of its implications can be extended and which cannot.

The opening tableau, with its self-conscious emphasis on solemnity and loneliness, helps define the conditions of the test. A stranger both to his ship and to himself, the narrator wonders whether he will measure up to the "ideal conception of one's own personality every man sets up for himself secretly." Although the crew is briefly differentiated at the start, the main emphasis is on the captain's relationship to the ship. Compare this to the opening of "Heart of Darkness," in which the brooding silence also serves to introduce the story of a test, and certain dramatic differences become obvious. From the start, Marlow's story has an elaborate social and historical context. He speaks to an audience and his earliest remarks link his adventures to those of Romans in ancient Britain. In "The Secret Sharer," the captain's situation more closely resembles that of Marlow in "Youth," for both men are natural egoists anxious to prove themselves against an exacting private challenge. The captain is, of course, more reflective than the young Marlow; but by admitting his willingness to take the adequacy of the crew for granted, he defines his self-absorption and the narrow range of the test.

Leggatt's spectacular entrance raises the first interpretive problem of the story. Faced with a "green cadaverous glow," a body that resembles "a headless corpse!" and a "ghastly, silvery fish," the Captain feels "a horrid, frost-bound sensation" grip his chest. This, however, passes quickly and the two men talk with the quiet assurance of well-bred strangers at the boat harbor of a fashionable club. Although the identification is established immediately (and reinforced beyond bearing for the rest of the tale), it is not easy to define the factors on which the tie is based. Because the captain alternates between an insistent, incantatory rhetoric and prosaic understatement, readers seem to find a mandate to look for analogues either in Jung or in the Seaman's Code. Primal symbolism seems to count for a good deal. The double comes up like a fish from the dark sea to wear the captain's sleeping suit; and yet the men communicate on the basis of experiences as mundane and "as identical as our clothes"—on one hand, primitive archetypes and, on the other, Conrad's statement that the story "deals with what may be called the 'esprit de corps,' the deep fellowship of two young seamen meeting for the first time." Yet, if the captain's responses are studied closely, the teasing symbolism turns out to be decorative, suspenseful, and inconclusive; at times, rather Poe-like. The less esoteric reading accounts more satisfactorily for the main thrust of the tale, if not for all its details.

The first two conversations between the captain and Leggatt establish sympathetic identification and provide clues to the nature of the crime. In every conceivable way, the murder is minimized. The victim had been a peevish malingerer, "half-crazed with funk," and by killing him Leggatt acted instinctively to help save the ship. No doubt crosses the narrator's mind, and Leggatt himself refers casually to the murder as a disagreeable necessity. His insistence that the price of exile is enough to pay "for an Abel of that sort" gains the admiration of the captain and should gain ours.

By minimizing the murder in these opening scenes, the narrator introduces a major theme of the story. When catastrophe threatens aboard ship, the life of someone who seriously interferes with seamanship may be legitimately sacrificed for the safety of the crew. Situations in which certain basic imperatives emerge as stronger than the traditional codes of the law are common in Conrad's fiction. A similar predicament faces the crew of the *Narcissus*, and Leggatt himself resembles Falk, who committed cannibalism in order to survive. In the context of their particular dilemmas, both men win respect for the ruthless force of their natural egoism. Oddly enough, a passage from the early part of "The Secret Sharer," which is usually read ironically, can be seen to have literal truth. Despite the anxiety caused by Leggatt's arrival and concealment, the drama of the *Sephora* does strike the captain by its "elemental moral beauty" and the "absolute straightforwardness of its appeal."

Once the captain has heard the facts of the case, he pays little attention to the murder. Nor, it should be emphasized, does he reflect at any length on the similarity between himself and the fugitive. Although he strains excessively to convey the drama of the identification, he fails to probe its meaning, concentrating instead on hiding Leggatt and assuming responsibilities on the ship. The fright of constantly seeing double does not prevent him from giving his first order and staying on deck to see it carried out. Leggatt's presence may be worrisome, but his self-possession continues to "induce a corresponding state in myself."

The opening scene of Part II, in which the captain plays host to Archbold with Leggatt hiding a few feet away, further strengthens the loyalties already established. Archbold, skittish and easily out of temper, is a foil to Leggatt and to the captain as well. Throughout the interview, he gives off an air of fussy distraction, and in his most authoritative act sticks out his tongue to imitate the death mask of Leggatt's victim. Archbold's solemnity is contrasted with the playfulness of the captain, who fakes being deaf and happily leads his guest on a futile search of the ship. For a man quick to confess his dislocation, the captain is remarkably self-assured. In a revealing exchange, he catches Archbold distorting his own action during the crisis on the *Sephora*:

"*That reefed foresail saved you,*" I threw in.

"*Under God—it did,*" he exclaimed fervently. "*It was by a special mercy, I firmly believe, that it stood some of those hurricane squalls.*"

"*It was the setting of that sail which—*" I began.

"*God's own hand in it,*" he interrupted me. "*Nothing less could have done it. I don't mind telling you that I hardly dared give the order. It seemed impossible that we could touch anything without losing it, and then our last hope would have been gone.*"

The terror of that gale was on him yet. I let him go on for a bit, then said, casually—as if returning to a minor subject:

"*You were very anxious to give up your mate to the shore people, I believe?*"

He was. To the law. His obscure tenacity on that point had in it something incomprehensible and a little awful; something, as it were, mystical, quite apart from his anxiety that he should not be suspected of 'countenancing any doings of that sort.' Seven-and-thirty virtuous years at sea, of which over twenty of immaculate command, and the last fifteen in the Sephora, seemed to have laid him under some pitiless obligation.[59]

According to the scale of values sketched earlier, Archbold is clearly the villain of "The Secret Sharer." Personally inadequate against the pressure of the storm, he refuses to admit Leggatt's heroic role and retreats to an unthinking reliance on Providence. Instead of responding flexibly to the exceptional circumstances of the murder, he becomes increasingly more rigid and more mystical. Archbold's failure of imagination, his inability to see that the moment called for charity not intransigence, testifies to the correctness and decency of the captain's response. Conrad, often scathing about sentimental benevolence, here gives Leggatt the benefit of every doubt and makes him worthy of pity in a way that a James Wait is not.

When the captain hears Leggatt confirm Archbold's fecklessness, he makes his final judgment of the affair: " 'I quite understand,' I conveyed that sincere assurance into his ear. . . . It was all very simple. The same strung-up force which had given twenty-four men a chance, at least, for their lives, had, in a sort of recoil, crushed an unworthy mutinous existence."[60] His response follows a familiar pattern. After a forceful conversation with Leggatt, he can spare "no leisure to weigh the merits of the matter," but goes out "to make the acquaintance of my ship."

Despite this renewed effort, the captain's self-mastery remains for a time incomplete. Unable to forget Leggett or the suspicions of his crew, he admits that he requires deliberation to perform acts that for a confident commander would be instinctive. At each new threat of exposure, he becomes increasingly apprehensive, while Leggatt continues "perfectly self-controlled, more than calm—almost invulnerable." When the steward opens the door of the bathroom in which Leggatt is hiding, the captain nearly swoons with terror; and before he learns of Leggatt's safety, he automatically stresses the inexplicable, nightmarish quality of the events. But once again, when he learns the mundane truth, he marvels at "something unyielding" in Leggatt's character "which was carrying him through so finely."

Much has been made of the severity of the captain's self-division at this point in the tale, though not enough, I think, of the comic quality of the action. The adventures that throw the Captain into fits of nervous anxiety are hardly sinister. He startles the steward who thought he had been below and then sends him around the ship on incomprehensible errands. How can one speak solemnly about dark nights of the soul when the antic disposition is so reminiscent of *Room Service?*

Following the narrow escape in the bathroom, Leggatt asks to be marooned, and after an initial protest the Captain accepts the challenge. There is no need to probe the unconscious to understand his ambivalent motives: he recognizes the value of getting rid of Leggatt, but is frightened of losing the man who so vividly inspires confidence. Once he accepts the inevitability of Leggatt's departure, the captain begins to conform more closely to the ideal of the perfect commander. Decisiveness becomes a matter of instinct as he fulfills Coleridge's formula for maturity: "act spontaneously, not with reflection; but it is your duty to study, inform yourself, and reflect so that you progressively become the kind of person whose spontaneous reflection is wise." Just before the climactic moment, he gives the fugitive three soverigns and, on "sudden thought, rams his floppy hat on Leggatt's head to protect him from the sun. To insure Leggatt's safety, and as a gesture of self-assertion, he sails dangerously close to shore. As Leggatt goes over the side, the Captain—with the hat as a marker—executes the daring maneuver which puts him back on course, in "perfect communion" with his first command.

What, then, has Leggatt meant to the captain? Exemplary but not necessary ideal, Leggatt represents a kind of behavior, a physical stance so to speak, which inspires the captain to act boldly himself. Having profited from his presence, the captain is now a better and luckier man than Leggatt, who—despite the declamatory ending— is faced with an uncertain future. The description of the fugitive in the final lines is still another index to the weakness of "The Secret Sharer." To call Leggatt "a free man, a swimmer striking out for a new destiny" is a triumph of grandiloquence over the facts of the case. Whatever one might say about Leggatt's resolution in the past, his future can hardly at this point be cause for celebration. An exile, swimming in the darkness toward an unknown island, his destiny may be new but not exactly enviable. The pretentious romanticism at the close has a revealing analogue in a later Conrad story. When Geoffrey Renouard, in "The Planter of Malata," commits suicide by swimming out to sea, the narrator remarks: "Nothing was ever found—and Renouard's disappearance remained in the main inexplicable. For to whom could it have occurred that a man would set out calmly to swim beyond the confines of life—with a steady stroke—his eyes fixed on a star!"[61] The high-coloring here and in the last line of "The Secret Sharer" recalls "Gaspar Ruiz," not "Heart of Darkness."

Some of the rhetorical embroidery in "The Secret Sharer" is surely temperamental (none of Conrad's major works is wholly free from it); but some is due to the uneasy relationship between Conrad and the magazine audience. The story's excessive length may have been the result of *Harper's* rigid yardstick (it fit neatly into two issues in the summer of 1910); and the three dozen synonyms for "double" seem designed to accentuate a dramatic point for fear of having it missed. Although the repetition reassured readers in 1910, it has proven fatal to critics since then. Because of its insistent promptings and seductive detail, "The Secret Sharer" has become everybody's Rorschach test. But its psychology remains elementary; its finest effects are explicit and traditionally moral.

"A SMILE OF FORTUNE"

A short time after finishing "The Secret Sharer," Conrad suffered a physical collapse precipitated by overwork, financial anxiety, and a disturbing quarrel with Pinker. As one might expect, the three stories written in the summer and fall of 1910 did not engage his full powers. Since two of the group add nothing new to our knowledge of Conrad's achievement as a short story writer, they do not call for discussion here. "The Partner," melodramatically similar to "The Brute," treats a plot to wreck a ship for insurance money; while "Prince Roman," which describes a Polish nobleman Conrad met as a boy, is of interest mainly as spiritual autobiography. *

"A Smile of Fortune," the first of this group, is another matter. Few of Conrad's stories are so fatally divided against themselves and few tell us more about the debilitating effect of his need "to make it salable." In its concern with the trial of a young captain on his first command, "A Smile of Fortune" has much in common with Conrad's best-known fiction. Here, however, the conditions of the test are significantly different, for instead of having his courage judged at sea, the captain is tested for sexual prowess and business skill on land.

When his ship docks at Mauritius in the Indian Ocean, he becomes involved with Alfred Jacobus, a disreputable chandler who offers to supply stores and later to procure some scarce bags for the packing of sugar. Jacobus' favors are linked with his desire to interest the captain in his illegitimate daughter, Alice, a petulant girl in a flimsy robe who lives isolated from the outside world. Although the captain returns often to see this "snarling and superb . . . wild animal," he spends most of his time teasing her and doesn't give any reliable sign of his feelings until ready to leave the island. When the girl responds with interest, he recoils, feels hopelessly detached, and wants only to escape her presence. Knowing that the compromised captain cannot now refuse to trade, Jacobus resumes negotiations for a huge shipment of potatoes. The captain grudgingly buys the cargo he cannot use; at the close, however, fortune smiles and he is able to sell it at a profit. Even this happy turn of events is not enough to erase discomforting memories of the girl. Since he has neither the courage nor the conscience to "go back to fan that fatal spark with my cold breath," he resigns the command and sails home.

* Jessie Conrad claimed that Conrad would not have included "Prince Roman" in *Tales of Hearsay* "had he lived." (*Joseph Conrad as I Knew Him*, p. 159.)

On its face, the raw material of "A Smile of Fortune" is promising. The peculiar patterns of motivation and the absorbing alliance between sex and money offer Conrad an opportunity to make some forceful points about the varieties of cupidity and lust. Unfortunately, he fails to follow up the unpalatable implications of the subject matter and tries to treat mercantilism and sexuality in conventional ways. Rather than explore the way one world subverts the other, he describes the love affair in the fervid vocabulary of romance and the corruptions of trade realistically. The striking tonal differences separate the two subjects and lead to moments of unintentional and almost ruinous comedy.

In the early part of the story, the humor is intentional and neatly managed. Fresh from an uneventful sea journey, the captain wonders if his adventures on the island will be "as luckily exceptional as this beautiful, dreamlike vision" of the coast which meets him as he approaches land. The lyric mood is quickly dispelled by the arrival of Jacobus, friendly yet tenacious, a businessman who invariably gets what he goes after. Although eager to spend other people's money, Jacobus conceals his assertiveness behind a mask of placidity and deference, and after a time his quiet authority is overwhelming. Despite suspicions of "some dark design against my commercial innocence," the captain develops "a sort of shady, intimate understanding" with the older man.

The scenes in which Jacobus responds with measured manipulation to the captain's fear of being hoodwinked are amusing pieces of social observation; the conflict between nautical innocence and commercial experience is treated with a playfulness rare in Conrad's fiction. After a while, however, facts are revealed that give Jacobus an interest extending beyond the range of light comedy. Years earlier, he had deserted his wife for a circus performer and, when the affair broke up, returned to Mauritius with his illegitimate daughter. From time to time, Jacobus' unorthodox love life is mentioned only to be marveled at with a mild joke: "The grotesque image of a fat, pushing ship-chandler, enslaved by an unholy love-spell, fascinated me; and I listened rather open-mouthed to the tale as old as the world, a tale which had been the subject of legend, of moral fables, of poems, but which so ludicrously failed to fit the personality. What a strange victim for the gods!"[62] Conrad's failure to go more deeply into the motivations of the man he liked to call "the impure Jacobus" is the most obvious missed opportunity in the early part of the story.

His failure with Alice is different and more harmful. The mysteries of Alfred Jacobus are in the past and playfully minimized; the mysteries of his daughter are in the present and exaggerated beyond credibility. Barred by birth from local society, she stays close to her father's opulent garden, silently nursing her grievances to keep them tender. With magnificent black eyes, a quivering, supple body, and a choked inarticulateness, she responds to provocation with "Won't," "Shan't," or "Don't care," a passivity so laughable as to forfeit sympathy and interest. The narrator's insistence that her peevish dejection has "an obscurely tragic flavour" does not exactly inspire confidence.

The vacancy of Alice need not have been fatal had Conrad elaborated on the captain's response to her. By the middle of the action, when he is delayed by the scarcity of packing sacks, the captain has become so involved in "business—the sacred business" that he is unable to react in a normal way to another human being. Thus his encounter with Alice is the second important stage in his test. At their early meetings, he finds her seductive and keeps returning to the house; but failing to break through her sullen distrust, he becomes fascinated by her contempt for him: "I cared for the girl in a particular way, seduced by the moody expression of her face, by her obstinate silences, her rare, scornful words; the perpetual pout of her closed lips, the black depths of her fixed gaze turned slowly upon me as if in contemptuous provocation, only to be averted next moment with an exasperating indifference."[63] Seeing her every day, he experiences "a unique sensation which I indulged with dread, self-contempt, and deep pleasure, as if it were a secret vice bound to end in my undoing, like the habit of some drug or other which ruins and degrades its slaves."[64]

The enthrallment of the captain, linked to the debased passion of Jacobus for the circus rider and to the relationship of the men with one another, is the most engaging subject in "A Smile of Fortune." But Conrad lets more amiable things distract him. The comedy of the first mate, Burns; the passing commentary on island society; and particularly the details about the potato transaction deflect him from the theme that should have been his main concern. The captain does speak of "cruel self-knowledge," "moral poison," and "abject dread"; and after his windfall, he wakes up "callous with greed" from a dream in which the girl is buried in a mountainous grave of gold. But the anecdotal preoccupation at the end points up his gift for hyperbole rather than his guilt and keeps the lesson from having very much force. Ford Madox Ford's remark that this tale was "the only story of a *bonne fortune*" that he had ever heard Conrad tell, puts the emphasis in the right place.[65]

Conrad's evasion is understandable. In 1910, looking back to his life in the East for a marketable subject, he must have judged two episodes useful in the Mauritius affair: the unexpected sale of the potatoes and the stormy interlude with Alice. As the story grew, a hidden theme emerged; but since impotence, voyeurism, and the enervating power of sexual desire was hardly fit material for the *London Magazine*, he emphasized the more convivial aspects of realism and romance. The mixture worked, for as Conrad later said, "I have been patted on the back for it by most unexpected people . . . the chief of them of course being the editor of a popular illustrated magazine who published it serially in one mighty installment. Who will dare say after this that the change of air had not been an immense success."[66]

The *London Magazine*, subtitled *A Magazine of Human Interest*, published articles on geography, current events, pseudo-science, health cures, and sports. Fiction was generally light and profusely illustrated (witness Conrad's "The Black Mate" in April 1908). In the issue containing "A Smile of Fortune," the department "Entre Nous: the editor's monthly chat to his readers" included a note about Conrad's prodigious ability to write in a foreign language and a reminder that his adventure stories were also works that analyzed character and emotion. A photograph of Conrad and a fierce drawing of Alice Jacobus completed the package. The caption under the drawing is incorrectly quoted from the text.

"FREYA OF THE SEVEN ISLES"

The process of deterioration can be studied further in "Freya of the Seven Isles," finished in February 1911. One of the most clumsily protracted of all Conrad's stories, "Freya" customarily reduces critics to compassionate silence. But since its publication was the occasion of an instructive controversy, the tale and the facts of its appearance are worth reviewing.

Like "A Smile of Fortune," "Freya" begins on a casual note and soon erupts into a flamboyant melodrama. Years ago, while commanding a steamer in the Carimata Straits between Sumatra and Borneo, the narrator had observed the first part of a family drama of which he is now reminded by a letter from a friend. When old Nelson, a retired Danish trader, had been unsympathetic to the courtship of his daughter Freya and Jasper Allen, the couple planned to elope. The passionate, romantic girl loved Allen for himself but even more for the splendor of his brig, the *Bonito*, in which he performed outrageous feats to dazzle her. Shortly before the day of the elopement, the narrator was called back to England, but he learned later that the happiness of the lovers was shattered by the villainy of a Dutch lieutenant named Heemskirk. After Freya had forcefully rejected his rival suit, Heemskirk ruined Allen by having the *Bonito* smashed on a reef. The Englishman lost his sanity and Freya died of pneumonia. Some time later, when Nelson insists that the girl never loved Allen, the dumbfounded narrator cries out, "Man . . . don't you see that she died of it," and Nelson sobs, "I thought she was so sensible."

At the beginning of "Freya" the mood is light. Nelson, fussy and self-deluded, is the typical bumbling father of low comedy; his beautiful daughter is too good-humored to take her own passions tragically. Able to temper rashness with discretion, she seems equal to any challenge. But as the catastrophe approaches, everyone suddenly grows to twice the size of life. Heemskirk, at first merely sour and arrogant, is now a "grotesque specimen of mankind from some other planet," a "Prometheus in the bonds of an unholy desire"; Allen, the conventionally impulsive lover, stalks the beaches of Macassar like a demented Empedocles; and Freya, a model of Scandinavian exuberance, is stricken by lethargy and drifts toward death. Even if one were to judge the story by the canons of romance rather than realism, so sudden and so inconsistent a metamorphosis is impossible to take seriously.

The stylistic imprecision and structural mismanagement obvious in *A Set of Six* is ruinous here. Passages such as the following are not atypical:

To see her [the Bonito], his cherished possession, animated by something of his Freya's soul, the only foothold of two lives on the wide earth, the security of his passion, the companion of adventure, the power to snatch the calm adorable Freya to his breast, and carry her off to the end of the world; to see this beautiful thing embodying worthily his pride and his love, to see her captive at the end of a tow-rope was not indeed a pleasant experience. It had something nightmarish in it, as, for instance, the dream of a wild sea-bird loaded with chains.[67]

The awkward sentence patterns, the anticlimatic "pleasant experience," and the comical image of the entangled sea-bird are fatal to the effect of Allen's loss.

For a writer of Conrad's technical sophistication, the narrative blunders of "Freya" are also dismaying. The story is told by an authorial surrogate who claims to have been an intimate in the Nelson household. Opening with the receipt of the letter from the East, he recalls the early events in which he had participated. Then, after mentioning his sudden return to England, he tells the rest of the tale omnisciently. Only at the end are we given to understand how the details of the wreck came to him. Nelson, visiting London, told the climactic events in Freya's own words. Aside from being maladroit, the device is undermined by the facts of Nelson's character. If he has remained so fuddled and insensitive, how is he to be trusted to record Freya's story faithfully?

Another puzzling element here is that Freya seems to have been invented while Heemskirk and Allen were real. As Conrad explained to Garnett:

> It is the story of the Costa Rica which was not more than five years old when I was in Singapore. The man's name was Sutton. ... He was just about to go home to marry a girl (of whom he used to talk to everybody and anybody) and bring her out there when the ship was run on a reef by the commander of a Dutch gun-boat whom he had managed to offend in some way. He haunted the beach in Macassar for months and lies buried in the fort there.[68]

Since Conrad wished to have a love interest complement the adventure on the reef, the importing of Freya is understandable. But what did he expect to gain from the unnecessarily involved point of view?

Part of the clumsiness is the result of Conrad's effort to revise the magazine version of "Freya" for its appearance in *'Twixt Land and Sea*. The book version begins with a veiled reference to Captain Marris (the friend from the East) and a long description of old Nelson. The magazine copy begins three pages later with the words "Freya Nelson (or Nielson) was the kind of a girl one remembers," and it omits the section on her father. Later, Conrad added many other comments which generally group themselves in five categories: references to Nelson's character, descriptions of the *Bonito*, psychological analysis of Heemskirk, literate metaphors (such as one describing a servant as "the faithful camerista of Italian comedy"), and moral reflections by the narrator.

The most interesting aspect of Conrad's revision is his attempt to give the frail magazine version something of the elaborate structure which he used in his best early work. Old Nelson and the narrator are obviously moral reflectors controlling the reader's response to the violent events of the *Bonito* story. Although the magazine version was simply a tale of unhappy lovers, the book version has a further dimension; it shows how the father realizes his earlier blindness and gains bitter self-knowledge. Like Conrad's most noteworthy work, it is about something "lived through and remembered." Unfortunately, this change does not transform "Freya of the Seven Isles" into a successful piece of fiction. It is flawed in too many places to survive. Nevertheless, when development seemed possible, Conrad did try to strengthen a commercial story by giving it something of the amplitude of his earlier fiction. Occasionally, he even planned it that way. In a letter to Pinker about "The Humane Tomassov" (published later as "The Warrior's Soul"), Conrad wrote, "The story I believe is quite sufficiently developed for Mag^{ne} Pub^{on}. I'll work on it for book form."[69]

Conrad admitted that in writing "Freya of the Seven Isles" he was trying to "do a magazine-ish thing with some decency. Not a very high purpose; yet it seems I've failed even in that!"[70] On its early rounds of the periodicals, the story was refused by the *Century*, *Scribner's* and even *Blackwood's*, mainly on the ground of its bleakness.[71] To Pinker, Conrad made this objection:

"Unrelieved gloom" seems to me a bit too strong. Of course the story is not the stuff for a comic paper; but I've tried to keep the pathetic side of the tale in the background. The fate of the girl is just sketched in, hinted at rather than told. Jasper's breakup is merely alluded to, in fact slurred over. There was material there for a novel as long as Almayer's Folly—I mean psychologically. And anyhow the tragic consequences appear only in the last 5000 (or less) words of the story. So there could have been four or three fairly cheerful instalments.

Frankly I thought (given the subject) that I had done a rather delicate piece of work. But perhaps the tone of the writing itself the style of telling is gloomy? Of that I can form no opinion. I don't want to bother you with such a question but as you are the only person who has seen the story in England may I ask whether you think it is so. I certainly didn't mean it to be. It is the tone I wish to avoid for practical purposes.[72]

Subsequently, when someone suggested that Conrad make the story more acceptable by revising the last section, he told Garnett: "As to faking a 'sunny' ending to my story I would see all the American Magazines and all the American Editors damned in heaps before lifting my pen for that task. I have never been particularly anxious to rub shoulders with the piffle they print with touching consistency from year's end to year's end."[73]

Appropriately, "Freya of the Seven Isles" was finally published in a notable repository of "piffle," the *Metropolitan Magazine of New York*. Subtitled *The Liveliest Magazine in America*, the Metropolitan looked like the present-day *Saturday Evening Post* and had more than 300,000 readers. A typical issue would include an attack on Theodore Roosevelt, a profile of J. P. Morgan, a dispatch about Pancho Villa, and romantic stories by Frederick Tabor Cooper, Anthony Hope, or Booth Tarkington. The editor, Henry James Whigham, admitted that he could not show you how "to get rich quick," but he certainly could "prevent you from contributing to the riches of others"; and one of his proudest features was the monthly exposé entitled "The Sempiternal Sucker" or "Your Consumer Dollar."

The standards of the *Metropolitan* were so low that even Arnold Bennett had trouble writing for it. Although Whigham paid $1,500 for a Bennett story, he complained that the author "had not been able to grasp the requirements of big-circulation magazines."[74] Conrad, less versatile, called Whigham's product "that six penny rag," and spoke often of his stories being "much too good for the *Metropolitan*."[75] The most decisive expression of his attitude toward the magazine is penciled on the bottom of a letter from Carl Hovey to Alfred Knopf, then working for Doubleday, which Pinker had sent to Conrad. Hovey, an editor at the magazine, told Knopf:

I hope you will succeed in obtaining for us some of the work of Joseph Conrad. There is no other living writer for whom we have so great an enthusiasm. The Metropolitan would be both proud and happy to print everything that Mr. Conrad writes, if only the editorial difficulties that stand in the way could be removed. There are some of Mr. Conrad's stories which we can handle and others which, by the form in which they are written, are rendered impossible.

Short stories like "The Brute," "Amy Foster," "Tomorrow," and of course "Youth," or a longer story like "Typhoon" are perfectly feasible for use in a popular magazine. On the other hand, "Heart of Darkness," "Falk," or "Lord Jim" present varying degrees of difficulty from the nearly impossible to the absolutely impossible. I should say that the difference between these two sorts of writing was a matter of directness and compactness. A story like "Typhoon" moves from point to point in a simple and orderly manner. "Lord Jim" on the other hand is constructed in a fashion of a legal trial —that is, you are presented with the evidence of various witnesses or the testimony of various incidents, all bearing on the nature of Jim's soul. When the book is done, when the evidence is all in— to continue my commonplace figure—the reader's knowledge is then complete. It seems to me that there is no question but that "Lord Jim" is the greater book and that the style is the greater style. Yet for magazine serial purposes, this manner of creation will not work. We have a circulation of 400,000 and are read by at least a million readers. Great as our desire is to present really fine work, still we must first make sure of holding the interest of a very large proportion of our circulation. To accomplish this, it is necessary for us to give them things which are simple and direct in which the element of suspense is fairly obvious and is not too fine and psychological for them to grasp. . . . Practically all the fiction which we are able to publish in a magazine like the Metropolitan is journalistic and casual in its essence. No one possesses a greater desire than its editors to present something finer and more real. The problem is to do this and still reach our public. If we could have from Mr. Conrad another short story like "The Brute" we would reach our public with all the certainty in the world. None of our rough-and-ready writers could write a story that would appeal to our readers with greater readiness. Doubtless they would read it without realizing how good it was. A certain few would appreciate it and the rest would just enjoy it.

I know it is not to be expected that an artist like Joseph Conrad will sit down and try to produce a story which will help an American editor to solve his practical problems. The situation does not offer the right kind of motive. On the other hand, Mr. Conrad's work shows that he does enjoy considering certain themes in a way which exactly fits in with our needs. It might not be unwise, therefore, to present to him our side of the case.

Conrad's response, written angrily across the bottom of the letter, reads:

This is absurd. Those people crawl before Knopf and all the time they are getting my work from you! You may tell them since they are so anxious that Because of the Dollars will be something in the Brute style they are crying for but that Conrad wants special terms for prostituting his intellect to please the Metropolitan.[76]

Conrad seems to have gotten his "special terms." "Because of the Dollars" appeared in *The Metropolitan* during the following year, and six of his last nine stories made either their first or second appearance in the magazine.

* * *

Conrad's sudden popularity—which came with *Chance* in 1914—is not without its irony. Not only did he receive recognition long after his most impressive writing had been done, but the books that the public sought so eagerly have few of the qualities associated with best-selling fiction. Although Conrad tried to simplify his narrative and to temper gloominess with love, humor, and an occasional affirmation, he could not produce an exemplary commercial story. Sometimes, when he felt especially disheartened, he would read a few pages of Hall Caine or Marie Corelli; and Garnett reports how once, "throwing down some miserable novel by Guy Boothby,"

Conrad said, "I can't get the secret of this fellow's manner. It's beyond me, how he does it!"[77] Despite the element of jesting, the exasperation is real. Conrad lacked both the temperament and the special skills needed to write like Hall Caine or Boothby. *The Arrow of Gold* and *The Rover* must be among the most tedious best sellers ever written.

Luck and publicity, more than design, were the major factors in Conrad's success. Having been serialized in the *New York Herald* in 1912, *Chance* appeared brightly packaged by Doubleday in the spring of 1914 and became a moderate best seller. In America it sold 20,194 copies within five months of publication, and in England 13,200 copies in the first two years.[78] Since the total British sale for first editions of *Lord Jim*, *Nostromo*, *The Secret Agent*, and *Under Western Eyes* was little more than 10,000, the demand for *Chance* was extraordinary. To keep perspective, however, one should remember that another Doubleday product, Gene Stratton Porter's *Laddie*, sold 300,000 copies during the same five month period. *Chance* was twenty-first on American best-seller lists for 1914; *Victory* forty-second in 1916; *The Arrow of Gold* second in 1919; and *The Rover* third in 1923.

Even so, none of Conrad's books was successful enough to be included among the one hundred best-selling books for the period 1895–1925, a group headed by *Quo Vadis*, *Beside the Bonnie Briar Bush*, *The Four Horsemen of the Apocalypse*, *Main Street*, and *If Winter Comes*. Yet Conrad's reputation among general readers seems to have been much higher than the actual sales of his novels would lead one to expect. In 1924 *Publisher's Weekly* printed the results of a poll in which nearly 2,000 readers voted for their favorite authors. Conrad placed eighth behind H. G. Wells, Blasco-Ibáñez, A. S. M. Hutchinson, the American Winston Churchill, Edward Bok, Giovanni Papini, and Booth Tarkington. All these men had at least one book among the one hundred best sellers, and Churchill had nine.

Although luck and publicity were the main factors in Conrad's good fortune, the optimistic qualities of his later works at least gave the publishers something to advertise. As usual, novel enthusiasts preferred affirmation, and Mrs. Porter (whose books sold nearly eight million copies in ten years) speaks for the common reader: "Personally, it is difficult for me to understand why characters that should not be admitted into a home or a family circle in person on any consideration should be allowed to come there between the covers of a book."[79] With a pretty girl on the dust jacket, *Chance* was widely advertised as a tender romance. Heyst's dying words in *Victory* ("woe to the man whose heart has not learned while young to hope, to love,—and to put its trust in life!") were quoted by many reviewers as the sum of Conrad's mature wisdom. And *The Arrow of Gold* delighted more than one critic "as one of the big love stories of the world of books, a story that simply refuses to be forgotten and that leaves a vague heart-ache, a lingering elusive fragrance behind it."[80]

Conrad's yearly income from writing passed £2,000 in 1917, and increased steadily until his death in 1924. Prosperity had a simple effect on his short stories: he stopped writing them. But before this occurred, he did produce five tales that reveal something distinct and final about the nature of his short fiction.*

---

* "The Inn of the Two Witches," written before *Chance*, is an anecdote about a British soldier who is nearly murdered in a huge bed with a false canopy that can be manipulated to suffocate its victims. It does not require discussion.

5
Last Tales

In the three years following the publication of *Chance* in 1913, Conrad wrote *Victory* and his last five short stories; then, for the remaining eight years of his life, he produced a handful of critical essays, two plays, and four long novels. These climactic novels, *The Arrow of Gold*, *The Rescue*, *The Rover*, and the fragment of *Suspense* are generally admitted to be failures of a fatigued imagination: prolix, platitudinous, and unconvincing, enlivened only by occasional flashes of brilliant writing. The five stories, however, are not fatally marred by these weaknesses; for within their deliberately circumscribed range they express engaging ideas without seeming interminable. Their relative ease and freedom from strain suggest that in one sense Conrad's apprenticeship to magazine fiction had positive value. He learned to write simple tales of adventure, romance, or life at sea in a swift and unpretentious way. Four of the last stories are among his most proficient potboilers, while one—which combines a straightforward story line with analysis and a memorable style—is his last great work.

"BECAUSE OF THE DOLLARS"

The first of the group, "Because of the Dollars," is an obvious pendant to *Victory*, the book that occupied Conrad during 1913 and early 1914.* In fact, the fate of "the good Captain Davidson" was

---

* Since Conrad worked on "Because of the Dollars" and "The Planter of Malata" interchangeably during the late fall and winter of 1913–1914, it is difficult to determine the exact order of composition. Although he seems to have started "Because of the Dollars" first, the manuscript of an early version in the Rosenbach collection is dated January 15, 1914, a month later than the manuscript of "The Planter" at Yale (December 14, 1913). "The Planter" was published in June-July 1914, "Because of the Dollars" in September.

originally planned to be the subject of the long novel but ultimately took second place to the more absorbing adventures of Axel Heyst. The short story describes Davidson's attempt to transport government dollars while moving a shipment of goods for an old acquaintance, the reformed prostitute Laughing Anne. Anne's lover, the feckless swindler Bamtz, conspires with three other rogues to rob the money from the anchored steamer. Warned in time by Anne, Davidson scares the men away in an exchange of gunfire; but the ringleader, a frightful Frenchman without hands, recognizes the woman's complicity and crushes her head with an iron weight. Davidson, oppressed by Anne's sacrifice, promises to support her young son; his charitable impulse, however, eventually causes him further grief. His wife, a "fool of the silent, hopeless kind," accuses him of having had a sordid affair and takes their daughter home to mother. The orphan grows up and decides to become a missionary, leaving the melancholy Davidson "to go downhill without a single human affection near him because of those old dollars."

The parallels with *Victory* are obvious: an isolated hero is set upon by a theatrical band of robbers and, after a savage denouement, a befriended woman dies for him. At times, there are even verbal similarities. In the story Conrad remarks, "The best of Chinamen as employers is that they have such gentlemanly instincts. Once they have become convinced that you are a straight man, they give you their unbounded confidence." In the novel, this comment is changed only slightly: "To serve a Chinese firm is not so bad. Once they become convinced you deal straight by them, their confidence becomes unlimited."

Although Schopenhauer and Villiers de L'Isle-Adam are not lurking in the background, Davidson's dilemma does suggest a familiar Conradian theme: the perils of simpleminded altruism. After having made much of his unobtrusive sympathy, the second narrator concludes that Davidson might have been spared his isolation had "he been less of a good fellow." Yet on the basis of the facts reported in the story, the captain is more obviously a victim of other people's malice and plain bad luck than of a notable failure of character. Admittedly, if he had not tried to help Laughing Anne, there would have been neither robbery nor murder; but in the light of the story's brutal determinism, Davidson's mild charity hardly seems crime enough for the punishment. Then, too, so much energy is spent getting all the combatants to their proper places for the gun battle that the reader becomes less concerned about Davidson's soiled benevolence than about his marksmanship.

The simplicity of the story is reinforced by the narrative frame. At first, when a man named Hollis begins to describe Davidson's misfortune to an unnamed narrator, one expects the usual interplay of reflectors. But the author's surrogate never returns to comment on what he has heard, and the frame has little suggestiveness beyond its practical use in conveying a sailor's yarn. Making no claims to artfulness, Hollis keeps promising to order events more efficiently, but continually falls back on "I had better begin at the beginning" and "You shall hear this presently." Luckily, the story's intrinsic interest offsets the shapelessness of his presentation.*

"Because of the Dollars" has pacing rather than profundity, and Conrad seems to have been pleased with its commercial value. In 1920, having already printed the piece in the *Metropolitan* and in *Within the Tides*, he still thought it had sufficient life to make a two-act play. Retaining the magazine title "Laughing Anne," he dropped the captain's sullen wife and emphasized the gothic elements in the criminal conspiracy. As the curtain falls, Davidson addresses the dead girl: "You are on my conscience, but your boy will have his chance." Since this is the only hint that Davidson's behavior has placed him under a spiritual shadow, the play has even less substance than the story.

"THE PLANTER OF MALATA"

"Because of the Dollars" is an unassuming, neatly ordered tale of adventure. "The Planter of Malata," written at the same time,

---

* Hollis played an important role in "Karain." In an early manuscript of "Because of the Dollars" (now in the Lilly Library), Conrad spoke of "the resourceful fellow who once saved the sanity and perhaps the life of a certain splendid Malay adventurer by hanging a Jubilee sixpence on his neck." For some unknown reason, Conrad cut this sentence from the final version.

makes a more varied claim for attention. The basic idea came from Stephen Crane, who tried, in 1899, to tease his older friend into collaborating on a play. Years later, Conrad described the occasion in an introduction to the Thomas Beer biography of Crane:

The general subject consisted in a man personating his "predecessor" (who had died) in the hope of winning a girl's heart. The scenes were to include a ranch at the foot of the Rocky Mountains, I remember, and the action, I fear, would have been frankly melodramatic. Crane insisted that one of the situations should present the man and the girl on a boundless plain standing by their dead ponies after a furious ride.... Thirteen years afterwards I made use, half consciously, of the shadow of the primary idea of "The Predecessor" in one of my short tales which were serialized in the Metropolitan Magazine. But in that tale the dead man in the background is not a Predecessor but merely an assistant on a lonely plantation; and instead of the ranch, the mountains, and the plains, there is a cloud-capped island, a bird-haunted reef, and the sea.[1]

Conrad's version takes place in the East.* On a visit to the mainland from his lonely island plantation, Geoffrey Renouard learns that a Professor Moorsam and his daughter have arrived from London to look for the girl's missing fiancée. The young man had run off in the wake of a financial scandal; when he was later proven innocent, the girl felt obligated to seek him out. The object of the search is soon identified as Renouard's assistant, but the planter conceals the fact that the fellow had died on the island a few days before. Having fallen wildly in love with Felicia Moorsam, Renouard allows the group to sail for Malata to prevent her from returning home. Once Felicia hears the truth, however, she is so disappointed at her failure and so shocked at his duplicity that she scornfully turns him away. The family sails back to the city, and Renuoard swims calmly to his death in the sea.

---

* The manuscript mentions Sydney, but the printed version keeps the exact locality obscure.

A familiar thematic contrast emerges early in "The Planter of Malata." Renouard's destructive passion for the shapely Miss Moorsam takes place in the context of low-keyed, dispassionate society life. While he burns, the other people go casually about their business; and the contrast between realism and romance takes on increasingly ironical significance. The opening scene, in which Renouard tells an editor friend of his first encounter with the Moorsams, is paradigmatic. The editor, a high priest in the "temple of publicity," is practical, prosaic, eminently sane, a man who believes that "the only really honest writing is to be found in newspapers and nowhere else." Renouard remains unconvinced, and his guarded, essentially journalistic description of Felicia (adopted especially for this audience) is skillfully alternated with his inflammable thoughts of the girl who "kindled in him an astonished admiration."

The more we learn about the planter, the more ironical his situation appears. Because he is most famous for energy and daring, Renouard is quickly typed as "the fellow that doesn't count the cost." A tactiturn adventurer who represents the prestige of the unknown, his rumored cruelty to his subordinates is matched only by his experimental success with silk plants on Malata as a subject for fascinated town gossip. Yet his physical and intellectual achievements make him a figure of authority as well as interest.

When this self-confident empiricist becomes the helpless victim of a love that he can hardly even declare, the shock is great; and in the description of this process Conrad achieves both the best and the worst effects in the story. The best things occur when Renouard's silent passion is set against the mundane activities of mainland social life: the platitudinous chatter of the editor, the frivolity of daily dinner parties, and the mechanical deliberation of a young businessman who, when he reads letters, "hunches his shoulders up to his ugly ears, and brings his long nose and his thick lips on it like a sucking apparatus. A commercial monster." The more infatuated Renouard becomes, the more superficial his associates appear to him. When Professor Moorsam suggests that the planter should throw a little cold water on his daughter's enthusiasm for the search, Renouard cannot imagine Felicia being "subjugated by something common."

The finest irony comes when Felicia turns out to be a frigid girl whose life in Europe had been a mindless round of partygoing. Trifling in sentimental images, she had planned to marry the rescued suitor less from a desire to do him justice than from a need to play the fated heroine and quiet public opinion. Her unanswerable response to Renouard's expression of overwhelming love is "Assez! J'ai horreur de tout cela."

The shallow egotism of Felicia Moorsam has its counterpart in the puzzlement of the editor on the last page of the story. Earlier, the newspaper man had any number of facile explanations of the mystery of Geoffrey Renouard. Now, having found the clothes at the water's edge, he refuses to admit the truth but insists instead that his friend had been drowned. Since adoration has no meaning in the world of fashion and finance, Renouard's tempestuous passion is met only with incomprehension by the drab people around him.

Unfortunately, once one looks past the ironical juxtaposition and concentrates on the passion itself, trouble begins. Renouard's infatuation is supposed to be both admirable and absurd: his proud withdrawal from society has intensified his heroic gift for dreaming of "love's infinite grace," but it has also made him foolishly vulnerable to the attractions of a hollow goddess. The subject is promising, but Conrad is unable to make the passion convincing in its own terms. In an effort to communicate the force of Felicia's presence, he relies on a pretentious pattern of classical allusion. The trivial society girl appears as "something pagan," a "tragic Venus," with an ivory forehead, a complexion "fairer than Parian marble," and hair like "a helmet of burnished copper." Speaking in "an unknown voice, like the voice of oracles," she brings "everlasting unrest" to the planter of Malata. To convey her effect on the powerful Renouard, Conrad raids the vocabulary of romantic melodrama with devastating results. Sitting near the girl, Renouard feels "fire in his breast, a humming in his ears, and a complete disorder in his mind." When he learns she may leave, the "menace of separation fell on his head like a thunderbolt," and he nearly collapses into unconsciousness.

Since "The Planter of Malata" is a tale about the dangers of solitude and the loss of energy, the once-invincible Renouard is continually shown in moments of near paralysis. Early in the action, he is oppressed by the "weight of the irremediable," and concludes "there was no other course in this world for himself, for all mankind, but resignation." In a disturbing dream of Felicia, after lifting a bust of her head, he feels it crumble to pieces in his hands; and at their first and final kiss, fire runs through his veins and turns his passion to ashes leaving him "empty, without force—almost without desire."

Between the incredible praise for the vacant Miss Moorsam and the stress on Renouard's fatal depletion, the love story, too, remains empty, without force. But unlike "Freya of the Seven Isles," in which both the realistic social observation *and* the flamboyant romanticism are unconvincing, "The Planter" is at least convincing in one area. In this respect, it is similar to "A Smile of Fortune," the other long story of the period that is marred by a striking inequality between its two major elements. As Thomas Moser has shown in his study of the later fiction, Conrad often found the subject of love temperamentally uncongenial. Although Moser's argument is often simplistic and fails to account for *Chance*, it does hold true for Conrad's commercial stories. Invariably during this period, Conrad treats love with less subtlety than the psychological or moral aspects of masculine self-knowledge. Unhappily, the more he thought about the conditions of popularity, the more he felt the compulsion to write about romantic love. The uncongenial subject became at last the essential subject—a fact of great importance in Conrad's later decline as a novelist.

"THE SHADOW–LINE"

The rights to *Victory* brought Conrad more than £2,000 in 1914 alone, and he spoke for the first time of his head resting safely above water. After an eventful visit to Poland at the end of the year, he began to retell the story of his first command, which he finished—despite illness and anxiety about the war—by December 1915. The relief at being temporarily free from the obligations of comedy and romance can be seen on every page of "The Shadow-Line," one of the last and most memorable of his tales and a work that neatly summarizes the qualities of his finest short fiction.

Most typical is the way autobiographical facts are arranged and colored for the purposes of art. For years readers have taken at face value Conrad's remark that the story is "exact autobiography," but the investigations of Norman Sherry and others have undermined the authority of the assertion.* Sherry's meticulous research has made it possible to see how Conrad embroidered fact to intensify his psychological insights and to heighten narrative suspense. The unnamed ship left so impulsively by the young first mate at the opening of "The Shadow-Line" was, of course, the *Vidar*, the steamer that had taken Conrad to the settlements of Borneo where Charles Olmeijer lived. But the narrator's insistence that "the past eighteen months of new and varied experience appeared a dreary, prosaic waste of days" is clearly an exaggeration. Conrad spent only four-and-a-half months on the *Vidar* and only ten-and-a-half in the area itself. That the brief period which introduced him to so much of the material for his early fiction should, in the winter of 1888, have seemed prosaic reinforces sharply the irony of the impulsive gesture. That it should have seemed, in the winter of 1915, too brief and in need of extension reveals Conrad's desire to make the narrator's motivation more convincing.

Another suggestive change concerns the crew members Conrad left behind on the *Vidar*. In the story, when John Nieven, a second engineer, chides the young mate for going home to marry some silly girl, Conrad playfully calls him a "fierce misogynist." Yet despite

* Much of what is now known about the facts behind the action of "The Shadow-Line" was discovered by Sherry, whose book *Conrad's Eastern World* (Cambridge, 1966) solves more puzzles than one would have thought possible at this distance in time. However, Sherry does not record Conrad's own contradictory statement on the subject. Less than a month after telling Sidney Colvin that the story was "exact autobiography," he changed his mind: "No. I don't really want the little piece to be recognised formally as autobiographical. Its tone is not. But as to the underfeeling I think there can be no mistake."

the attempt to qualify Nieven's aggression by insisting that "no-body but a friend could be so angry as that," the image remains tart. That this, too, was a heightened response is suggested by a modest letter the engineer wrote Conrad in 1923, thirty-five years after they sailed together on the *Vidar*:

Dear Mr. Conrad,
You will no doubt ere this have forgotten your old shipmates on the S. S. Vidar, but we are all alive and in this country, we send you our sincere congratulations on your great accomplishments. With kindest regards,
Yours sincerely,
John C. Niven, late 2nd Engineer
For   Capt James Craig   late
        James Allan   late 1st Eng.[2]

Most of the calendar alterations were minor, designed mainly to stretch time to make it more oppressive. However, the change in the relationship between the young captain and his predecessor on the *Otago* is a splendid example of Conrad's distinctive use of auto-biographical fact for fiction. In the story, the former master of the *Otago* is described as a demented womanizer of sixty-five, whose hobbies were passionate violin playing and the writing of dirty verse. On land, he fell effortlessly into the hands of some "professional sorceress from the slums," and refused for weeks to move from the Haiphong harbor. Once at sea, he exposed his ship to unnecessary hazards, kept the crew in a frightful state of despondency, and in a last demonic act threw his violin into the Gulf of Siam. The passages in which the first mate, Burns, describes the old man's death and burial at sea are among the most vivid in Conrad's fiction, and the mate's obsession that the ghost will haunt the ship is an important element in the rising suspense of the story.

As a result of Sherry's investigations, the former master of the *Otago* turned out to be a moody but rather ordinary individual named John Snadden, who did not expose his ship to danger and who was, in fact, on reasonably decent terms with his crew. Nearly every detail now known about Snadden was the basis for some theatrical exaggeration in Conrad's tale. In "The Shadow-Line," the captain dies of a "mysterious illness"; in real life, Snadden collapsed of a heart attack. In the story, he throws his violin overboard; in reality, it went home in a box with the rest of his belongings. In the story, the first mate is terrified by the ghost hovering at the burial spot near the mouth of the gulf; in real life, the *Otago* sailed far from the place where Snadden's corpse had been deposited.

Conrad seems to have made similar changes in the portrait of Mr. Burns. Although Sherry has not been able to uncover as many facts about the mate as he did about the captain, it is now reasonably certain that their relationship was not unfriendly. Nor was Burns's fever as debilitating as Conrad makes it out to be in the story. Yet whatever the severity of Burns's obsession, he was to *some* degree unsettled by the death of the old captain. A letter from Conrad to a friend confirms this point:

Strangely enough, you know, I never either meant or "felt" the supernatural aspect of the story while writing it. It came out somehow and my readers pointed it out to me. I must tell you that it is a piece of as strict autobiography as the form allowed,— I mean, the need of slight dramatization to make the thing actual. Very slight. For the rest, not a fact or sensation is "invented." What did worry me in reality was not the "supernatural" character, but the fact of Mr. Burns's craziness. For only think: my first command, a sinister, slowly developing situation from which one couldn't see any issue that one could try for: and the only man on board (second in command) to whom I could open my mind, not quite sane,—not to be depended on for any sort of moral support.[3]

The so-called supernatural aspect (which seems to have bothered a good many readers) was the result, in part, of Conrad's manipulation of autobiographical fact. Since much of the "slight dramatization" concerned the increasingly mysterious relationship between a dead man and his crew, a reader might be excused for evoking the miraculous. Once again, however, Conrad's own contradictory remarks on the subject cloud the issue, and his insistence that he did not notice the strong supernatural element is hard to take seriously. Not only does he refer to the sinister element many times in the tale itself, but by eliminating the following passage from the final draft of the story, he calls attention to his fear of being misunderstood.*

I was oppressed by my lonely responsibility; weighed down by it in that cabin, gloomy with the lamp turned down and where my predecessor had expired under the eyes of a few awed seamen.

The passage of death made of it like a vast solitude. I took refuge from it in my state-room where nobody had died as far as I knew. After all the passion of anger and indignation I had thrown into my activities on shore the unpeopled stillness of that gulf weighed on my shaken confidence like a mere artifice of some inimical force—I upbraided myself for the very existence of that unwholesome sensation. I resisted it. But that resistance itself was a manifestation of a self-consciousness which was to me a strange experience, distasteful and disquieting. I welcomed a great wave of fatigue that all at once overwhelmed me from head to foot [in my] struggle against morbidity.

Without taking off any of my clothing—not even removing my cap from my head—I ensconced myself in the corner of the couch and crossing my arms on my breast fell into a profound slumber.

I dreamt of the Bull of Bashan. He was roaring beyond all reason on his side of a very high fence striking it with his forehoof and also rattling his horns against it from time to time. On my side of the fence my purpose was (in my dream) to lead a contemplative existence. I despised the brute, but gradually a fear woke up in me that he would end by breaking through—not through

---

* Remarkable despite its roughness, the passage appears in the manuscript at Yale but not in the printed version. It comes at the end of section III, just after the words "Enough to get under way with, he said," on p. 75 of the collected edition.

the fence—through my purpose. A horrible fear. I tried to fight against it and mainly to keep it down with my hands. But it got the better of me like a powerful compressed spring might have done—violently.*

I found myself on my feet, very scared by my dream and in addition appalled by the apparition of the late captain in front of my open door. For what else could be that dim figure in the halflight of the cuddy, featureless, still malevolently silent, not to be mistaken for anything earthly.

Before my teeth began to rattle however the apparition spoke in a hoarse apologetic voice which no ghost would have thought it necessary to adopt. Certainly not the ghost of that savage overbearing old sinner who would have liked to take his ship out of the world with him.

It was but the voice of the seaman on watch who had come down to tell me that there were faint airs off the land. Enough he thought to get underway with.

I told him to call all hands to man the windlass. Before he left the cabin it occurred to me to ask him whether he had much trouble to wake me up.

"You were very sound off Sir" he said with much feeling as he retired. That was it! He must have had to shout pretty loud. He was the Bull of Bashan of my dream, so detailed, so vivid, so concrete as to be more real than the great shadowy peace which met me when I came on deck.

Although Conrad provides a concrete explanation for the narrator's vision, so much has already been made of spirits and demons that the ghost remains far more distinct than his apologetic human counterpart. The decision to eliminate this striking episode may have been motivated by Conrad's fear that the miraculous element was becoming too dominant. He disliked the supernatural in fic-

---

* The Bulls of Bashan are mentioned several times in the Old Testament, most memorably in the twenty-second Psalm: "They open wide their mouth against me / As a ravening and a roaring lion." They often symbolize cruel and noisy oppressors.

tion, as the author's note to "The Shadow-Line," makes clear: "all my moral and intellectual being is penetrated by an invincible conviction that whatever falls under the dominion of our senses must be in nature. ... I am too firm in my consciousness of the marvellous to be ever fascinated by the mere supernatural. ..."[4]

On the whole, however, the mixture of prosaic fact and theatrical exaggeration is kept within credible limits in "The Shadow-Line." The menace of the dead captain, the hallucination of Burns, and the dismay of the narrator have psychological rather than transcendental origins and help make "The Shadow-Line" more than the story of a calm-haunted ship. Yet the distinctive use of autobiographical materials is not the only link to Conrad's best early work. Here, for the first time in many years, he returns to the conflict between egoism and altruism as the basic theme of a short story.

As I have suggested earlier, there is usually a direct correlation between Conrad's handling of this thematic contrast and the successes of a particular piece of fiction. In "Heart of Darkness" and *Nostromo*, the subject is complex and expressive; in the best short fiction of 1904–1914, "Il Conde" and "The Secret Sharer," it is uncomplicated but graphic; whereas in the potboilers of the same period, it is never more than fragmentary. The subject of "The Shadow-Line," however, is the education of a young egoist, and among his teachers are all the figures in Conrad's gallery of the self-forgetful and the self-absorbed.

The young mate, fleeing the responsibilities of the *Vidar*, feels detached from "the forms and colours of the world" and sensitive only to the vibrations of his own ego. Bored with the past, restless in the present, and uncertain of the future, he wants to get "a bit of one's own"; but when pressed to define the goal, he nearly dissolves into tears. As a victim of the "green sickness of late youth," he is a familiar prodigy of inarticulate self-concern. Yet he is an attractive figure, despite his callowness. Just as the naïve posturings of the twenty-year-old Marlow in "Youth" are admirable, so the quixotic confusions of the hero in "The Shadow-Line" gain our sympathy and understanding. Certainly, everyone in the port at Singapore is concerned when he throws up his berth. Each member of the *Vidar* crew has an explanation of the impulsive gesture, and Captain Kent expresses the consensus opinion when he tells the mate "that he hoped I would find what I was so anxious to go and look for." The concern of others, based on the genuine decency and talent of the boy himself (and the universality of his dilemma), keeps the reader from becoming impatient with his self-indulgence and immaturity.

A good part of the delicate comedy of the early chapters comes from the mate's blindness to the attractive solicitations of other people. Sailors in port are inevitably "dreary, unimaginative fellows," and the most preposterous is Captain Giles. A substitute pilot in the harbor at Singapore, Giles is an expert on the perils of land and water; in his head are the details of every maritime intrigue and the images of all the rocks at sea. To the capricious mate, however, he is a stuffy old bore, a church warden or sanctimonious uncle, from whom benevolence radiates "ridiculously, mildly, impressively." Giles, of course, is the prime mover in the story, since only at his insistence does the narrator follow up the letter that carries news of his first command. The old pilot helps him make the most critical decision of his life; and he is humane in small matters as well. When the mate confesses a desire to torment the miserable steward who conspired against him, Giles goes off at once to put the man's mind at ease. The mate's failure to see that Giles's pomposity is a mannerism concealing genuine intelligence and wisdom proves the comic limitations of his egotism. Only at the end of the story does he suggest that there was a complex side to Giles's intrusive benevolence. When the old man puffs moodily on a cigar after speaking of hard work and duty, the narrator remarks: "It was as if a ponderous curtain had rolled up disclosing an unexpected Captain Giles. . . . We rose, left the hotel, and parted from each other in the street with a warm handshake, just as he began to interest me for the first time in our intercourse."[5]

Because his main concern in "The Shadow-Line" is elsewhere, Conrad does nothing with the more tantalizing elements in the personality of Giles, but he does hint that inside the complacent fat man is a complex altruist prepared to come out. Early in the tale, Giles is credited "with some wonderful adventures and with some mysterious tragedy in his life." One of the definitive marks of the mature altruist—Mrs. Gould, Dr. Kennedy, Stein, Monygham, or Marlow—is the scar of bitter personal failure. But since this strain in Giles's history is never developed, he remains a humour figure, slightly ludicrous and impressively wise.

The old pilot is the first of three altruistic figures the young mate encounters during his initiation. Once in command, he is also tutored by the legation's medical officer and by Ransome, his own cook. "A doctor," the narrator remarks, "is humane by definition. But that man was so in reality." When a fever-stricken crew prevents the ship from leaving Bangkok, the doctor brings not only professional skill but a sympathetic ear. His entrance line—"I am really sorry to see you worried like this"—is called "the only humane speech I used to hear at that time"; and by later coming aboard for an occasional chat, he shows a compassion equaled by no one else in the port. Like Giles, the doctor offers advice which his young friend is too impatient to take; but unlike the older man, he knows enough to hold his tongue. After Burns is felled by fever, the doctor cautiously suggests that a replacement be sought from Singapore, but the captain refuses:

"Not a day," I said. The very thought gave me the shivers. The hands seemed fairly fit, all of them, and this was the time to get them away. Once at sea I was not afraid of facing anything. . . .

The doctor's glasses were directed at me like two lamps searching the genuineness of my resolution. He opened his lips as if to argue further, but shut them again without saying anything. . . .

"Look here," I said. "Unless you tell me officially that the man must not be moved I'll make arrangements to have him brought on board tomorrow. . . ."

"Oh! I'll make all the arrangements myself," said the doctor at once. "I spoke as I did only as a friend—as a well-wisher, and that sort of thing."

He rose in his dignified simplicity and gave me a warm handshake, rather solemnly, I thought. But he was as good as his word.[6]

Once the ship is out to sea, the captain goes below to prepare quinine for the stricken crew and unexpectedly finds a note from the physician in the medicine cabinet. Beginning "My dear Captain," the "good, sympathetic man" warns him not to trust too much in the beneficial effects of a sea change. Interestingly enough, the letter that Conrad actually received in February 1888 (now in the Keating Collection) is more impersonal, beginning "Dear Sir," and testifying that Conrad did everything possible to get the *Otago* away from the pestilential port. The fictional liberty increases the intimacy of the relationship and makes the physician seem more humane.

Later, discovering that the treasured quinine has been mysteriously replaced with a worthless powder, the captain instinctively rages against the doctor:

Instead of writing that warning letter, the very refinement of sympathy, why didn't the man make a proper inspection? But, as a matter of fact, it was hardly fair to blame the doctor. The fittings were in order and the medicine chest is an officially arranged affair. There was nothing really to arouse the slightest suspicion. The person I could never forgive was myself. Nothing should ever be taken for granted.[7]

Despite the captain's quickness to assume responsibility for the error, his initial anger is not entirely unjust. The doctor's friendly letter cannot wholly excuse his failure to inspect the quinine, an oversight which suggests that his benevolence, like Giles's, is not without just a touch of complacency. Nevertheless, he remains an influential figure in the narrator's moral development. A model of good nature at the time of crisis, he also reinforces an important maritime commandment: never take anything for granted.

Ransome is more memorable. Compelled by a weak heart to sign up as the cook, he quickly gains respect as the most versatile sailor on the ship; and his first speech reveals the trait for which he is most exemplary: "I am afraid, Sir, I won't be able to give the mate all the attention he's likely to need." Yet despite his modesty, Ransome does give the crew such attention. Serving coffee at 4:00 A.M., running up with a vital piece of equipment, reminding the captain to open the compressors or to put on his coat, he "sheds comfort around him as he moves." When the new master becomes susceptible to Burns's delirium and speaks of "fever devils," Ransome's quick, intelligent glance of disapproval brings him back to his senses. The most striking instance of Ransome's benevolent power comes just after the captain has confessed to his diary that he is too frightened to take his place of command:

At that moment, or, perhaps, the moment after, I became aware of Ransome standing in the cabin. Something in his expression startled me. It had a meaning which I could not make out. I exclaimed:

"Somebody's dead."

It was his turn then to look startled.

"Dead? Not that I know of, sir. I have been in the forecastle only ten minutes ago and there was no dead man there then. . . ."

Ransome lingered in the cabin as if he had something to do there, but hesitated about doing it. I said suddenly:

"You think I ought to be on deck?"

He answered at once but without any particular emphasis or accent: "I do, sir."

I got to my feet briskly, and he made way for me to go out.[8]

Later, whenever Ransome disappears from sight, the unsteady captain feels as if some vital support had been withdrawn. But the ship survives its ordeal by calm and storm, and he gets the chance to thank Ransome at an attractively symbolic moment. As the cook stands relief at the helm, the captain says, "I, and the ship, and everyone on board of her, are very much indebted to you, Ransome." And the narrator adds, "He made as though he had not heard me, and steered in silence till I was ready to relieve him."

Ransome's finest moment occurs at the end of the story. In the face of the captain's desire to keep him on board, he powerfully asserts his right to place reasonable self-regard above loyalty to others. "Life was a boon to him—this precarious hard life—and he was thoroughly alarmed about himself." Thus, one of the most effective of Conrad's selfless seamen is last observed walking cautiously up the companion stairs in "a blue funk about his heart." The benevolent actions of Giles, Ransome, and the legation's doctor are countered by the behavior of three different egoists: the former master of the *Otago*, the first mate Burns, and the chief steward of the Officers' Home at Singapore. The steward, a sour, cowardly man who hoards cardboard boxes in his tiny room, schemes to get the command of the *Otago* for an unemployed sailor named Hamilton. Characteristically, the motive is self-interest. Hamilton has been running up a large bill at the Home, and the steward wants to get the luckless fellow off his hands. Thanks to Giles's kindly interference, the narrator spoils the ploy by locating the decisive letter which is properly his. The steward and Hamilton connive for personal gain, but their fecklessness and transparency make them easy to thwart. Since Conrad found greed most absorbing when it was touched by a powerful fanaticism, these feeble conspirators are given only minor roles in the story.

Burns and the old captain are more forceful and dangerous to the narrator's welfare. Instead of carrying out his owner's orders, the former master of the *Otago* preferred to keep the ship drifting about while he played wildly on his violin. On those rare occasions when he left the cabin, he would curse the ship by praying for its loss at sea. In his most celebrated escapade—the three-week assignation with the enchantress from Haiphong—he kept the crew idle in a sweltering harbor; and by selling the quinine to pay for his wenching, he directly endangered several human lives. Although his adventures may be tales of hearsay, the old man is one of the most memorable sequestered egoists in Conrad's fiction.

The new captain feels the menace of his predecessor soon after he takes command. Before learning of the old man's predilections, he sits back in the captain's chair to reflect on his own position in a dynasty, "a dynasty, continuous not in blood, indeed, but in its experience, in its training, in its conception of duty, and in the blessed simplicity of its traditional view on life." But moments later,

hearing the wretched story from the lips of Burns, he is shocked
at the betrayal of a tradition which had once seemed "as imperative
as any guide on earth could be."

Yet the example of the old man's treachery would hardly be so
unnerving were it not for Mr. Burns. Burns, after all, is the source
of everything the narrator knows about his predecessor; and when
the mate is paralyzed by fright of the dead man's ghost, the captain's own morale is affected. The captain looks for human support
at the start of a difficult challenge. Occasionally, Burns provides it;
but more often he undermines unity by insisting on the urgency of
his demonic message. This alternating pattern of support and sub-
version is established soon after the first meeting of master and
mate; and the conflict between Burns's disabling obsession and his
desire to help the ship in its need eventually becomes a major
tension in the story. The following passage is typical of the way it
operates:

In the evening, under the crude glare of his lamp, Mr. Burns
seemed to have come more to the surface of his bedding. It was
as if a depressing hand had been lifted off him. He answered my
few words by a comparatively long, connected speech. He asserted
himself strongly. If he escaped being smothered by this stagnant
heat, he said, he was confident that in a very few days he would
be able to come up on deck and help me.

While he was speaking I trembled lest this effort of energy
should leave him lifeless before my eyes. But I cannot deny that
there was something comforting in his willingness. I made a suitable
reply, but pointed out to him that the only thing that could really
help us was wind—a fair wind.

He rolled his head impatiently on the pillow. And it was not
comforting in the least to hear him begin to mutter crazily about
the late captain, that old man buried in latitude 8° 20', right in
our way. . . .

I felt the inexpugnable strength of common sense being insid-
iously menaced by this gruesome, by this insane delusion. . . .

"Now, not a word more," I said, stepping in and laying my hand on his cool forehead. It proved to me that this atrocious absurdity was rooted in the man himself and not in the disease, which, apparently, had emptied him of every power, mental and physical, except that one fixed idea.[9]

Given the peculiarity of the winds and the ship's odd immobility, Burns's continual stress on unearthly forces is hard to laugh off. At times, it even gains support from the elements. Just after the captain admits that Burns's talk is "not exactly wholesome for my resolution," an inexplicable wind drives the ship off its course and within five minutes dies out completely. Not for the first time, the troubled captain adopts Burns's terminology to complain that "only purposeful malevolence" could account for the travesty.

Although his fanaticism weakens the captain's resolve, Burns is not without his moments of splendid lucidity. He suspects that the captain's remorse about the loss of the quinine is a form of self-pity and chides him for being foolish. From time to time, he can even support and subvert in the same breath. At the captain's query about the possibility of changing the ship's course, Burns screams: "No, no, no. Don't do that, sir. You mustn't for a moment give up facing that old ruffian. If you do he will get the upper hand of us." Exasperated, the captain walks away, but not before he admits to himself that "his protest, however, was essentially sound."

The high point of Burns's influence comes during the torrential rainstorm. The huge, bear-like object that trips the captain in the darkness on deck is Burns crawling from his sick bed to help his mates. But instead of aid, he brings disquiet, droning away again at his familiar complaint about ghostly persecution. Before the crew can get down below, the raving mate exhorts them all to "Laugh! Laugh—I tell you. Now then—all together. One, two, three—laugh!" Much to everyone's surprise and relief, Burns faints, and soon the tension is eased. The breeze continues and the crisis is over.

The next time Burns comes on deck, the captain feels a natural dread at having to deal with a lunatic while trying to steer a ship full of stricken men. But the obsession (which earlier seemed rooted in the man and not in the illness) turns out to be "a symptom of his disease." The fancy passes with the fever, but not before "the exorcising virtue of Mr. Burns' awful laugh" helps lay "the spectre" and remove "the curse."

Burns's recovery is related to the overall success of the captain's first test. If his obsession is remedial, so are the problems that face his master. As Ian Watt has argued about the story as a whole: "conceit and error and guilt are universal, but their consequences, it seems, are not irredeemable; we are all in the same boat with them, and with sickness and death, but if we seize our fleeting and partial opportunities, we can steer."[10] As usual, the victory is hard won and Conrad's optimism is cautionary.

The lessons taught both by the altruists and the egoists support the argument that "The Shadow-Line" is the communal counterpart of "The Secret Sharer."* A good part of the earlier story is concerned with a young initiate unsure of his powers. Here, however, the captain (whatever his other confusions) knows the range of his talent, and when he is threatened by "moral dissolution," it is his incorrigible "seaman's instinct" that saves him. Confident enough of his ability, he compares himself to a mad carpenter making a box: "were he ever so convinced that he was King of Jerusalem, the box he would make would be a sane box." The major threat to the captain's well-being comes not from any serious personal flaw, but from a youthful inability to evaluate other people. His imagination is too easily inflamed by the sound of Burns's frenzy and too quick to dismiss as tiresome the conventional wisdom of Giles. With the help of Ransome, however, the captain learns to appreciate his dependence on others, and his gradual passage from self-absorption to an awareness of his place in an elaborate human continuum is the basic subject of the story.

* See Carl Benson, "Conrad's Two Stories of Initiation," *PMLA*, LXIX (March 1954), 46–56; and Watt's "Story and Idea in Conrad's 'The Shadow-Line,'" *Critical Quarterly*, II (summer 1960), 133–148.

"THE WARRIOR'S SOUL" AND "THE TALE"

Conrad's last two stories, "The Warrior's Soul" and "The Tale," are slight "war-time products," written when he was too weary "to sit down and invent fairy tales."[11] "It seems," he once told a friend, "almost criminal levity to talk at this time of books, stories, publications. This war attends my uneasy pillow like a nightmare."[12] Between 1915 and 1917, Conrad wrote very little, and the only work he found relatively easy to finish, "The Shadow-Line," looked back thirty years for an example of human solidarity in time of stress. "The Warrior's Soul" and "The Tale" are less confident both in impulse and in execution. In the subjects they choose to examine and in the elements they decide to leave out, they are oddly reminiscent of Conrad at full- and half-strength, of "Heart of Darkness" and "Gaspar Ruiz," of "The Secret Sharer" and "An Anarchist."*

The basic materials are unmistakably Conradian. In "The Warrior's Soul," an old Russian officer tells a group of young men about a drama of obsessive loyalty, murder, and self-exile during Napoleon's retreat from Moscow. In "The Tale," a naval officer describes to his mistress his own moral dilemma when he caused the wreck of a Scandinavian oil tanker during the first World War.

Tomassov, the hero of the Russian story, falls in love with a society woman while serving as an attaché in Paris on the eve of the war. The woman, who has learned that the French plan to arrest the entire Russian delegation, asks her lover—a French officer named De Castel—to warn the affectionate Tomassov to escape. Overwhelmed with gratitude, the Russian swears to his adversary, "You may command my life." Later, on the battlefield outside Moscow, Tomassov—notorious for his tender sensibilities—is caught in an agonizing predicament. De Castel, battered and

---

* "The Warrior's Soul," finished in March 1916, is based on an anecdote in the memoirs of Philippe de Ségur. "The Tale," written in October 1916, was a product of visits Conrad paid to ships sweeping for mines and repairing torpedo defenses off the English coast.

disgraced, insists that the humane Tomassov honor the earlier pledge by obeying an order to kill him. At first, the Russian refuses; when the Frenchman calls him a coward, however, he manfully pays his debt by releasing De Castel "from a fate worse than death—the loss of all faith and courage." Reprimanded afterward for shooting an unarmed prisoner, Tomassov resigns his commission and exiles himself in "the depths of his province."

The commanding officer of a British warship in "The Tale" prowls the coast looking for neutral ships suspected of refueling enemy submarines. Noticing an empty barrel on the water, he realizes that a submarine must have met a tanker very near this spot; before he can take action, a great cover of fog forces him to drop anchor in a large cove. A crewman brings news that another ship is nearby; the commanding officer immediately wonders why, when his ship entered, the other did not make itself known. Eventually, he boards the ship and quickly becomes convinced that its captain, identified only as the Northman and a neutral, was a "moral cannibal," guilty of profiting from the horrors of war. The Northman denies all conspiratorial knowledge and claims only to have become lost by blundering into the area. Although he cannot confirm his suspicions, the commanding officer—giving the Northman a set of bearings—orders the neutral ship to leave the cove in the denseness of the fog. The directions are false: if the Northman follows them he will wreck his ship; but if he knows the way and avoids the rocks, he will confirm his own guilt and the British will track him down. The ship sinks and the officer is torn by uncertainty: did he commit "stern retribution or murder?"

Like so many of Conrad's stories, "The Warrior's Soul" and "The Tale" dramatize the ordeal of a hero pressed to choose when every choice is frightful. Tomassov's test is straightforward; he can commit treachery or murder. The crisis of the commanding officer is less clear; he is compelled to act with partial knowledge and can never be sure of the moral consequences of his action. Like Marlow, Tomassov has the dubious pleasure of being loyal to a nightmare of his own choosing; the officer is left in ethical limbo. Characteristically bitter and unavoidable, these tests also turn on a typical

Conradian conflict between egoism and altruism brought about by some fatal weakness of character. "Full of compassion for all forms of mankind's misery," Tomassov is a simple-minded altruist betrayed by his own theatrical and thoughtless self-assertion ("You may command my life!"). Although quick to sympathize with suffering, he takes a human life. The commanding officer, a patriot repelled by all forms of hypocrisy, is victimized by his own moral rigidity. Alert to the slightest sign of duplicity, he lies and destroys a ship and its crew.

Both stories are also characteristic in the way they are told. Except for three short sentences at the start, "The Warrior's Soul" is entirely in the Russian's voice. "The Tale," like "Youth" and "Heart of Darkness," uses the omniscient narrator to introduce and later to punctuate the remarks of the commanding officer. In both cases the intimate byplay between the audience and the narrator is supposed to add suggestiveness to the events being described. For the old Russian, Tomassov's history is an exemplary tale designed to answer his listeners' deprecatory remarks about the Slavic capacity for heroism. For the commanding officer, the moral ambiguity of an encounter at sea might explain the mood of melancholy depletion that hangs over his love affair on land.

The trouble begins, however, with the way each narrator performs his function. In Conrad's finest work, the invented speaker is in part the author's surrogate, a man sensitive to the need for focus and composition in the telling of tales. Marlow, Dr. Kennedy, and the captain in "Falk" are always conscious of the capacity of the audience when they shape their narratives. Although Conrad uses narrators with great variety, only twice before "The Warrior's Soul" did he invent a persona who did not in some important way resemble himself. In "Gaspar Ruiz" he forfeited much of the narration to General Santierra, whose fervid romanticism destroyed the plausibility of that story of heroism and betrayal. In "The Informer," Conrad has Mr. X (the greatest rebel of modern times) tell the main story to a first narrator, a collector of *objects d'art*, whose incomprehension is supposed to lend the exchange a certain cumulative irony.

The old Russian officer in "The Warrior's Soul" resembles General Santierra and the collector of porcelain and bronze. Characterized through his opening statements as a vigorous, opinionated man of some subtlety and quickness of mind, he soon degenerates into the kind of narrator so familiar from *A Set of Six*. Once he gets past the introductory tableau in which Napoleon's army is seen engraved against the frozen landscape, he starts begging questions and emphasizing his own inability to understand the fascinating events he is trying to describe. Tomassov, he claims, was saved from being a fool by a "dose of poetry" in his nature; but the officer—by his own admission—has only a poor share of "common shrewdness." As we learn more about Tomassov, we begin to feel that common shrewdness could provide no satisfactory clue to his conduct. According to the old man, a human being "is like the sea whose movements are too complicated to explain, and whose depths may bring up God knows what at any moment." But instead of moving toward these unknown territories, the officer continually harps on his own inadequate powers of explanation. Motives that cannot be analyzed and qualities that escape definition mount as the story continues, and he closes with the most striking refusal of all: "Yes. He had done it. And what was it? One warrior's soul paying its debt a hundredfold to another warrior's soul. . . . You may look on it that way. I don't know. And perhaps Tomassov did not know himself."[13] Despite having been Tomassov's confidant, the old man finds his young friend totally enigmatic, but enigmatic in the way Gaspar was to Santierra, not Jim to Marlow.

The officer's advocacy raises another critical problem. Although he describes Tomassov as a fascinating mixture of innocent good nature, poetic imagination, and just a touch of Russian barbarism, the old man depicts him only when he is incapacitated by love, admiration, or the moral complexity of his situation. Because of the special narrative point of view, Tomassov says almost nothing; and on the rare occasions when his conversation is reported, it belies his reputation for passion and nobility. In the following exchange, De Castel speaks first:

"Pay it, I say, with one liberating shot. You are a man of honor.
I have not even a broken sabre. All my being recoils from my own
degradation. You know me."

Tomassov said nothing.

"Haven't you got the soul of a warrior?" the Frenchman asked
in an angry whisper, but with something of a mocking intention
in it.

"I don't know," said poor Tomassov.[14]

As the story ends, we last see the hero bending over his lifeless
adversary "in a tenderly contemplative attitude. And his young,
ingenuous face, with lowered eyelids, expressed no grief, on stern-
ness, no horror—but was set in the repose of a profound, as if
endless and endlessly silent meditation." Unfortunately, neither the
narrator nor the reader ever learns what Tomassov had on his mind.

The commanding officer in "The Tale" labors under a similar
disability. The only one of Conrad's narrators who has a woman
for an audience, he is praised for having told "simple and—and
professional—tales very well at one time. . . . You had a—a sort of
art—in the days before the war." However accomplished his technique was in the past, it is sadly impoverished now. Instead of providing the kind of rich substantiality upon which the more generalized meanings of *Lord Jim* might rest, he opts for allegory from the
start: "there was once upon a time a Commanding Officer and a
Northman. Put in the capitals, please, because they had no other
names." As he moves into the story itself, the narrator continues to
neglect the specificity of his encounter with the Northman to emphasize his hatred for duplicity, his nostalgia for a world in which
loyalties are more serviceable, and his inability to probe the consequences of his final action. Most of the story takes place in darkness or in suffocating mist, and characters remain vague to the point
of nullity. The narrator, so obsessed with the enfeebling power of
treachery, drains all force from an occasional homily on the need
for Frankness, Sincerity, and Passion. Like the Russian in "The
Warrior's Soul," he ends by confessing, "I shall never know."

The worst that can be said of Conrad in "The Warrior's Soul" and "The Tale" is that, through narrative sophistication and insistent symbolism, he makes claims for greater suggestiveness than the stories actually embody. But by staying clear of comedy, exotic adventure, and an easy optimism, he at least never sinks to the transparent falseness of his weakest commercial stories. At a time when he might have reaffirmed his belief in "les valeurs idéales" by turning to the more tractable and consoling materials of romance (as he did a year later in *The Arrow of Gold*), he wrote two tales in which he refuses to bypass the ambiguous springs of human conduct. To memorialize a "warrior's soul," he describes a young man fated to die in the obscurity of exile after violating the commandment by which he had governed his life. In his only fictional commentary on modern warfare, he records the history of an officer betrayed at sea by his devotion to an unsatisfactory idea of service. Even at half-strength, and partly against his will, Conrad remains the historian of moral compromise.

* * *

The history of Conrad's career as a short story writer has its moments of melancholy as well as bitterness and triumph. Few writers capable of achieving the concentration and power of "Heart of Darkness" ever descended to the dismal fabrication of "The Inn of the Two Witches"; and no collection of a major writer brackets a story like "The Secret Sharer" between works of such different quality as "A Smile of Fortune" and "Freya of the Seven Isles." Perhaps the most painful part of tracing Conrad's career as a story writer is to have watched an elegant, aristocratic man of genius try, from necessity, to learn the formulaic secrets of commercial fiction—and fail. Few potboilers have been as tepid as "To-morrow."

But time, which has forgiven Ford for *The New Humpty-Dumpty* and Dickens for *Master Humphrey's Clock*, will forgive Conrad for "Gaspar Ruiz." "Youth," "Heart of Darkness," "Typhoon," "The Secret Sharer," and "The Shadow-Line"—the stories on which his claim to classic standing rests—avoid romance, sentimentality, hollow humor, and an unconvincing affirmative ethic.

Most of Conrad's finest fiction belongs to the genre of the masculine adventure story in which violence, physical peril, and natural disaster dictate the course of events. But instead of putting his emphasis on the violence, Conrad is preeminently concerned with man's response to the hazards of circumstance or to the unexplored vulnerability of his own nature. In his preoccupation with the moral ramifications of experience, Conrad, like James, steps away from most of his contemporaries in the short story genre and moves toward the discoveries of Joyce, Lawrence, Hemingway, and Faulkner. Speaking of Kipling's work, Conrad once told his French translator: "Son intérêt est dans le sujet, l'intérêt de mon oeuvre est *dans l'effet* qu'elle produit."[15]

In his best stories, Conrad's major aim was to find new ways to give a work "a sinister resonance, a tonality of its own, a continued vibration that, I hoped, would hang in the air and dwell on the ear after the last note had been struck." The desire for tonality—the need to be intense, skeptical, excursive—brought Conrad into conflict with the more casual and concise demands of popular magazines. At the close of his critical study, Albert Guerard wondered if "Conrad would have been a still more original and even greater writer had he been freed from commercial pressures and ambitions; had he shared, for instance, Gide's money and Gide's literary connections."[16] Such speculation is, of course, futile; but given the circumstances of the case, inevitable; and the image it projects is golden.

Appendix

A Chronology of
Conrad's Short Stories

Story and No. of Words	Completion	First Serialization	Book Publication
"The Black Mate" (12,000)	ca. 1886 (rewritten 1908)	London Magazine, April 1908	Tales of Hearsay, 1925
"The Idiots" (10,000)	May 1896	The Savoy, Oct. 1896	Tales of Unrest, 1898
"An Outpost of Progress" (9,750)	July 1896	Cosmopolis, June–July 1897	"
"The Lagoon" (5,700)	Aug. 1896	The Cornhill, Jan. 1897	"
"Karain" (14,500)	April 1897	Blackwood's, Nov. 1897	"
"The Return" (20,000)	Sept. 1897	[Never serialized]	"

"Youth" (13,000)	June 1898	*Blackwood's,* Sept. 1898	*Youth, A Narrative; and Two Other Stories,* 1902
"Heart of Darkness" (38,000)	Feb. 1899	*Blackwood's,* Feb.–April 1899	"
"Typhoon" (28,000)	Jan. 1901	*Pall Mall Magazine,* Jan.–March 1902	*Typhoon, and Other Stories,* 1903
"Falk" (26,000)	May 1901	[Never serialized]	"
"Amy Foster" (11,000)	June 1901	*Illustrated London, News,* Dec. 1901	"
"Tomorrow" (9,000)	Jan. 1902	*Pall Mall Magazine,* Aug. 1902	"
"The End of the Tether" (47,000)	Oct. 1902	*Blackwood's,* July–Dec., 1902	*Youth, A Narrative,* 1902

Story and No. of Words	Completion	First Serialization	Book Publication
"Gaspar Ruiz" (18,700)	Nov. 1905	Pall Mall Magazine, July–Oct. 1906	A Set of Six, 1908
"The Brute" (8,000)	ca. Dec. 1905	Daily Chronicle, Dec. 5, 1906	"
"An Anarchist" (8,000)	Nov.–Dec. 1905	Harper's Magazine, Aug. 1906	"
"The Informer" (8,500)	Dec.–Jan. 1905–06	Harper's Magazine, Dec. 1906	"
"Il Conde" (7,000)	Dec. 1906	Cassell's Magazine, Aug. 1908	"
"The Duel" (30,000)	April 1907	Pall Mall Magazine, Jan.–May 1908	"
"The Secret Sharer" (15,500)	Dec. 1909	Harper's Magazine, Aug.–Sept. 1910	'Twixt Land and Sea, 1912

"A Smile of Fortune" (24,000)	Aug. 1910	*London Magazine,* Feb. 1911	
"Prince Roman" (8,000)	Sep.–Oct. 1910	*Oxford and Cambridge Review,* Oct. 1911; also *Metropolitan Magazine,* Jan. 1912, under title of "The Aristocrat"	*Tales of Hearsay,* 1925
"The Partner" (11,500)	Oct.–Nov. 1910	*Harper's Magazine,* Nov. 1911	*Within the Tides,* 1915
"Freya of the Seven Isles" (26,000)	Feb. 1911	*Metropolitan Magazine,* April 1912; also *London Mag.,* July 1912	*'Twixt Land and Sea,* 1912
"The Inn of the Two Witches" (10,000)	Dec. 1912	*Pall Mall Magazine,* March 1913; also *Metropolitan,* May 1913	*Within the Tides,* 1915

Story and No. of Words	Completion	First Serialization	Book Publication
"Because of the Dollars" (12,000)	Dec. 1913 or Jan. 1914	Metropolitan Magazine, Sept. 1914	"
"The Planter of Malata" (23,000)	Dec. 1913	Metropolitan Magazine, June–July 1914	"
"The Shadow-Line" (45,000)	Dec. 1915	English Review, Sept. 1916–March 1917; also Metropolitan, Oct. 1916	The Shadow-Line 1917
"The Warrior's Soul" (7,500)	March 1916	Land and Water, March 29, 1917	Tales of Hearsay, 1925
"The Tale" (6,500)	Oct. 1916	Strand Magazine, Oct. 1917	"

Notes

[References to Conrad's writings are to volumes in *The Collected Edition of the Works of Joseph Conrad* (London: J. M. Dent, 1946–   ). Complete authors' names, titles, and publication dates are given in the bibliography, pp. 215–218.]

1. FIRST TALES

[1] John A. Gee and Paul J. Sturm, *Letters of Joseph Conrad to Marguerite Poradowska, 1890–1920*, p. 91.

[2] "Alphonse Daudet," in *Notes on Life and Letters*, p. 20.

[3] Letters dated December 4, 1907, January 1908, and February 1908 (Gordan Collection).

[4] Gee and Sturm, *Letters to Marguerite Poradowska*, p. 84.

[5] Edward Garnett, *Letters from Joseph Conrad, 1895–1924*, pp. 137–138.

[6] G. J. Worth, "Conrad's Debt to Maupassant in the Preface to *The Nigger of the 'Narcissus,'*" *Journal of English and Germanic Philology*, LIV (October 1955), 700–704. See also Paul Kirschner, "Conrad and Maupassant," *A Review of English Literature*, VI (October 1965), 37–51.

[7] Letter, October 1, 1903 (Yale University Library).

[8] *Notes on Life and Letters*, p. 26.

[9] *Tales of Unrest*, p. vii. See also Milton Chaikin, "Zola and Conrad's 'The Idiots,'" *Studies in Philology*, LII, 3 (July 1955), 502–507.

[10] *Tales of Unrest*, pp. 57–58.

[11] Garnett, *Letters from Conrad*, p. 66.

[12] Gerard Jean-Aubry, *Joseph Conrad: Life and Letters*, I, 264.

[13] *Ibid.*, p. 228.

[14] *Ibid.*, p. 209.

2. COMING TO BLACKWOOD'S

[1] April 9, 1896, Jean-Aubry, I, 164.

[2] December 5, 1897, Garnett, *Letters from Conrad*, p. 120.

[3] Letter from Garnett to Conrad, June 2, 1896, quoted in Carolyn Heilbrun's *The Garnett Family*, p. 111.

[4] June 3, 1896 (Lilly Library, University of Indiana).

[5] June 7, 1896 (Yale University Library).

[6] July 22, 1896 (Yale University Library).

[7] November 21, 1896, Jean-Aubry, I, 197.

[8] August 14, 1896, Garnett, *Letters from Conrad*, pp. 67–68.

[9] *Ibid.*, p. 103. S. S. Pawling was a partner in the firm of William Heinemann, publishers of *The Nigger of the "Narcissus."*

10 Jean-Aubry, I, 206.
11 William Blackburn, ed., *Joseph Conrad: Letters to William Blackwood and David S. Meldrum*, p. 140.
12 *Ibid.*, p. 144.
13 *Ibid.*, p. 141.
14 Jean-Aubry, I, 277.
15 Blackburn, *Letters to Blackwood*, p. 25.
16 *Ibid.*, pp. 152–156. Conrad's break with *Blackwood's* was gradual and a result partly of the quarrel, but also Conrad's reliance on J. B. Pinker.
17 Letter to Pinker, November 1911 (Gordan Collection).
18 March 28, 1912 (Berg Collection, N.Y.P.L.).
19 Blackburn, *Letters to Blackwood*, p. 3.
20 *Ibid.*, p. 172.
21 *Ibid.*, p. 86.
22 *Ibid.*, p. 46.
23 Letter to Pinker, October 16, 1913 (Gordan Collection).
24 The argument can be followed in these essays: F. A. D., "Conrad's 'The Lagoon,' " *Explicator*, IX (1951), item 7; Gullason, *Explicator*, XIV (January 1956), 23; Sickels, *Explicator*, XV (December 1956), 17; Gleckner, *Explicator*, XVI (March 1958), 33; McCann, *Explicator*, XVIII (October 1959), 3; and Owen, *Explicator*, XVIII (May 1960), 47.
25 The *Cornhill*, LXXV (January 1897), p. 71; *Tales of Unrest*, p. 204.
26 Thomas Moser, *Joseph Conrad*, p. 70.
27 Garnett, *Letters from Conrad*, p. 88.
28 Albert Guerard, *Conrad, the Novelist*, pp. 90–92.
29 *Tales of Unrest*, pp. 53–55.
30 *Ibid.*, p. 48.
31 Jean-Aubry, I, 234.
32 *Tales of Unrest*, p. 49.
33 Blackburn, *Letters to Blackwood*, p. 154.
34 Guerard, p. 96.
35 Blackburn, *Letters to Blackwood*, p. 8.
36 Garnett, *Letters from Conrad*, p. 106.
37 *Ibid.*, p. 107.
38 *Ibid.*, p. 129.
39 *Tales of Unrest*, p. viii.
40 *Bookman*, LXVI (January 1928), 495.
41 *The Academy*, LVI (March 11, 1899), p. 282.
42 John D. Gordan, *Joseph Conrad*, p. 258.
43 January 7, 1898 (Berg Collection, N.Y.P.L.).
44 See Guerard, pp. 96–98; Moser, pp. 71–78; and Gordan, pp. 252–59.
45 Gee and Sturm, *Letters to Marguerite Poradowska*, p. 72.
46 Elizabeth Bowen, *The Faber Book of Modern Stories*, p. 8.
47 Zdzislaw Najder, *Conrad's Polish Background*, p. 219.

3. THE MAJOR STORIES

1 *The New York Times*, August 24, 1901, p. 603.
2 Schopenhauer, *The Complete Essays*, ed. T. S. Saunders, p. 102. See also Tadeusz Bobrowski's letter to Conrad, October 28, 1891, in Najder, *Conrad's Polish Background*, pp. 152–156.
3 *Youth*, p. 126.
4 *The World as Will and Idea* (New York, 1961), p. 380.

5 Gee and Sturm, *Letters to Marguerite Poradowska,* pp. 84–85.
6 *An Outcast of the Islands,* p. 13.
7 Moser, *Joseph Conrad,* p. 146.
8 Ian Watt, "Conrad Criticism and *The Nigger of the 'Narcissus,' "* *Nineteenth-Century Fiction,* XII (March 1958), 275.
9 *The Nigger of the "Narcissus,"* p. 140.
10 *Ibid.,* pp. 83–84.
11 *Ibid.,* p. 41.
12 Guerard, *Conrad, the Novelist,* pp. 104, 124.
13 *Youth,* p. 21.
14 "Conrad's 'Youth,' " *College English,* XX (March 1959), 276.
15 *Youth,* pp. v–vi.
16 Najder, *Conrad's Polish Background,* pp. 16–17.
17 Walter Allen, *The English Novel,* p. 365.
18 *Youth,* p. 28.
19 *The Nigger of the "Narcissus,"* pp. 162–163.
20 *Youth,* p. 55.
21 *The Times Literary Supplement,* I, 48 (December 12, 1902).
22 *Bookman,* XVIII (1903), 311.
23 Marvin Mudrick, "The Originality of Conrad," *Hudson Review,* XI, 4 (winter 1958–59), 553.
24 More pages of commentary have been devoted to "Heart of Darkness" than any piece of prose fiction of equal length in English with the possible exception of "The Turn of the Screw." Relevant essays are collected in the following anthologies: Bruce Harkness, *Conrad's Heart of Darkness and the Critics* (San Francisco, 1960); Leonard Dean, *Joseph Conrad's Heart of Darkness* (New Jersey, 1960); and Robert Kimbrough, *Heart of Darkness* (New York, 1963).
25 Seymour Gross has had the best of a three-way argument that began in *Modern Fiction Studies* (summer 1957), pp. 167–170, and which has been reprinted in Robert W. Stallmann's *Joseph Conrad: A Critical Symposium* (East Lansing, Michigan, 1960).
26 *Youth,* p. vii.
27 *Ibid.,* p. 90.
28 *Ibid.,* p. 113–114.
29 *Ibid.,* p. 119.
30 *Ibid.,* p. 144.
31 January 7, 1902, Blackburn, *Letters to Blackwood,* p. 138.
32 August 22, 1899, *ibid.,* p. 62.
33 *Pall Mall Magazine* (May 1914), p. 575.
34 *Ibid.,* p. 579.
35 *Ibid.,* p. 640.
36 Blackburn, *Letters to Blackwood,* p. 130.
37 *Pall Mall Magazine* (March 1899), p. 307.
38 *Pall Mall Magazine* (April 1899), p. 482.
39 Blackburn, *Letters to Blackwood,* pp. 56, 81.
40 *Ibid.,* p. 111.
41 *Ibid.,* pp. 115–116.
42 *Ibid.,* p. 118.
43 *Typhoon,* pp. 40, 56.
44 *Ibid.,* p. 15.
45 *Ibid.,* pp. 42–43.
46 E. M. Forster, *Abinger Harvest* (New York, 1936), p. 140.

[47] See Ian Watt, "Conrad Criticism and *The Nigger of the 'Narcissus,'*" *Nineteenth-Century Fiction*, XII (March 1958), 257–283.

[48] Richard Curle, *The Last Twelve Years of Joseph Conrad*, p. 87.

[49] Blackburn, *Letters to Blackwood*, pp. 135–136.

[50] *Ibid.*, p. 140.

[51] Jean-Aubry, I, 314.

[52] *Typhoon*, p. vii.

[53] *Ibid.*, pp. 145–147.

[54] *Ibid.*, pp. 198–99.

[55] Ford, *Joseph Conrad*, p. 140.

[56] Jessie Conrad, *Joseph Conrad as I Knew Him*, p. 118.

[57] "The Genesis of Conrad's 'Amy Foster,'" *Studies in Philology*, LVII (July 1960), 549–566.

[58] *Typhoon*, p. 109.

[59] Baines, *Joseph Conrad*, p. 269.

[60] *Typhoon*, pp. 270–271.

[61] *Ibid.*, p. 276.

[62] Manuscript in Berg Collection, N.Y.P.L., p. 8.

[63] Baines, p. 268.

[64] January 28, 1902, Blackburn, *Letters to Blackwood*, p. 140.

[65] August 29, 1902, *ibid.*, p. 164.

[66] October 30, 1902, *ibid.*, p. 167.

[67] *Ibid.*, p. 169.

[68] July 29, 1911, Garnett, *Letters from Conrad*, p. 230.

[69] June 1, 1901, Blackburn, *Letters to Blackwood*, p. 127.

[70] Garnett, *Letters from Conrad*, p. 184.

[71] M. C. Bradbrook has claimed that "the old man, simple, heroic in his integrity, is ruined only in a material sense." *Joseph Conrad, England's Polish Genius*, p. 27. Oliver Warner, ignoring Conrad's indignation, insists again that the captain is "one of Conrad's noble portraits. . . . No flaw marks Whalley's character or intentions. Conrad portrayed many good men, but none who appeal more directly to the heart. . . ." *Joseph Conrad*, p. 143. And Paul Wiley sees the old man's betrayal as "due rather to circumstance than to any inherent weakness of nerve or will." *Conrad's Measure of Man*, p. 64. An essay which challenges these readings is William Moynihan's "The End of the Tether," *Modern Fiction Studies*, IV (summer 1958), 186–191.

[72] Blackburn, *Letters to Blackwood*, pp. 169–170.

[73] *Youth*, p. 324.

[74] Letter quoted by Douglas Goldring, *The Last Pre-Raphaelite* (London, 1948), p. 82. The letter is undated but from internal evidence seems to have been written in March 1902, just before Conrad began "The End of the Tether."

[75] *Youth*, p. viii.

[76] G. W. Whiting, "Conrad's Revision of Six of his Short Stories," *PMLA* XLVIII (June 1933), 552–557; and H. T. Webster, "Conrad's Changes in Narrative Conception in the Manuscripts of *Typhoon* and *Victory*," *PMLA* LXIV (December 1949), 953–962.

[77] Whiting, p. 557.

[78] Jean-Aubry, II, 29.

4. STORIES DURING THE YEARS OF THE GREAT NOVELS

[1] George Keating, *A Conrad Memorial Library*, opposite p. 150.

[2] Jean-Aubry, *Joseph Conrad*, II, 66.

3 *A Set of Six*, title page.
4 Blackburn, *Letters to Blackwood*, p. 37.
5 Curle, *Conrad to a Friend*, pp. 116–117.
6 See Basil Hall, *Extracts from a Journal Written on the Coasts of Chile, Peru, and Mexico* (1824); and Paul Kirschner, "Conrad's Strong Man," *Modern Fiction Studies*, X, 1 (spring 1964), 31–36. The original Gaspar was a bandit named Benavides. Conrad took the name Gaspar Ruiz from a sergeant-major who was one of Benavides' victims.
7 *A Set of Six*, p. 4.
8 *Ibid.*, p. vi.
9 *Ibid.*, pp. 68–69.
10 *Ibid.*, p. 70.
11 *Ibid.*, p. 62.
12 Garnett, *Letters from Joseph Conrad*, p. 212.
13 Curle, *Conrad to a Friend*, pp. 87–8.
14 The scenario for the film of "Gaspar Ruiz" at Yale describes Ruiz as "a Samson with a docile soul which he gave into the keeping of a noble woman."
15 *A Set of Six*, p. 105.
16 *Ibid.*, p. 131.
17 Jean-Aubry, II, 317.
18 April 25, 1906, Blackburn, *Letters to Blackwood*, pp. 188–189.
19 Richard Ludwig, *Letters of Ford Madox Ford* (Princeton, 1965), p. 23.
20 *A Set of Six*, pp. 160–161.
21 *Ibid.*, pp. 145, 161.
22 *Ibid.*, p. 144.
23 Blackburn, *Letters to Blackwood*, p. 178.
24 Letter, April 15, 1904 (Harvard University Library).
25 Letter, October 6, 1905 (Gordan Collection).
26 Letter to Pinker, April 1909 (Gordan Collection).
27 Letter, November 1911 (Gordan Collection).
28 Letter to Pinker, March 28, 1912 (Gordan Collection).
29 *Harper's*, C (May 1900), 950.
30 *Ibid.*, June 1910, p. 42.
31 Letter to Austin Harrison, March 28, 1912 (Berg Collection).
32 *Harper's*, CXIII (August 1906), pp. 406–407.
33 *A Set of Six*, p. 77.
34 *Ibid.*
35 *Ibid.*, p. 81.
36 *Ibid.*, pp. 101–102.
37 Jean-Aubry, II, 74.
38 *A Set of Six*, p. v.
39 *Ibid.*, p. 281.
40 *Ibid.*, p. 288.
41 *Modern Fiction Studies*, I, 1 (1955), 22–25.
42 "The Pathos of 'Il Conde,'" *Studies in Short Fiction*, III, 1 (fall 1965), 31–38.
43 *A Set of Six*, p. 281.
44 *Ibid.*, p. 289.
45 Frederick R. Karl, *A Reader's Guide to Joseph Conrad*, pp. 206–207.
46 January 25, 1907, Jean-Aubry, II, 41.
47 DeLancey Ferguson, "The Plot of Conrad's 'The Duel,'" *Modern Language Notes*, L (June 1935), 385–390.
48 *A Set of Six*, pp. 224, 230.
49 Garnett, pp. 211–212.

[50] Letter to the author, May 31, 1961.
[51] Letter to the author, August 28, 1961.
[52] Letter, Friday, September 1907, Jean-Aubry, II, 56.
[53] Jean-Aubry, II, 65.
[54] Letter, May 1909 (Gordan Collection).
[55] Jean-Aubry, II, 103.
[56] Stallman, "Conrad and 'The Secret Sharer,' " in *The Art of Joseph Conrad* (East Lansing, 1960), pp. 275–288; Guerard, *Conrad the Novelist*, pp. 14–33; J. L. Simmons, "The Dual Morality in Conrad's 'Secret Sharer,' " *Studies in Short Fiction* (spring 1965), pp. 209–220; Curley, "Legate of the Ideal," *Conrad's "Secret Sharer" and the Critics*, edited by Bruce Harkness (Belmont, California, 1962), pp. 75–82. An amusing spoof of critical extravagance is Bruce Harkness' "The Secret of 'The Secret Sharer' Bared," *College English*, XXVII (1965), 55–61.
[57] Karl, pp. 230–236; Baines, pp. 354–359.
[58] "Story and Idea in Conrad's 'The Shadow-Line,' " *Critical Quarterly*, II (summer 1960), 133–148.
[59] *'Twixt Land and Sea*, pp. 118–119.
[60] *Ibid.*, pp. 124–125.
[61] *Within the Tides*, p. 85.
[62] *'Twixt Land and Sea*, p. 36.
[63] *Ibid.*, pp. 56–57.
[64] *Ibid.*, p. 62.
[65] Ford, *Joseph Conrad: A Personal Remembrance*, p. 74.
[66] *'Twixt Land and Sea*, p. viii.
[67] *Ibid.*, p. 218.
[68] Garnett, *Letters from Conrad*, p. 231.
[69] Letter, April 1916 (Gordan Collection).
[70] Garnett, p. 230.
[71] Garnett, p. 230; and Blackburn, *Letters from Blackwood*, p. 197.
[72] Letter, Saturday, March 1911 (Gordan Collection).
[73] Garnett, p. 231.
[74] Bennett, *Letters to J. B. Pinker* (Oxford, 1966), p. 221.
[75] Baines, p. 409. Conrad had first appeared in the *Metropolitan* in January 1912 with "The Aristocrat," which was later called "Prince Roman."
[76] Letter, December 16, 1913 (Gordan Collection).
[77] *Letters from Conrad*, p. 25.
[78] Baines, p. 382; and *Publishers' Weekly* (September 26, 1914), p. 876.
[79] Quoted in the *New Republic*, March 1924.
[80] F. T. Cooper, *Publishers' Weekly* (April 19, 1919), p. 1129.

5. LAST TALES

[1] *Last Essays*, pp. 115–116, 118.
[2] Letter, December 3, 1923 (Lilly Library, University of Indiana).
[3] Jean-Aubry, II, 195.
[4] *The Shadow-Line*, p. v.
[5] *Ibid.*, p. 132.
[6] *Ibid.*, pp. 71–72.
[7] *Ibid.*, p. 95.
[8] *Ibid.*, pp. 107–108.
[9] *Ibid.*, pp. 81–82.

[10] Ian Watt, "Story and Idea in Conrad's 'The Shadow-Line,' "*Critical Quarterly* II (summer 1960), 145.

[11] Baines, p. 406; and Jean-Aubry, II, 182.

[12] Jean-Aubry, II, 168.

[13] *Tales of Hearsay*, p. 26.

[14] *Ibid.*, p. 23.

[15] Joseph Conrad, *Lettres françaises*, ed. Jean-Aubry (Paris, 1930), p. 87.

[16] Guerard, p. 301.

Selected Bibliography

GENERAL STUDIES

Allen, Jerry. *The Sea Years of Joseph Conrad*. New York, 1965.
————. *The Thunder and the Sunshine*. New York, 1958.
Allen, Walter. *The English Novel*. New York, 1954.
Andreas, Osborne. *Joseph Conrad: A Study in Non-Conformity*. New York, 1959.
Aubry. See Jean-Aubry.
Baines, Jocelyn. *Joseph Conrad: A Critical Biography*. London, 1960.
Bancroft, W. W. *Joseph Conrad*. Philadelphia, 1931.
Blackburn, William, ed. *Joseph Conrad: Letters to William Blackwood and David S. Meldrum*. Durham, North Carolina, 1958.
Bradbrook, M. C. *Joseph Conrad: Poland's English Genius*. Cambridge, 1942.
Brown, Douglas. "From *Heart of Darkness* to *Nostromo*: An Approach to Conrad," in Boris Ford, ed., *The Modern Age*, Pelican Guide to English Literature, VII (Baltimore, 1961), 119–137.
Conrad, Jessie. *Joseph Conrad as I Knew Him*. London, 1926.
————. *Joseph Conrad and His Circle*. London, 1935.
Crankshaw, Edward. *Joseph Conrad: Some Aspects of the Art of the Novel*. London, 1936.
Curle, Richard. *The Last Twelve Years of Joseph Conrad*. New York, 1928.
————. *Conrad to A Friend*. New York, 1928.
Fleishman, Avrom. *Conrad's Politics*. Baltimore, 1967.
Ford, Ford Madox. *Joseph Conrad: A Personal Remembrance*. Boston, 1924.

Forster, E. M. *Abinger Harvest*. New York, 1936, pp. 136–141.

Garnett, Edward. *Letters from Joseph Conrad, 1895–1924*. Indianapolis, 1928.

Gee, John A., and Paul J. Sturm. *Letters of Joseph Conrad to Marguerite Poradowska, 1890–1920*. New Haven, 1940.

Gillon, Adam. *The Eternal Solitary: A Study of Joseph Conrad*. New York, 1960.

Gordan, John D. *Joseph Conrad: The Making of a Novelist*. Cambridge, Mass., 1940.

Guerard, Albert J. *Joseph Conrad*. New York, 1947.

———. *Conrad the Novelist*. Cambridge, Mass., 1958.

Gurko, Leo. *Joseph Conrad: Giant in Exile*. New York, 1962.

Haugh, Robert. *Joseph Conrad: Discovery in Design*. Oklahoma, 1957.

Hay, Eloise Knapp. *The Political Novels of Joseph Conrad*. Chicago, 1963.

Heilbrun, Carolyn. *The Garnett Family*. New York, 1961.

Hewitt, Douglas. *Conrad: A Reassessment*. Cambridge, 1952.

Hicks, John H. "Conrad's *Almayer's Folly*: Structure, Theme, and Critics," *Nineteenth-Century Fiction*, XIX (June 1964), 17–31.

Hopkinson, Tom. "The Short Stories," *London Magazine*, IV (November 1957), 36–41.

Jean-Aubry, Gerard. *Joseph Conrad: Life and Letters*. New York, 1927.

———. *The Sea-Dreamer*. New York, 1957.

Karl, Frederick R. *A Reader's Guide to Joseph Conrad*. New York, 1960.

Keating, George T. *A Conrad Memorial Library*. New York, 1929.

Kirschner, Paul. "Conrad and Maupassant," *Review of English Literature*, VI, iv (1965), 37–51.

———. "Conrad and Maupassant: Moral Solitude and 'A Smile of Fortune,' " *REL*, VII, iii (1966), 62–77.

Krieger, Murray. "Joseph Conrad: Action, Inaction, and Extremity," *The Tragic Vision*. New York, 1960, pp. 154–194.

Krzyanowski, Ludwik. *Joseph Conrad: Centennial Essays*. New York, 1960.

Leavis, F. R. *The Great Tradition*. London, 1948.

Lohf, Kenneth A., and Eugene P. Sheehy. *Joseph Conrad at Mid-Century: Editions and Studies, 1896–1955*. Minneapolis, 1957.

Megroz, R. L. *Joseph Conrad's Mind and Method*. London, 1931.

Meyer, Bernard. *Joseph Conrad: A Psychoanalytic Biography*. Princeton, 1967.

Miller, J. H. *Poets of Reality*. Cambridge, Mass., 1965, pp. 13–67.

Morf, Gustav. *The Polish Heritage of Joseph Conrad*. New York, 1931.

Morris, Robert L. "The Classical Reference in Conrad's Fiction," *College English*, VII (March 1946), 312–318.

Moser, Thomas. *Joseph Conrad: Achievement and Decline*. Cambridge, Mass., 1957.

Mudrick, Marvin. *Conrad: A Collection of Critical Essays*. Englewood Cliffs, N. J., 1966.

———. "Conrad and the Terms of Modern Criticism," *Hudson Review*, VII (autumn 1954), 419–426.

———. "The Originality of Conrad," *Hudson Review*, XI (winter 1958–59), 545–553.

Najder, Zdzislaw. *Conrad's Polish Background*. Oxford, 1964.

Retinger, J. H. *Conrad and his Contemporaries*. New York, 1943.

Rosenfield, Claire. *Paradise of Snakes*. Chicago, 1967.

Said, Edward. *Joseph Conrad and the Fiction of Autobiography*. Cambridge, Mass., 1966.

Sherry, Norman. *Conrad's Eastern World*. Cambridge, 1966.

Stallman, Robert W. *Joseph Conrad: A Critical Symposium*. East Lansing, Michigan, 1960.

Stewart, J. I. M. "Joseph Conrad," *Eight Modern Writers*. Oxford, 1963, pp. 184–222.

Unger, Leonard. "LaForgue, Conrad, and T. S. Eliot," *The Man in the Name*. Minneapolis, 1956, pp. 190–242.

Visiak, E. H. *The Mirror of Conrad*. New York, 1956.

Warner, Oliver. *Joseph Conrad*. London, 1951.

Watt, Ian. "Conrad Criticism and *The Nigger of the 'Narcissus,'* " *Nineteenth-Century Fiction*, XII (March 1958), 257–283.

Webster, H. T. "Conrad's Changes in Narrative Conception in the Manuscripts of *Typhoon and Other Stories* and *Victory*, *PMLA*, LXIV (Dec. 1949), 953–962.

Whiting, G. W. "Conrad's Revision of Six of His Short Stories," *PMLA*, XLVIII (June 1933), 552–557.

Wiley, Paul L. *Conrad's Measure of Man*. Madison, Wisconsin, 1954.

Worth, George J. "Conrad's Debt to Maupassant in the Preface to *The Nigger of the 'Narcissus,'* " *Journal of English and Germanic Philology*, LIV (Oct. 1955), 700–704.

Wright, Walter F. *Romance and Tragedy in Joseph Conrad*. Lincoln, Nebraska, 1949.

Zabel, Morton D., ed. "Introduction," *The Portable Conrad*. New York, 1947.

——. "Introduction," *Joseph Conrad: Tales of the East*. Garden City, 1961.

——. "Introduction," *Joseph Conrad: Tales of Heroes and History*. Garden City, 1960.

——. "Introduction," *The Shadow-Line and Two Other Tales*. Garden City, 1959.

——. "Introduction," *Youth: A Narrative and Two Other Stories*. Garden City, 1959.

SELECTED CRITICISM OF INDIVIDUAL SHORT STORIES

AMY FOSTER

Andreach, Robert J. "The Two Narrators of 'Amy Foster,' " *Studies in Short Fiction*, II (1965), 262–269.

Andreas, 70–72.

Baines, 265–267.

Gross, Seymour L. "Conrad's Revision of 'Amy Foster,' " *Notes and Queries*, X (April 1963), 144–146.

Guerard, *Conrad the Novelist*, 49–51.

Gurko, 210–212.

Herndon, Richard. "The Genesis of Conrad's 'Amy Foster,'" *Studies in Philology*, LVII (July 1960), 549–566.

Meyer, passim.

Morf, 167–176.

Moser, 86–87.

Mudrick, "Conrad and the Terms of Modern Criticism," 422–424.

Said, 113–114, 149–150.

Schorer, Mark. *The Story* (New York, 1950), 243–246.

Stallman, Robert W., and R. E. Watters. *The Creative Reader* (New York, 1954), 326–328.

Wasiolek, Edward. "Yanko Goorall: A Note on Name Symbolism in Conrad's 'Amy Foster,'" *Modern Language Notes*, XVII (June 1956), 418–419.

Wright, 165–166.

AN ANARCHIST

Andreas, 124–126.

Baines, 323–324.

Gurko, 164–165.

Megroz, 202–204.

Said, 153.

Zabel, *Tales of Heroes and History*, xxxvii–xxxviii.

BECAUSE OF THE DOLLARS

Andreas, 159–160.

Meyer, 356.

Wright, 162–163.

Zabel, *Tales of the East*, 35–36.

THE BLACK MATE

Andreas, 1–4.

Baines, 84–85.

Graver, Lawrence. "Conrad's First Story," *Studies in Short Fiction*, II, 2 (winter 1965), 164–169.

Meyer, 54, 317.

THE BRUTE

Andreas, 121–123.
Meyer, 293n.

THE DUEL

Andreas, 107–112.
Ferguson, J. D. "The Plot of Conrad's 'The Duel,'" *Modern Language Notes*, L (June 1935), 385–390.
Meyer, 198–201.
Wiley, 92–94.
Wright, 31–32.
Zabel, *Tales of Heroes and History*, xxix–xxxi.

THE END OF THE TETHER

Andreas, 82–85.
Baines, 278–281.
Bancroft, 84–87.
Blackburn, 169–170.
Graver, Lawrence. "Critical Confusion and Conrad's 'The End of the Tether,'" *Modern Fiction Studies*, IX (winter 1963–64), 390–393.
Guerard, Albert J. "Introduction," *The Nigger of the "Narcissus"* (New York, Dell, 1960).
Gurko, 82–85.
Karl, 140–141.
Meyer, passim.
Moynihan, W. T. "Conrad's 'The End of the Tether': A New Reading," *Modern Fiction Studies*, IV (summer 1958), 173–177.
Said, passim.
Sherry, passim.
Warner, 143–144.
Whiting, 556–557.
Wiley, 64–69.
Wright, 96–97.
Zabel, *Youth*, passim.

FALK

Andreas, 73–77.

Baines, 261–265.

Crankshaw, 92–95.

Guerard, *Conrad the Novelist*, 20–21.

Hewitt, 40–45.

Meyer, passim.

Moser, 99–100.

Said, passim.

Sherry, passim.

Webster, H. T. "Conrad's Changes . . . ," 954–955.

———. "Conrad's 'Falk,' " *Explicator*, VII (June 1949), item 56.

FREYA OF THE SEVEN ISLES

Andreas, 145–148.

Baines, 375–378.

Bancroft, 53–55.

Garnett, 231–232.

Meyer, passim.

Moser, 100–101.

Said, 160–161.

Wiley, 139–141.

Wright, 163–165.

GASPAR RUIZ

Andreas, 113–118.

Kirschner, Paul. "Conrad's Strong Man," *Modern Fiction Studies*, X (spring 1964), 31–36.

Wright, 90–92.

Zabel, *Tales of Heroes and History*, xxxi–xxxii.

HEART OF DARKNESS

Andreas, 46–54.

Baines, 223–230.

Baskett, Sam S. "Jack London's Heart of Darkness," *American Quarterly*, X (spring 1958), 72–76.

Benson, Donald R. " 'Heart of Darkness': The Grounds of Civilization in an Alien Universe," *Texas Studies in Language and Literature*, VII (1966), 339–347.

Bernard, Kenneth. "The Significance of the Roman Parallel in 'Heart of Darkness,' " *Ball State Teachers College Forum*, V, 2 (1964), 29–31.

Blackburn, 36–56.

Boyle, Ted. "Marlow's 'Lie,' " *Studies in Short Fiction*, I (winter 1964), 159–163.

Bradbrook, 27–33.

Brady, Marion B. "Conrad's Whited Sepulcher," *College English*, XXIV (October 1962), 24–29.

Brown, 122–137.

Bruffee, Kenneth A. "The Lesser Nightmare: Marlow's Lie," *Modern Language Quarterly*, XXV (1964), 322–329.

Burgess, C. F. "Conrad's Pesky Russian," *Nineteenth-Century Fiction*, XVIII (Sept. 1963), 189–193.

Clifford, Hugh. "The Art of Joseph Conrad," *Spectator*, LXXXIX (1902), 827–828.

Collins, Harold R. "Kurtz, the Cannibals, and the Second-rate Helmsman," *Western Humanities Review*, VIII (autumn 1954), 299–310.

Crews, Frederick C. "The Power of Darkness," *Partisan Review*, XXXIV, 4 (fall 1967), 507–525.

Curle, Richard. "Conrad's Diary," *Yale Review*, XV (Jan. 1926), 254–266.

Daiches, David. *White Man in the Tropics* (New York, 1962), 3–16.

D'Avanzo, Mario L. "Conrad's Motley as an Organizing Metaphor in 'Heart of Darkness,' " *College Language Association Journal*, IX (1966), 289–291.

Dean, Leonard. "Tragic Pattern in 'Heart of Darkness,' " *College English*, XVI (Nov. 1944), 100–104.

———. *Heart of Darkness: Backgrounds and Criticism* (New Jersey, 1960).

Dowden, Wilfred S. "The Light and the Dark: Imagery and Thematic Development in Conrad's 'Heart of Darkness,' " *Rice Institute Pamphlet,* XLIV (April 1957), 33–51.

Evans, Robert O. "Conrad's Underworld," *Modern Fiction Studies,* II (May 1956), 56–62.

———. "Further Comments on 'Heart of Darkness,' " *Modern Fiction Studies,* III (winter, 1957–58), 358–360.

Farmer, Norman. "Conrad's 'Heart of Darkness,' " *Explicator,* XXII (1964), item 51.

Feder, Lillian. "Marlow's Descent into Hell," *Nineteenth Century Fiction,* IX (March 1955), 280–292.

Gillon, 106–108.

Gordan, 266–268.

Gross, Harvey. "Aschenbach and Kurtz: The Cost of Civilization," *Centennial Review,* VI (spring 1962), 131–143.

Gross, Seymour. "A Further Note on the Function of the Frame in 'Heart of Darkness,' " *Modern Fiction Studies,* III (1957), 167–170.

Guerard, *Conrad the Novelist,* 33–48.

———. "Introduction," *Heart of Darkness and The Secret Sharer* (New York, Signet Books, 1950).

Guetti, James. " 'Heart of Darkness' and the Failure of the Imagination," *Sewanee Review,* LXXIII (1965), 488–504.

Gurko, 148–153.

Halle, Louis. "Joseph Conrad: An Enigma Decoded," *Saturday Review of Literature,* XXX (May 22, 1949), 7–8.

Harkness, Bruce. *Conrad's 'Heart of Darkness' and the Critics* (San Francisco, 1960).

Harper, George M. "Conrad's Knitters and Homer's Cave of the Nymphs," *English Language Notes,* I (Sept. 1963), 53–57.

Haugh, 35–55.

Hay, 109–158.

Hewitt, 31–39.

Hoffman, Stanton de Voren. "Comedy and Theme in 'Heart of Darkness,' " *Studies in Short Fiction,* II (1965), 113–123.

Hollingsworth, Alan. "Freud, Conrad, and the Future of an Illusion," *Literature and Psychology,* V (1955), 78–82.

224   *Bibliography*

Hopkinson, 37–38.

Karl, 133–140.

Kettle, Arnold. "The Greatness of Joseph Conrad," *Modern Quarterly*, III (summer 1948), 64–70.

Kimbrough, Robert. *Heart of Darkness: Text, Sources, Criticism* (New York, Norton, 1963).

Krieger, 154–165.

Leavis, 174–183.

McConnell, Daniel J. "The 'Heart of Darkness' in T. S. Eliot's 'The Hollow Men,'" *Texas Studies in Language and Literature*, IV (summer 1962), 141–153.

Masefield, John. "Deep Sea Yarns: *Youth, a Narrative*," *Speaker*, XXXIV (January 31, 1903), 20–24.

Meyer, passim.

Morris, 312–318.

Moser, 78–81.

Mudrick, "The Originality of Conrad," passim.

Ober, Warren. " 'Heart of Darkness': 'The Ancient Mariner' a Hundred Years Later," *Dalhousie Review*, XLV (1965), 333–337.

Owen, Guy. "A Note on 'Heart of Darkness,' " *Nineteenth Century Fiction*, XII (1957), 168–169.

Owen, R. J. "Two Books," *Notes and Queries*, V (June 1958), 260.

Powys, Llewelyn. "Youth," in Keating, *A Conrad Memorial Library* (New York, 1929), 88–93.

Raskin, Jonah. " 'Heart of Darkness': The Manuscript Revisions," *Review of English Studies*, XVIII (Feb. 1967), 30–39.

Rawson, C. J. "Conrad's 'Heart of Darkness,' " *Notes and Queries*, VI (March 1959), 110–111.

Reid, Stephen. "The 'Unspeakable Rites' in 'Heart of Darkness,' " *Modern Fiction Studies*, IX (winter 1963–64), 347–356.

Ridley, Florence H. "The Ultimate Meaning of 'Heart of Darkness,' " *Nineteenth-Century Fiction*, XVIII (June 1963), 43–53.

Rosenfield, Claire. "The Shadow Within," *Daedalus*, XCII (1963), 333.

Said, passim.

Sanders, Charles. "Conrad's 'Heart of Darkness,'" *Explicator*, XXIV (1965), item 2.

Spinner, Kaspar. "Embracing the Universe: Some Annotations to Conrad's 'Heart of Darkness,'" *English Studies*, XLIII (October 1962), 420–423.

Stein, William Bysshe. "The Lotus Posture and 'Heart of Darkness,'" *Modern Fiction Studies*, II (winter 1956–57), 235–237.

———. "Buddhism and 'Heart of Darkness,'" *Western Humanities Review*, XI (summer 1957), 281–285.

———. " 'Heart of Darkness': Bodhisattva Scenario," *Orient West*, IX (1964), 37–46.

Stewart, 193–197.

Thale, Jerome. "Marlow's Quest," *University of Toronto Quarterly*, XXIV (1955), 351–358.

———. "The Narrator as Hero," *Twentieth Century Literature*, III (1957), 69–73.

Tick, Stanley. "Conrad's 'Heart of Darkness,'" *Explicator*, XXI (April 1963), item 67.

Tindall, William York. *The Literary Symbol* (New York, 1955), 85–91.

Unger, 194–218.

Visiak, 224–231.

Warner, 138–142.

Whiting, 555–556.

Wilcox, Stewart C. "Conrad's 'Complicated Presentations' of Symbolic Imagery in 'Heart of Darkness,'" *Philological Quarterly*, XXXIX (January 1960), 1–17.

Wiley, 61–64.

———. "Conrad's Skein of Ironies," in Kimbrough's *Heart of Darkness: Text, Sources, Criticism*, 223–227.

Williams, George W. "The Turn of the Tide in 'Heart of Darkness,'" *Modern Fiction Studies*, IX (summer 1963), 171–173.

Wimsatt, W. K. *The Verbal Icon* (Kentucky, 1954), 196–197.

Wright, 143–160.

Zabel, *Youth*, passim.

THE IDIOTS

Andreas, 23–25.

Chaikin, Milton. "Zola and Conrad's 'The Idiots,'" *Studies in Philology*, LII, 3 (July 1955), 502–507.

Gordan, 219–226.

Guerard, *Conrad the Novelist*, 94–96.

Meyer, passim.

Wright, 169–171.

IL CONDE

Andreas, 119–120.

Baines, 340–341.

Bancroft, 37–38.

Hagopian, John. "The Pathos of 'Il Conde,'" *Studies in Short Fiction*, III (1965), 31–38.

Karl, 206–209.

Megroz, 118–122.

Meyer, 196–197.

Wiley, 89–90.

Wills, John H. "Adam, Axel, and 'Il Conde,'" *Modern Fiction Studies*, I (Feb. 1955), 22–25.

Wright, 167–168.

THE INFORMER

Andreas, 97–101.

Bancroft, 18–19.

Howe, Irving. *Politics and the Novel* (New York, 1957), 85.

Karl, 209–210.

Walton, James. "Mr. X's 'Little Joke': The Design of 'The Informer,'" *Studies in Short Fiction*, IV (summer 1967), 322–333.

Zabel, *Tales of Heroes and History*, xxxviii–xl.

THE INN OF THE TWO WITCHES

Andreas, 157–158.

Baum, P. F. "A Source," *Modern Language Notes*, XXXIII (May 1918), 312–314.

Meyer, passim.

KARAIN

Andreas, 31–34.
Baines, 189–190.
Gordan, 248–252.
Guerard, *Conrad the Novelist*, 90–92.
Whiting, 554.
Wright, 25–27.
Zabel, *Tales of the East*, 32–34.

THE LAGOON

Andreas, 40–42.
D., F. A. "Conrad's 'The Lagoon,'" *Explicator*, IX (1951), item 7.
George, Gerald A. "Conrad's 'The Lagoon,'" *Explicator*, XXIV (1965), item 23.
Gleckner, Robert F. "Conrad's 'The Lagoon,'" *Explicator*, XVI (March 1958), item 33.
Gordan, 224–247.
Graver, Lawrence. "Conrad's 'The Lagoon,'" *Explicator*, XXI (May 1963), item 70.
Guerard, *Conrad the Novelist*, 65–68.
Gullason, Thomas A. "Conrad's 'The Lagoon,'" *Explicator* XIV (Jan. 1956), item 23.
Levy, Milton A. "Conrad's 'The Lagoon,'" *Explicator*, XXIII (1965), item 35.
McCann, Charles J. "Conrad's 'The Lagoon,'" *Explicator* XVIII (October 1959), item 3.
Millett, Fred B. *Reading Fiction* (New York, 1950), 175–177.
Mroczkowski, Przemyslaw. "A Glance Back at the Romantic Conrad: 'The Lagoon,'" in Krzyzanowski, *Joseph Conrad: Centennial Essays* (New York, 1960), 73–83.
Meyer, passim.
Owen, Guy. "Conrad's 'The Lagoon,'" *Explicator*, XVIII (May, 1960), item 47.
Rehder, Jessie. *The Story at Work* (New York, 1963), 254–255.
Said, passim.

Sickels, Eleanor. "Conrad's 'The Lagoon,'" *Explicator* XV (Dec. 1956), item 17.

Williams, George W. "Conrad's 'The Lagoon," *Explicator*, XXIII (1964), items 1, 51.

Wright, 92–93.

Zabel, *Tales of the East*, 32–34.

AN *OUTPOST OF PROGRESS*

Andreas, 26–30.

Bancroft, 80–83.

Baskett, Sam S. "Jack London's Heart of Darkness," *American Quarterly*, X (spring 1958), 67–70.

Garnett, 66–67.

Gillon, 104–106.

Gordan, 240–244.

Meyer, passim.

Said, passim.

Tolley, A. T. "Conrad's Favorite Story," *Studies in Short Fiction*, III (1966), 314–320.

Unger, 232–234.

Whiting, 553.

Wright, 131–134.

Zabel, *Tales of Heroes and History*, xxxv–xxxvii.

THE *PARTNER*

Andreas, 149–150.

Baines, 373.

THE *PLANTER OF MALATA*

Andreas, 161–162.

Baines, 392–394.

Karl, 270–272.

Meyer, passim.

Moser, 144–145.

Said, 133–136, 161–163.

Wiley, 158–162.

Zabel, *Tales of the East*, 36–38.

PRINCE ROMAN

Andreas, 151–152.

Krzyzanowski, Ludwik. *Joseph Conrad: Centennial Essays*, 27–72.

Said, 132–133.

Zabel, *Tales of Heroes and History*, xxx–xxxi.

THE RETURN

Andreas, 35–39.

Garnett, 107–109.

Gordan, 252–259.

Guerard, *Conrad the Novelist*, 96–99.

Hopkinson, 39–40.

Meyer, passim.

Moser, 71–78.

Said, passim.

Wiley, 25–28.

THE SECRET SHARER

Andreas, 135–138.

Baines, 354–359.

Benson, Carl. "Conrad's Two Stories of Initiation," *PMLA*, LXIX (March 1954), 46–56.

Burton, Dwight L. "Teaching 'The Secret Sharer' to High School Students," *English Journal*, XLVII (May 1958), 263–266.

Curley, Daniel. "Legate of the Ideal," in Harkness, *Conrad's Secret Sharer and the Critics*, 75–82.

———. "The Writer and His Use of Material: The Case of 'The Secret Sharer,'" *Modern Fiction Studies*, XIII, 2 (summer 1967), 179–194.

Day, Robert A. "The Rebirth of Leggatt," *Literature and Psychology*, XIII (summer 1963), 74–81.

Evans, Robert O. "Conrad: A Nautical Image," *Modern Language Notes*, LXII (Feb. 1957), 98–99.

Gettman, Royal, and Bruce Harkness. "Morality and Psychology in 'The Secret Sharer,'" in Harkness, *Conrad's Secret Sharer and the Critics*, 125–132.

Gilley, Leonard. "Conrad's 'The Secret Sharer,'" *Midwest Quarterly*, VIII (summer 1967), 319–350.

Guerard, *Joseph Conrad*, 38–42.

———. *Conrad the Novelist*, 13–33.

———. Introduction to *Heart of Darkness and The Secret Sharer* (New York, Signet, 1950).

Gurko, 91–94.

Harkness, Bruce. *Conrad's Secret Sharer and the Critics* (Belmont, Calif., Wadsworth, 1962).

———. "The Secret of 'The Secret Sharer' Bared," *College English*, XXVII (1965), 55–61.

Hewitt, 70–79 and passim.

Hoffman, Charles G. "Point of View in 'The Secret Sharer,'" *College English*, XXIII (May 1962), 651–654.

Haugh, 78–82.

Karl, 230–236.

Leiter, Louis H. "Echo Structures: Conrad's 'The Secret Sharer,'" *Twentieth-Century Literature*, V (Jan. 1960), 159–175.

Meyer, passim.

Moser, 138–141.

Mudrick, "Conrad and the Terms of Modern Criticism," 424–426.

O'Hara, J. D. "Unlearned Lessons in 'The Secret Sharer,'" *College English*, XXVI (1965), 444–450.

Robinson, E. Arthur. "Conrad's 'The Secret Sharer,'" *Explicator*, XVIII (Feb. 1960), item 28.

Ryan, Alvan S. *Insight II*, ed. J. V. Hagopian (Frankfurt, 1964), 70–76.

Said, passim.

Simmons, J. L. "The Duel Morality in Conrad's 'The Secret Sharer,'" *Studies in Short Fiction*, II (spring 1965), 209–220.

Stallmann, Robert W. "Life, Art and 'The Secret Sharer,'" in W. V. O'Connor's *Forms of Modern Fiction* (Minneapolis, 1948), 229–242.

———. "Conrad and 'The Secret Sharer,'" *Accent*, IX (spring 1949), 131–144.

Trilling, Lionel. *The Experience of Literature* (New York, 1967), 621–623.

Walcott, Charles C. "Interpreting the Symbol," *College English*, XIV (May 1953), 452–454.

Wiley, 94–97.
Williams, Porter, Jr. "The Brand of Cain in 'The Secret Sharer,' " *Modern Fiction Studies,* X (spring 1964), 27–30.
———. "The Matter of Conscience in Conrad's 'The Secret Sharer,' " *PMLA,* LXXIX (1964), 626–630.
Wills, John H. "Conrad's 'The Secret Sharer,' " *University of Kansas City Review,* XXVIII (1961), 115–126.
Wright, 48–50, 112–113.
Zabel, *The Shadow-Line,* 24–27.

THE SHADOW-LINE

Andreas, 169–170.
Benson, Carl. "Conrad's Two Stories of Initiation," *PMLA,* LXIX (March 1954), 46–56.
Bone, David. "The Shadow-Line," in Keating, *A Conrad Memorial Library* (New York, 1929), 255–261.
Leavis, *The Great Tradition,* passim.
———. "Joseph Conrad," *Sewanee Review,* LXVI (1958), 179–200.
Moser, 137–140.
Newman, "Joseph Conrad and the Ancient Mariner," *Kansas Magazine* (1960), 79–83.
Said, passim.
Stewart, 185–186.
Unger, 237–239.
Watt, Ian. "Story and Idea in Conrad's 'The Shadow-Line,' " *Critical Quarterly,* II (summer 1960), 133–148.
Waugh, Arthur. "Mr. Joseph Conrad and the Discipline of Fear," *Tradition and Change* (New York, 1919), 276–284.
Wiley, 199–214.
Wright, 19–21, 45–48.
Zabel, The Shadow-Line, 24–27.

A SMILE OF FORTUNE

Andreas, 139–144.
Baines, 374–375.
Bancroft, 77–78.
Guerard, *Conrad the Novelist,* 51–54.

Kirschner, Paul. "Conrad and Maupassant: Moral Solitude and 'A Smile of Fortune,' " *Review of English Literature*, VII (1966), 62–77.

Meyer, passim.

Moser, 96–98.

Said, 158–160.

Wright, 134–137.

Zabel, *Tales of the East*, 34–35.

Zuckerman, Jerome. " 'A Smile of Fortune': Conrad's Interesting Failure," *Studies in Short Fiction*, I (winter 1964), 99–102.

THE TALE

Andreas, 173–174.

Meyer, 230, 237–238.

Wright, 94–96.

Zabel, *Tales of Heroes and History*, xl–xlii.

TO-MORROW

Andreas, 78–81.

Wright, 166–167.

TYPHOON

Allen, Walter. *Six Great Novelists* (London, 1955), 172–175.

Andreas, 66–69.

Austin, Mary. "Typhoon," in Keating, *A Conrad Memorial Library*, 103–110.

Baines, 256–261.

Clay, N. L., ed. *Typhoon and Youth* (San Francisco, 1963).

Connolly, Francis. *The Types of Literature* (New York, 1955) 712–715.

Garnett, 18–19.

Graver, Lawrence. " 'Typhoon': A Profusion of Similes,' " *College English*, XXIV (October 1962), 62–64.

Guerard, *Conrad the Novelist*, 294–299.

———. *Joseph Conrad*, 53–54.

Gurko, 86–91.

Haugh, 25–31.
Hewitt, 112–117.
Hopkinson, 36–37.
Leavis, 183–187.
Sister M. Martin. "Typhoon," *Explicator*, XVIII (June 1960), item 57.
Meyer, passim.
Ward, A. C. *Aspects of the Mosern Short Story* (London, 1924), 145–157.
Webster, 953–962.
Weigand, Herman. *Insight II*, ed. J. V. Hagopian (Frankfurt, 1964), 49–58.
Wiley, 69–74.
Wills, John H. "Conrad's 'Typhoon': A Triumph of Organic Art," *North Dakota Quarterly*, XXX (1962), 62–70.
Wright, 12–17, 44–45, 62–65.
Zabel, *The Shadow-Line*, 19–22.

THE WARRIOR'S SOUL
Andreas, 171–172.
Wright, 168–169.
Zabel, *Tales of Heroes and History*, xxx–xxxi.

YOUTH
Andreas, 43–45.
Baines, 210–212.
Buckler, W. E. and A. B. Sklare, eds. "A Suggested Interpretation," in *Stories from Six Authors* (New York, 1960), 509–511.
Clay, N. L., ed. *Typhoon and Youth* (San Francisco, 1963).
Davis, Robert G. "Instructor's Manual for *Ten Modern Masters*," (New York, 1953), 33–34.
Garnett, 12–13.
Gonzalez, N. V. M. "Time as Sovereign: A Reading of Conrad's 'Youth,'" *Literary Apprentice* (University of the Philippines, 1954), 106–122.
Gordan, 264–266.
Gurko, 79–82.

Haugh, 20–24.

Karl, 131–133.

Krieger, Murray. "Conrad's 'Youth': A Naive Opening to Art and Life," *College English*, XX (March 1959), 275–280.

Meyer, passim.

Moser, 43–49.

Owen, Guy. "Crane's 'The Open Boat' and Conrad's 'Youth,'" *Renascence*, XVI (fall 1963), 22–28.

Said, passim.

Smith, J. Oates. "The Existential Comedy of Conrad's 'Youth,'" *Renascence*, XVI (fall 1963), 22–28.

Unger, 240–242.

Welker, Robert and Herschel Gower, eds. *The Sense of Fiction* (Englewood Cliffs, New Jersey, 1966), 193–196.

Whiting, 554–555.

Wills, J. H. "A Neglected Masterpiece: Conrad's 'Youth,'" *Texas Studies in Language and Literature*, IV (spring 1963), 591–601.

Wright, 9–12.

Zabel, *Youth*, 1–27.

———. *Tales of the East*, 9–13.

Index